D0867191

Interest Groups
and the Bureaucracy

JOHN E. CHUBB

Interest Groups
and the Bureaucracy

THE POLITICS OF ENERGY

STANFORD UNIVERSITY PRESS
Stanford, California   1983

Stanford University Press
Stanford, California
© 1983 by the Board of Trustees of the
Leland Stanford Junior University
Printed in the United States of America
ISBN 0-8047-1158-5
LC 82-60106

To Joyce

ACKNOWLEDGMENTS

While working on this book I had the benefit of considerable advice and support—only the latter of which I always accepted. I am grateful for all this help, but a few individuals and institutions merit special thanks.

Robert B. Kvavik and Gary Wynia aroused my curiosity in interest groups, bureaucracy, and the relationships between them; convinced me of their importance in modern policy making; and introduced me to an alternative way of looking at them. Because of their influence, the book's perspective—however far it may be from the Scandinavian and Latin American views they provided—is different from traditional American approaches. W. Phillips Shively, who advised me through several years of advanced training in quantitative methods at the University of Minnesota, encouraged me to take the analytical risks of exploratory and qualitative field research in Washington, D.C. Without his guidance I might have finished my doctoral dissertation a year sooner, but I would not have collected the novel data that, I think, distinguish this book. Data collection was also facilitated by the Brookings Institution, which supported me as a Research Fellow in 1977–78 and, through its high reputation in Washington, gained me access to major energy interest groups.

Once the data were collected, Herbert Kaufman offered wise advice on their interpretation, and Paul Sniderman contributed good sense on their presentation. Terry Moe's careful criticism of my theoretical work made Part I of the book more logical than it might otherwise have been. My colleagues in the Department of Political Science at Stanford University reinforced my decision to report this research as a book, and stimulated my thinking throughout its writing. The University generously covered the costs of a fast and accurate private typist, Gaye Passell, and a remarkable technical typist, Elizabeth Gretz; I am grateful for the relief they provided me from the tedium of manuscript preparation. Finally, Stanford University Press must be thanked for its patience and care, and especially for its editing—Madeleine Gleason is simply superb.

As important as this professional assistance has been, my greatest debts of gratitude are personal. My father and my grandfather, veterans of over sixty years in the oil industry, piqued my interest in the subject of energy—long before I knew what political science was—and my parents supported, in every sense of the word, my intellectual development—even when it turned to political science. My wife, Joyce, who had to live with this project for five years, sustained me through and through. To her I owe the greatest thanks.

J.E.C.

CONTENTS

TABLES AND FIGURES

PART I

THE THEORETICAL PERSPECTIVE

1

INTEREST GROUPS, BUREAUCRACY, AND THE ENERGY PROBLEM

For nearly a decade the energy problem has plagued the United States in fundamental and far-reaching ways. Energy scarcity is a major cause of both inflation and recession. The search for new energy supplies is a menace to the natural environment. The effective control of oil prices by the Organization of Petroleum Exporting Countries (OPEC) destabilizes international economic relations. Competition for oil in the politically volatile Middle East endangers world peace. While American oil imports have declined somewhat in the early 1980s, they retain more than double their market share of the early 1970s. With over 40 percent of American supplies coming from abroad, and much of that from politically unstable regimes, the United States is highly vulnerable to the panoply of problems associated with supply interruptions, price hikes, and domestic efforts to reverse the situation. Notwithstanding the world oil glut of 1982, the challenge of the energy future remains as ominous as ever.

What is perhaps most remarkable about the first decade of the energy crisis is the sustained failure of the government to improve the situation significantly. Since 1973 Americans have frequently viewed energy as one of the top problems facing the nation.[1] Congress has grappled extensively with the problem in every session. Each president has proposed a massive or radical program for conquering it once and for all. And literally hundreds of pages of energy legislation have been enacted. Yet none of this political attention— from Nixon's Project Independence, to Carter's National Energy Plan, to Reagan's rapid deregulation—has provided, nor does it promise, substantial relief. Why this has happened is a matter of considerable importance—both for the practical bearing it has on the work of policy makers and energy analysts and for the theoretical light it may shed on the apparent inability of the government to handle increasingly complex and chronic problems. Despite this, the political dimension of the energy problem remains poorly understood.

This may seem a rash appraisal in light of the many studies spawned by the energy crisis; however, very little of the work has a political emphasis. The preponderance of energy research has been done by economists and technical specialists. This work usually acknowledges the obvious difficulties that political conflict causes for innovative policy proposals. But even the most sophisticated studies analyze only superficially the operation and consequences of politics.[2] The few studies by political scientists are only beginning to fill this important gap and remain quite inadequate in elucidating energy politics at the national level. What we know about the role of politics in federal energy policy is mostly fragmentary, speculative, and impressionistic.[3]

Energy Politics: The Prevailing Perspective

The crux of the energy policy dilemma, in the view of many political observers, is an emergent conflict between a well-established set of segregated policy subsystems and a diversity of new demands for a policy that requires considerable interest integration.[4] Historically, energy politics *per se* did not exist. The major conflicts in the field centered around individual fuels. Coal politics, for example, was limited traditionally to labor wage and safety issues. A separate contest over domestic petroleum prices constituted oil politics. And, prototypically, enthusiasts of private nuclear power fought their own quiet battles with cautious government guardians of the atom and with fledgling environmentalists. The substantive energy issues were effectively independent. The policy-making arenas were institutionally distinct: coal had the Bureau of Mines, oil the Office of Oil and Gas, and nuclear power the Joint Committee on Atomic Energy. The contemporary dilemma arises from the tension between this established pattern of subsystem policy making and a newly perceived need to manage energy comprehensively.

The old subsystems flourished because they were consistent with the larger interests of the government and not grossly inconsistent with the particular interests of excluded groups. The producers of the fuels at the centers of the subsystems desired promotional policies and insured profitability. The government, for its part in any bargain, wanted a steady supply of fairly inexpensive energy to stimulate constant gains in productivity and living standards. Potential opponents of these government-producer "partnerships" were easily mollified as long as energy remained abundant relative to short-term domestic needs. Producer-endorsed compromises on prices, safety, environmental quality, and the like were costs that nonproducers willingly accepted in exchange for economic growth. Over time producer-dominated subsystems became the firmly established mode of energy policy making. Today, however, these established means cannot provide an easily accepted route out of the energy problem.

Traditional supply-promoting policies cannot satisfy the domestic shortfall in energy either soon enough or at costs society will complacently bear. Policies to limit demand and stimulate nontraditional supplies are widely acknowledged necessities.[5] In the long run renewable energy supplies will become physically and economically mandatory.[6] In the shorter run the policy challenge is as substantial as it is clear. The government will be pressed to ensure that progress toward some renewable energy future be made without severe economic disruptions, physical discomforts, or other social costs associated with market failure. This challenge is substantial in two important and reinforcing ways. First, because of the increasing tightness of traditional energy markets, new supplies will become available only at swiftly escalating internal and external costs. The government has therefore lost the basis for an easy partnership with traditional energy producers. Policies promoting the fossil fuels cannot be exchanged for cheap energy, minor externalities, and economic growth. Difficult value trade-offs must be resolved. Second, the system of institutions and political relationships through which these conflicts are supposed to be mediated has little experience with the problem. While it is adept at resolving the simpler, segregated problems of traditional fuels, it only exacerbates the substantial challenge of modern energy problems.

It is this clash between the existence of entrenched, producer-dominated, supply-oriented policy subsystems and the substantive need for realigned, multi-interest, supply-and-demand-oriented policy systems that is most commonly stressed as the political root of the energy problem. It contributes to policy stalemate, impedes the development of consistent energy programs, interferes with the promotion of alternative energy supplies, discourages conservation, and generally sustains an ominous gap between domestic energy consumption and production.

Unanswered Questions

The historical evidence for this political dilemma is strong, and the logic of its consequences is almost intuitive. Segregated policy subsystems were undoubtedly the traditional means of energy policy-making, and the frustrating effects of their struggle with new demands seem obvious.[7] When we move beyond the intuitive level of understanding, or begin to evaluate the explanation against recent political events, however, the weaknesses of the prevailing political perspective stand out. Its inadequacies are, in short, empirical and theoretical.

The empirical flaws are most evident. If the traditional producer-dominated subsystems continue to exert near controlling influence over energy policy, a number of recent occurrences represent serious anomalies. The most obvious discrepancy between tradition and current events lies in the reorganization of institutions responsible for energy policy. On the executive side the Atomic Energy Commission was split, in response to charges of producer favoritism, into an ostensibly unbiased Nuclear Regulatory Commission and a promotional Energy Research and Development Administration. The latter's responsibilities for encouraging alternative energy technologies were more diverse than those of its predecessor, including the gamut of non-nuclear options. Executive control over oil policy was also substantially reorganized. Oil prices became regulated against OPEC price increases in 1973, and an independent Federal Energy Administration was soon established to administer the program in coordination with broader energy policy objectives. Its creation spelled the end of that inveterate friend of the oil industry, Interior's Office of Oil and Gas. The subsystem orientation of the executive energy establishment was finally shaken by the new Department of Energy, which in 1977 consolidated ERDA, FEA, the Federal Power Commission, and portions of five other agencies. On their face, at least, these reorganizations are inconsistent with the domination of the political arena by producer groups in tenacious command of their subsystems.

Similar blows to the old organization structure have been struck in Congress. The Joint Committee on Atomic Energy, the sole legislative custodian of nuclear power for two decades, was disbanded in 1976, and its regulatory jurisdiction was assigned to less sympathetic environmental committees. The Senate took a significant stride toward energy centralization by establishing a standing committee on Energy and Natural Resources. The House has been reluctant to restructure its fragmented apparatus, but it did construct an *ad hoc* Select Committee on Energy to facilitate passage of Carter's National Energy Plan in 1977. Congress is by no means organized for comprehensive energy policy making but, like the executive branch, it has reorganized sufficiently to raise serious questions about the strength of traditional subsystems.

The old ways are also inconsistent with certain policy innovations of the 1970s. After maintaining oil prices above free market levels for fifty years, the government initiated a regulatory program to depress domestic prices.[8] The creation of this program can be attributed to the exigencies of the OPEC embargo, but its continuation after the emergency challenges the simple notion of industry dominance. Likewise, the termination of the oil depletion allowance, for half a century the symbol of petroleum promotionalism, strongly suggests slippage in the industry's political stronghold.[9] Skepticism about the prospects for substantial conservation legislation must also be questioned. The 1975 Energy Policy and Conservation Act mandated more than a doubling in automobile fuel efficiency by 1985— a goal that is being implemented without the anticipated delays. President Carter's National Energy Plan was also unprecedented, not only in its emphasis on conservation but also in its comprehensiveness. This is not to say that the policy indicators are moving only in this nontraditional direction. Oil price deregulation occurred nine months ahead of schedule in January 1981; natural gas price deregulation is underway against Carter's original wishes; and nuclear power commands the lion's share of government research and development expenditures. But the policies of the last decade indisputably challenge the prevailing assumption of producer domination.

When we try to account for these deviations in the substance and organization of energy policy, the theoretical superficiality of the conventional view becomes apparent. At best it offers a general, pluralist interpretation. Established modes of political conduct have been thrown into conflict with each other, and with novel demands, by sharp changes in the country's energy situation. The result is an indeterminate mixture of the old and the new, of parochialism and comprehensiveness, reflecting a host of private interests. The model of producer-dominated subsystems cannot offer more precise explanations because it is largely a descriptive model. It identifies regular, historical, subsystemic patterns of policy making but fails to account theoretically for their persistence. It recognizes the contemporary strains on the subsystems but offers little theoretical guidance for assessing their consequences. Without propositions accounting for the apparent resilience of policy subsystems over time, it is impossible to understand the effects of recent physical, economic, and political changes upon them.

At best the prevailing perspective leaves important questions of energy politics to conjecture. What, for example, is the policy significance of bureaucratic or congressional reorganization? How serious a threat to government-producer relationships is posed by the activity of newly organized interests, or by the economics of energy scarcity? Once the political turmoil of the past decade subsides, what patterns of political accommodation are likely to dominate energy policy making? And how will these political transformations affect the future course of energy production and consumption? These are difficult questions, and progressively so, but we cannot hope for satisfactory answers until we move from historical description to a mode of analysis that seeks general explanations and predictive theory.

An Organizational Approach

The descriptive studies have shown us the clearest feature of past energy politics in the United States and other industrial nations: that it permitted the development of policy through cooperation, on a segregated basis, between the government and producer groups.[10] Often this cooperation was institutionalized in administrative bureaucracies, responsible for implementing and reformulating sectoral policies, in which producer groups enjoyed informal privileged access or nearly direct participation through advisory committees. The relationship between the Office of Oil and Gas and the National Petroleum Council, an advisory committee dominated by major oil companies, was perhaps the most routinized and best known of these arrangements.[11] Similar ties of mutual support also bound such agencies as the Bureau of Land Management, the Atomic Energy Commission, the Federal Power Commission, and the Rural Electrification Administration to producer clienteles.[12] These relationships were the major manifestation of the most salient feature of energy politics past.

The most salient feature of contemporary energy politics is the battle being fought against the cooperative mode of policy making, and against the public and private organizations that carried it out. The new combatants are the legions of environmental groups, consumer lobbies, labor unions, and commercial energy users that now find their interests threatened by the old political ways and the new problem situation. Their lobbying has been at least partially rewarded in legislation such as the Strip Mining Act of 1977, the Natural Gas Act of 1978, and the "Windfall Profits" Tax of 1980. It also made inroads in the bureaucracy with appointments by President Carter to executive posts. The considerable scope of this recent challenge to status quo energy politics is undeniable.

Identifying a key dynamic of energy politics and developing a general explanation of that dynamic are, however, two very different things. The ultimate objective of this book is essentially the latter. I seek a theoretical understanding of the political relationships underpinning energy policy making that will explain the conditions under which energy policy changes. To that end the dynamic that emerges so clearly and centrally in descriptive studies provides the starting point. That is, I take as problematic the relationship between the government and private interests, as manifested in its most organized form—the relationships between the bureaucracy and interest groups.

The decision to focus on these relationships is justified by the particular history of energy politics and the prominence of interest groups and the executive establishment in current energy events; however, this is partly fortuitous. General, theoretical considerations most compel the focus. It is easy to be led by the recent swirl of congressional activism, the spate of lobbying, and the perplexing inconsistency of legislation to pronounce energy politics a pluralist policy arena. So it may be. However, it is almost inevitable that, as energy ebbs and flows in public salience over the next several years, more stable patterns of political accommodation will emerge.[13] In the energy field stable relationships have always developed between the executive bureaucracy and producer groups, with the assent of congressional committees. There is good reason to believe that politically influential ties will continue to involve these organizations.

Interest groups and bureaucratic agencies have important sources of natural affinity for each other. Compared to other major actors in the political system—congressmen, the courts, the president and his executive office—agencies and groups are policy specialists. On a day-to-day basis they are the participants most involved with particular policies. Also, by virtue of formal organization they bring to the process greater expertise and permanence than do other actors. Theoretically they constitute the durable core of any policy arena. If we can explain the dynamics of relationships between them, and how the relationships are affected by other actors in the policy process, we have a strong foundation for understanding the politics of a problem area generally.

For reasons of theory and history, then, we approach sounder knowledge of energy politics by studying the relationships between its major organizations—its interest groups and its executive bureaucracies. This clarifies our first task. We must identify the theoretical tools that will permit us to construct explanations not only of the political behavior of these organizations individually, but also of their relationships with each other.

Turning the Theoretical Table

The theoretical literature on both interest groups and bureaucracy provides a number of promising approaches for understanding the behavior of each of these forms of organization.[14] The theoretical puzzle, however, is not how to approach these organizational forms independently, but how to understand the relationship between them. Most existing research is not very helpful because it simply does not take their relationship as problematic. Public policy research is particularly deficient in this respect; interest group behavior and bureaucratic politics are commonly studied as independent causes of policy rather than as variables to be explained.

Since the seminal work of Bentley early in this century, interest groups have been conceptualized as exogenous variables in the policy process. In his "attempt to fashion a tool" Bentley suggested that all of politics could be understood through the complete description of organized and unorganized groups. Nearly a half-century later Truman eloquently reiterated the approach with a social psychological theory of group formation and an equilibrium theory of politics. Analytical pluralism, as this approach had come to be known in the 1950s, found empirical expression in a spate of policy-making case studies, frequently focused on congressional lobbying, that invariably employed interest group activity as an explanatory variable.[15] The accumulated wisdom of these case studies indicated that group influence was a product of private resources, communication skills, and pressure tactics or strategies. The pluralist perspective has also been prominent in studies of the role of bureaucracy in the policy process. Its prevailing "bureaucratic politics" model explains presidential and executive policy making in terms of competition between interested agencies.[16] In essence, the roles of interest groups and bureaucracies have been perceived quite similarly: they supply competitive inputs to the political system and independent variables in explanations of policy outputs.

Venerable as this tradition has been in American political science, it has long had detractors. Students of other advanced industrial systems do not usually interpret the behavior of interest groups or of the bureaucracy in pluralist terms. Research on Western European countries, for example, does not find extensive competition among interest groups for access to decision makers, nor regular parliamentary lobbying in order to influence legislators.[17] The dominant means by which organized interests appear to be transmitted to public authorities is formal group participation on planning committees, advisory boards, administrative councils, and the like.[18] Interest groups are incorporated into the policy process within the bureaucracy where they assist ministers and bureaucrats in drafting legislation to be recommended to parliament, and in implementing laws once they are enacted. Their contribution is therefore not determined exclusively by their organizational or economic resources; it is also manipulated directly by the state to suit government goals. Similar characteristics have been identified in American group politics and bureaucratic behavior. In fact, relationships between interest groups and the administration are often used to support critiques of pluralist theories of American politics. Grant McConnell, an early critic of pluralism, offers a wealth of illustrations of "privileged" group access to administrative agencies—energy cases being prominent. Many scholars have documented the proclivity of regulatory agencies to become public mouthpieces for private interests.[19] Theodore Lowi explains American policy in the 1970s as government by "permanent receivership." That is, through a variety of administrative arrangements such as economic regulation, subsidy programs, and loan guarantees the government is underwriting the stability of society's largest interest groups and sharing its policy-making authority with them.[20]

Emerging in part from these American studies, but chiefly from European research, is an alternative school of thought on the fundamental issues of private interest representation and public authority. Known generically as *corporatism*, this proto-theory is gaining the same intellectual status vis-à-vis many European political systems as pluralism has traditionally had in relation to American politics. To draw the comparison briefly: pluralism envisages a society with a multiplicity of voluntary competitive groups; corporatism idealizes a limited number of compulsory, noncompetitive groups, hierarchically ordered so that single peak associations monopolize the representation of functional sectors. Pluralism assumes that private groups will compete with each other for access to government decision makers and influence over public policy; corporatism is based on official recognition of functional representatives and on formal incorporation of groups into the policy process.[21] Pluralism, finally, places faith in competition among a diversity of groups and in cross-cutting membership to achieve socially desirable policies; corporatism relies on state coordination of functionally organized interests, and on group cooperation to reach that end. If pluralism is the political analogue of a free market economy, corporatism is the political analogue of a cooperatively planned economy.

The United States hardly fits the mold of the archetypical corporatist system. The United States is not as thoroughly organized as the European cases of corporatism. For example, only about one-fourth of American workers are unionized while in Sweden over ninety percent are organized. Organizations are not hierarchically ordered into sectoral peak organizations in the United States, where even the AFL-CIO is quite imperfect, excluding such major unions as the International Brotherhood of Teamsters and the United Mine Workers. Business has three national peak associations that compete against one another, and a plethora of trade associations that engage in substantial political activity. The United States also lacks an institutional structure conducive to corporatism. Separation of powers provides the United States with an independent, vigorous Congress that is not likely to slip into complacent rubber-stamping of administration policy proposals.

It would be stretching a reasonable point, then, to classify the United States as a corporatist system—at least of the Western European form—and proceed with an analysis on those terms. At the same time, it taxes reason to accept the pluralist model of American group politics or bureaucratic behavior. The challenge to pluralist conceptions is particularly significant in the area of administration-interest group relations. Through "advisory" incorporation, selective cooperation, "biased" ground rules for participation, and outright co-optation, the administration structures group-access and influence as assuredly as does any so-called corporatist system. This is not to say that relations between the executive branch and interest groups are never open, competitive, and pluralistic. It is to say, rather, that our understanding of these relations is likely to profit if we shift our focus to the role the government plays in structuring them. Interest group activity should *not* be the exogenous variable in explanations of policy making. The equation should be reversed; the theoretical table should be turned. The influence of private interests should be studied as a dependent variable; the policy needs of the government and the actions of the administration in pursuit of them should become the primary explanatory candidate.

Interpreted in this manner the corporatist model provides the theoretical point of departure for this study. By simply underscoring an often overlooked fact of modern policy making, it suggests a way of resolving the theoretical problem of linking the behavior of interest groups and the bureaucracy. We may build on the recognition that the bureaucracy is not a passive recipient of group demands, but rather that it actively encourages, impedes, and otherwise manipulates group participation. In the next chapter I construct a framework-cum-theory to handle the new questions prompted by a corporatist perspective.

The Book in Brief

The largest systematic data source for this study is a survey of seventy-three interest groups that were active in national energy politics throughout the 1970s. In each of these interest groups (listed in Table 1.1) I identified a respondent who specialized in executive branch liaison. The respondents were interviewed from June to August 1978, following a detailed questionnaire (Appendix A), in personal meetings ranging in length from forty minutes to two hours.[22]

The sample is not random, but representative, based on eight "functional interests"—a concept I shall elaborate in the next chap-

TABLE 1.1
Participating Organizations by Function

Environmental Groups

Critical Mass
Environmental Action Incorporated
Environmental Policy Center
Friends of the Earth
National Parks and Conservation Association
Natural Resources Defense Council (NRDC)
Public Interest Research Group (PIRG)
Sierra Club
Union of Concerned Scientists (UCS)

Consumer and Public Interest Groups

Citizen-Labor Energy Coalition
Common Cause
Congress Watch
Consumers Union
Energy Action Committee
Energy Policy Task Force of the Consumer Federation of America (CFA)
National Taxpayers Union (NTU)
New Directions
Tax Reform Research Group

Petroleum and Natural Gas Industry

American Gas Association (AGA)
American Petroleum Institute (API)
American Petroleum Refiners Association (APRA)
Ashland Oil, Inc.
Clark Oil and Refining Corporation
Council of Active Independent Oil and Gas Producers
Exxon Corporation
Gulf Oil Corporation
Major International Oil Corporation (anonymous)
National Oil Jobbers Council (NOJC)
National Petroleum Refiners Association (NPRA)
Natural Gas Supply Committee
Shell Oil Company
Society of Independent Gas Marketers of America (SIGMA)
Standard Oil Company of California
Sun Company

Electric Power

American Mining Congress
American Nuclear Energy Council (ANEC)
American Public Power Association (APPA)
Atomic Industrial Forum (AIF)
Edison Electric Institute (EEI)
National Association of Electric Companies
National Association of Regulatory Utility Commissioners (NARUC)
National Coal Association (NCA)
National Rural Electric Cooperative Association (NRECA)

TABLE 1.1—*cont.*

Conservation and Renewable Energy

American Institute of Architects (AIA)
Consumer Action Now
Institute for Local Self-Reliance
National Association of Home Builders (NAHB)
National Congress for Community Economic Development
Solar Energy Industries Association (SEIA)
United Technologies, Inc.

Labor Unions

American Federation of Labor—Congress of Industrial Organizations (AFL-CIO)
American Federation of State, County and Municipal Employees
International Association of Machinists and Aerospace Workers
International Brotherhood of Teamsters, Chauffeurs, Warehousemen, and
    Helpers of America
Oil, Chemical, and Atomic Workers International Union
United Automobile, Aerospace and Agricultural Implement Workers:
    International Union (UAW)
United Mine Workers of America (UMW)
United Steel Workers of America

Commercial Energy Users

American Public Transit Association (APTA)
American Trucking Associations, Inc. (ATA)
Americans for Energy Independence
Association of American Railroads
Business Roundtable
Chamber of Commerce of the United States
Electricity Consumers Resource Council
Industrial Energy Users Forum
Motor Vehicle Manufacturers Association of the United States, Inc.
National Association of Manufacturers (NAM)
National Farmers Union (NFU)
Petrochemical Energy Group (PEG)
Transportation Association of America (TAA)

Financial Institutions

American Bankers Association
National Savings and Loan League

ter—that together embody most of the major lines of conflict in energy politics. The groups selected within each of these categories are representative in several senses. They always include the largest and most politically active groups in each sector—the American Petroleum Institute and the National Coal Association, for example. They represent exhaustively those categories, such as labor and environmentalists, with relatively small populations of groups concerned with energy matters. They are selected randomly from distinct sub-populations when the category has a large group population. The oil and gas industry, for example, is represented by at least eighty groups in Washington, of which many espouse very different interests. The sample provides for groups representing major oil corporations, independent oil producers, small refiners, distribution companies, gasoline stations, and other specialties. Finally, the sample's representativeness is enhanced by allowing the number in each category to vary according to the size of the active group population in the sector. These procedures, which are detailed completely in Appendix B, provide a sound empirical base for studying the group politics of energy.

In the next chapter I develop the general theoretical framework for explaining relationships between interest groups and the executive bureaucracy, and derive from it several general propositions regarding these relationships. The propositions are tested by way of an overview of the political behavior of the groups in the sample. The tests validate the theoretical approach for use in the remainder of the study. In Chapter 3 the theoretical model is integrated with the national energy policy-making system. The theory suggests that political relationships will vary predictably across executive policy-making activities. The many activities of the energy bureaucracy are therefore reduced to categories that theoretically ought to display significantly different political relationships. If these differences do in fact occur, and if they are adequately explained by the theory, we then have a general basis for understanding the organizational relationships that underpin executive policy making, and for predicting the conditions under which they are likely to change. In any event, the theory creates a manageable means for investigating and interpreting the complexity of energy politics.

Chapter 3 also introduces four executive energy functions—nuclear regulation, oil regulation, research and development subsidization, and energy planning—selected for further study because of their importance in ameliorating the energy problem and their utility in evaluating the theory. These functions organize the empirical analysis. In Chapter 4 nuclear power regulation by the Nuclear Regulatory Commission is examined. Chapter 5 investigates oil price and allocation regulation, administered first by the Federal Energy Administration and after October 1977 by the Department of Energy's Economic Regulatory Administration. Chapter 6 probes a nonregulatory function—policy making for research, development, and demonstration—handled first by the Energy Research and Development Administration and later by the Department of Energy. Chapter 7 takes a look at executive policy making on the grandest scale—the formulation of legislative policy proposals. Particular attention is focused on the development of President Carter's National Energy Plan.

Each of the case studies follows the same format. First, the relationships between the executive bureaucracy and the sample constituency of seventy-three groups are fully described. Then, the propositions generated by the theory are subjected to two different types of tests. One test evaluates explanations of group behavior and employs the principles of large N design and probabilistic inference. That is, variation across the sample in group behavior is explained by concomitant variation in independent variables across the groups. The other type of test is used primarily to explain bureaucratic behavior and is based on intensive longitudinal case study. Each case study examines the behavior of a bureaucracy over the five-year period, 1973–78. The longitudinal focus permits temporal variation in agency behavior and in the theoretical variables to be identified. Hypotheses relating bureaucratic behavior to the contextual variables are tested by identifying temporal covariation, and then "controlling" for other causes by comparing temporal patterns in other variables, and by intensive "process tracing."[23] Each case thus stands on its own as a test of the general theory. In the concluding chapter the cases are compared for consistent findings.

In the end we will do more than understand how recent decisions have been made in four important policy areas. We will also have uncovered more than the particular political relationships that characterize them. The larger objective is to have developed a general basis for predicting how the relationships among the most organized political actors will respond to various substantive and political changes. In accomplishing that objective we will have a sound theoretical foundation for anticipating where politics is likely to lead American policy in its response to the ominous energy gap.

2

AN ORGANIZATIONAL THEORY
OF POLITICAL INFLUENCE

The major premise of this book is that modern energy politics must be understood in terms of the relative influence of numerous groups contending for protection or promotion by the government. Historically, more parsimonious explanations were plausible. Market forces established the important contours of traditional energy politics.[1] Interdependence among energy interests was minimized, conflicts were limited in scope, and promotional policies were justified with the economic growth produced by cheap energy. Today the market does not provide an easy basis for cooperation between energy producers and the government. Instead, it creates a situation of complex political interdependence in which energy policy cannot be formulated or executed without resolving difficult tradeoffs. The policy compromises that have been and will be reached are not apparent in the structure of energy markets. To understand these compromises, and the politics that produces them, we must identify and explain the leverage exerted on the government by a host of private and social interests. The task is complicated, but the premise that necessitates it is compelling.

To simplify the task we should focus our attention on organizations. That is, we can reasonably hope to identify the core of energy politics in the behavior of, and relationships between, *organized* private and public interests. In particular, if we understand the mutual influence of interest groups and the bureaucracy we have a firm foundation for understanding energy politics generally. In its empirical focus, then, my approach to the puzzle of political influence posed in the major premise is organizational.

In its theoretical method the approach is also organizational. To explain the contributions of interest groups to energy politics I acknowledge first the potential significance of their organizational structures. Corporations, trade associations, labor unions, and environmental groups have very different organizational structures that help differentiate their relationships with the political process.[2] The theory of political influence I shall advance is therefore partly constructed with those tools of rational analysis that have been demonstrated to be useful in explaining the organization of interests.[3] I propose an explanation of interest group behavior that relates the policy stakes controlled by the government to the needs of groups as organized representatives of interests. This organizational method contrasts sharply with the prevalent pluralist approach that reifies groups, and studies interests as they inhere in society and the economy.[4]

To complete the theory of political influence I take as problematic the behavior of the government toward interest groups. Specifically, I ask: what use does the executive bureaucracy make of interest groups, and under what conditions? To answer the question I build on models of bureaucracy that likewise give organizational characteristics a central role.

Based on its major assumptions, then, this approach to the complicated problem of political influence should be understood as an organizational theory. It assumes, first, that the durable exercise of political influence is accomplished through formal organizations, among which interest groups and executive bureaucracies are likely to be the most important. And it assumes, second, that the political behavior of interest groups and bureaucracy can be best understood in terms of their individual and mutual organizational needs. This chapter is devoted to explicating an organizational theory of political influence, and generating preliminary propositions.

The Theoretical Framework

The assumptions that lead us to focus our study on political organizations may appear to simplify the study of political influence considerably, if not unreasonably. In reality the opportunities for political influence remain immense and the theoretical task complex. The executive bureaucracy—which I define to include all executive branch departments, agencies, and bureaus except the President's Office—is integrally involved in the entire policy process.

The suggestion that its activities are essentially administrative is implausible in theory and in practice. In most industrial nations the bureaucracy's impact on policy formulation is as unmistakable as its effect on implementation. Even the United States Congress, with its comparative political independence, has come to rely on the executive branch for policy proposals.[5] The bureaucracy holds a theoretical advantage in policy knowledge that naturally secures for it a role in designing new policy. This role is now institutionalized in most agencies and departments in offices of "planning and evaluation" or "policy analysis." In theory, the expertise gained from proximity to established programs is used to reformulate old legislation or to formulate new. Agencies also engage in legislative liaison to smooth the political road to enactment of their proposals. Add to this the political discretion inevitably exercised by the bureaucracy in implementing necessarily "incomplete" laws, and you find the bureaucracy either in control of or in a strong bargaining position vis-à-vis the gamut of values at stake in national policy making.

Because we seek to understand political influence generally, it is of course important that the bureaucracy control substantial political stakes. It does, however, complicate the development of theory. Interest groups and bureaucratic agencies have many modes and motivations for interacting with each other. Interactions may occur through formal adversarial procedures or through informal lobbying. Relationships may be advisory and utilize public committees, or they may be close partnerships enabling groups to exchange compliance for control over regulations.[6] The motives for interactions are similarly varied. Agencies consult with interest groups for reasons ranging from political support, to informational dependence, to statutory obligation. And interest groups approach agencies for such diverse rewards as legislative alliances, implementation benefits, and long-term working relationships. If these multifaceted relationships are to be analyzed and explained in general terms, it is plainly important to first describe their variations in a parsimonious yet theoretically meaningful way.

To begin, the relationships are conceptualized in terms of two purposive dimensions: interest group initiatives and bureaucratic strategies. Each of these dimensions summarizes the actions and intentions of the respective organizations toward each other. The intersection of the dimensions describes the relationship between the bureaucracy and its interest group constituency. Although this conceptualization may seem to skirt the putative interdependence between public and private organizations, it actually faces it squarely. Many of the causes of variation in each dimension are to be found, at least hypothetically, in characteristics of the opposing dimension.

Next, the various actions and intentions that occur along these dimensions must be conceptualized and measured. Since the central concern in this analysis is political influence in a democratically accountable bureaucracy, the one feature of each dimension that demands general description is its interest composition. That is, interest group initiatives and bureaucratic strategies must be measured in terms of their representativeness.[7] The most general standards for gauging representation are democratic (or geographic) and functional.[8] The former focuses on the weights given to different geographic constituencies (e.g., congressional districts) in bureaucratic decision making while the latter concentrates on the favor shown different social, economic, or political interests. This study employs a functional concept of representation, because interest groups are organized on that basis and energy policy has revolved historically around functional conflicts. The representativeness of the NRC, for example, will be described functionally in terms of electric power producers, nuclear equipment vendors, health- and safety-conscious citizens, and electricity consumers, and not in terms of the interests of congressional districts.

The final prerequisite for theory construction is a measure of functional representation that is general enough to describe the many types and mixtures of functions that can occur in bureaucratic arenas. For that purpose it will be useful to categorize all functional interests as beneficiaries, cost-bearers, or some combination thereof. Although this dichotomy greatly simplifies the concept of functional representation, it preserves probably the paramount basis of political conflict and cooperation. All public policies provide benefits to some members of society at the expense of others, and this dichotomy is often the basis for political conflict.[9] Since bureaucracies are established around substantive policies, it is often possible to distinguish their constituents as either functional beneficiaries or cost-bearers. The NRC, for example, has environmental and safety interests as its legally intended beneficiaries, and power companies and nuclear equipment vendors as its cost-bearers. The representativeness of bureaucratic decision-making can thus be described in terms of the balance among beneficiaries and cost-bearers.

Interest Group Initiatives

Interest group initiatives are assumed, at very little risk of over-simplification, to be undertaken with one overriding purpose in mind: to secure benefits of government policy for group supporters or leaders. Specific group actions, such as submitting technical data to a team of government policy analysts or educating a program manager on the finer points of an industrial project, may be initiated for reasons less ambitious than political influence in the immediate instance. But these cooperative efforts are intended to establish good will, and ultimately to sway government decision makers toward group perspectives. Variation in interest group initiatives is conceptualized along a single continuum that varies from a participatory pattern dominated by beneficiaries to a pattern dominated by cost-bearers. In the middle of the continuum is a mixed pattern in which both beneficiaries and cost-bearers participate effectively. The political significance of these patterns is similar to the economic significance of different configurations of producers and suppliers in a private market.

The beneficiaries of a public policy are in much the same position as buyers in a marketplace. Both consume a good (be it public or private) until its marginal utility is exceeded by its price. In economic theory the buyers are assumed to be so numerous that none can affect the price through individual decisions.[10] If the buyers are few, exchanges become suboptimal for producers and a condition of market failure is said to exist. The extreme condition, where only one buyer exists, is called monopsony. In a similar sense I label as *monopsonistic* any pattern of interest group initiatives in which a single benefiting group is virtually the sole bureaucratic participant. Under such conditions the major beneficiary, like the lone buyer in a private market, threatens to control the distribution of the goods or services. *Ceteris paribus*, costs might be ignored and allocations made inefficiently. With respect to both the representation standard of functional balance and the statutory objectives of the agency, this outcome is suboptimal.

At the other end of the constituency continuum is a pattern of group initiatives similar to that of an economic monopoly. In a private market an optimal exchange for both buyers and sellers also depends on the existence of enough sellers so that none can dictate prices. For a variety of reasons this condition is not always satisfied, and a single monopolist or several oligopolists are able to extract larger profits than a competitive market would allow.[11] In the production of public goods the cost-bearers are in a position analogous to that of private goods suppliers. The bureaucratic agency that is conventionally viewed as a supplier can usefully be viewed as an economic middleman managing transactions between beneficiaries and cost-bearers.[12] The ultimate suppliers of public goods are the cost-bearers, who change their behavior, incur direct costs, or pay money to the public treasury. For example, a coal user who installs stack scrubbers can be considered the supplier of the public good of clean air. If the organized constituency of an agency comes to be represented by a single cost-bearing group, the production of public goods runs the danger of being provided on terms established unilaterally by that group. The EPA, for example, might delay and relax air quality standards if the initiatives from its functional constituency were dominated by, say, the National Coal Association. In a descriptive as well as a theoretical sense, then, *monopolistic* initiative is the appropriate label for that end of the constituency continuum controlled by cost-bearing groups.

In the middle of the continuum is the condition of perfect competition. In economic analysis competition approaches perfection as, among other things, the numbers of buyers and sellers of private goods become large. In this political analysis competition approaches perfection as the initiatives of bureaucratic constituents become functionally representative. When the occurrence of interest group initiatives is functionally balanced among and between beneficiaries and cost-bearers, it will be labeled *competitive*. Theoretically, a competitive pattern of representation is conducive to the optimal production of public goods—i.e., to a distribution of costs and benefits that provides a proportional surplus to each participant. Whether the optimal outcome does occur depends on other factors, including most prominently the strategy of the bureaucracy. Whatever the outcome, competition is an apt description of functional balance among organized participants.

The constituency dimension describes a continuous pattern of change in group initiatives. As it extends from monopsony, to competition, to monopoly it describes smooth changes: from beneficiary domination, to increasing cost-bearer participation, to balanced representation, to decreasing beneficiary participation, to cost-bearer domination. To facilitate analysis, however, it is useful to divide the

BUREAUCRATIC STRATEGIES

	Corporatist	Pluralist	Co-optive
Monopsonistic	*Corporatism*		
Competitive		*Pluralism*	
Monopolistic			*Capture*

(Left axis label: INTEREST GROUP INITIATIVES)

Fig. 2.1. A Typology of Relationships Between Interest Groups and the Bureaucracy

continuum into three ordinal categories designated by their *extrema*. When cross-tabulated with the bureaucratic strategy dimension, also reduced to a trichotomy, a three-by-three typology of relationships between interest groups and the bureaucracy is produced (Figure 2.1).

Bureaucratic Strategies

To understand these relationships it is necessary first to understand the bureaucratic strategies that contribute to them. Among the political and programmatic motivations and the passive and active tactics for accommodating interest groups is a singular basis for distinguishing between various bureaucratic strategies, whose essence can be described by the interests being favored or disfavored. As with interest group initiatives, the concept of functional representation and the distinction between beneficiaries and cost-bearers will be used to measure interest representation. Bureaucratic strategies are conceptualized as a unidimensional variable that ranges from exclusive beneficiary representation to exclusive cost-bearer representation.

This continuum subsumes several discrete strategies that have been prominent in studies of bureaucratic politics, but have never been conceptualized in systematic relationship to one another. In theory an executive agency has an infinite variety of political strategies from which to choose. Innumerable combinations of beneficiary and cost-bearer groups can be attracted into political alliances with the bureaucracy: it is important, for descriptive accuracy, to recognize the rich variety of strategies that executives play, and it is essential, for explanatory purposes, to appreciate that these strategies can be arrayed along a continuum of functional representation. Heretofore the connections between disparate types of public-private cooperation have never been drawn. For analytic parsimony, however, it is useful also to divide this continuum into three segments identified by their *extrema*—labeled corporatist, pluralist and co-optive strategies, because they denote familiar forms of political accommodation. The strategic dimension should nonetheless be understood as a continuous variable defined independent of these convenient nominal concepts.

The left pole of the continuum is characterized by bureaucratic strategies that cater exclusively to beneficiary groups. In the extreme the executive agency believes that its goals can be best accomplished by striving for a cooperative relationship with those groups that are mandated to benefit, or that stand to benefit most, from executive policy making. In a classic political exchange the bureaucracy lures the major beneficiary into a mutually beneficial association by offering it considerable control over policy implementation and substantial input into new legislative proposals. In return the bureaucracy hopes to avoid conflict and delay in the administrative process, and to receive political support with the agency's sovereigns. No encouragement, and only pro forma access to bureaucratic policy channels, is offered cost-bearing groups. A well-known example of this pattern is, of course, the relationship between the Department of Interior's Office of Oil and Gas and the major oil companies represented through the National Petroleum Council.[13] In the extreme this strategy is labeled *corporatist* because it conforms, albeit on a smaller scale, to the method of political accommodation practiced by the quasi-corporatist states of northern Europe and Latin America. The state hopes to build support for the enactment and implementation of its policies by granting privileged participation to a sectoral interest group sufficiently powerful to deliver the support of its benefiting constituency.

As we move to the right along the continuum the bureaucracy diversifies its overtures toward interest groups, gradually providing more access to, and eventually accommodating, more cost-bearing groups. At the midpoint—when the executive finds it profitable, or essential, to appease all of its functional constituents—it assembles only temporary coalitions of interests and establishes few stable bonds with organized groups. It finds more advantage in a flexible approach to its constituency, and its alliances become fluid over time. The *pluralist* label aptly describes the central tendency of this middle portion of the continuum.

The right third of the continuum is characterized by diminishing executive attention toward beneficiaries, and increasing deference toward cost-bearers. This type of behavior seems to imply that the agency cannot accomplish its programmatic and political objectives without nullifying the opposition of its cost-bearing constituents. In the extreme the bureaucracy finds the support of beneficiaries to be comparatively unprofitable, and therefore wagers its future success (or survival) on a compromise with its natural opponents. Regulatory agencies, notably in the energy field, are most commonly accused of pursuing this political strategy. The AEC, for instance, was reorganized to combat precisely this method of accommodation. Nonregulatory agencies also find it necessary to appease cost-bearers. In fact, the *co-optive* label attached to this strategy was coined by Philip Selznick to describe the bureaucratic strategy devised by the Tennessee Valley Authority.[14]

Organizational Relationships

When the strategies of the bureaucracy interact with the initiatives of interest groups, clearly distinguishable relationships develop. In terms of the typology, at least nine different relationships are determined conjointly by the two dimensions. As long as we view the effects of each dimension on the relationships as *independent*, all of these combinations are theoretically plausible. For example, it is possible for a regulatory agency to try to co-opt its opposition, rather than court its supporters, in a competitive constituency—a possibility represented by the center, far-right cell of the typology. Likewise, it is conceivable that a planning agency with a diverse, competitive constituency might prefer the simplicity and stability offered by a corporatist strategy—a relationship found in the center, far-left cell. Because the two dimensions are continuous, countless combinations other than the nominal nine in the typology are possible.

What is theoretically possible and what is theoretically probable are, however, very different matters. The actions of the bureaucracy and interest groups are not independent; they are interdependent. It is therefore necessary to consider the *interactive* effects of these organizations on the relationships between them, which leads us to expect fewer than the nine major patterns to really exist—at least in the long run. The specific reasons for this expectation cannot be stated until we understand the causes of interest group and bureaucratic behavior, but the general logic is straightforward. Interest groups have great difficulty sustaining their participation in bureaucratic politics without government encouragement or cooperation, and executive agencies are constrained in their choice of strategies by the state of interest group organizing in their environment. For example, if the executive is intent on following a corporatist strategy, those groups in an originally competitive constituency not granted privileged access to the government will eventually diminish their interactions with that bureaucracy. Similarly, a bureaucratic agency that would like to associate in a corporatist manner with its constituency will have little success if the initiatives of interest groups are monopolized by cost-bearers. These interactive effects mean that our empirical attention will probably be directed to only a few types of relationships.

The relationships that are theoretically most likely to occur are those on the main diagonal of the typology. These are also the only relationships to be independently labeled. *Corporatism* denotes a cooperative relationship between the bureaucracy and a constituency represented by the major beneficiary organization(s). *Pluralism* denotes a fluid relationship associating many groups in temporary relationships with the bureaucracy. *Capture* denotes a bureaucratic agency collaborating with the cost-bearing organization that dominates its environment. In these three cells the structure of interest group initiatives and the strategy of the bureaucracy are consistent. That is, the actions of the groups and the bureaucracy are mutually supportive in an organizational sense.

As we move away from the main diagonal, tension develops between the organizations. For example, a regulatory agency pursuing a co-optive strategy would face fewer conflicts in a constituency effectively monopolized by cost-bearers than in one that was competitive. The conflictual situations represented by the four middle-outer cells are not unlikely, the theory will show, but neither are they as probable as the politically consistent patterns on the main diagonal. Finally, the most unlikely patterns are of course those described by the bottom-left and upper-right cells of the typology. Corporatist strategies cannot coexist for long with a monopolistic constituency, and co-optive strategies are completely at odds with monopsonistic constituencies. Eventually either the constituency will change shape or the bureaucracy will relent and change its strategy.

The two-dimensional typology of organizational relationships provides the framework for the subsequent analysis, enabling us to describe complex empirical relationships in a parsimonious, theoretically useful, and normatively significant fashion. The next task is to explain in general terms the conditions under which interest group initiatives take various shapes and bureaucratic strategies follow different lines. The relationships explained in the process are at the heart of an organizational understanding of the larger issue of political influence.

Explaining Interest Group Initiatives

Under what conditions will political interests take sufficient initiative to influence the bureaucracy? This analysis approaches that central theoretical question from an organizational perspective. That is, the theory attempts to understand interest group initiatives from the perspective of an organizational leader who seeks political influence with the aid of, and subject to the constraints of, members, contributors, employees, and/or stockholders. In the economic tradition of organization theory, the theory developed here conceptualizes interest groups as voluntary collectivities of rational, economically self-interested individuals (or firms). The leader of the interest group must therefore choose political initiatives consistent with the collective and selective interests of rational supporters. These assumptions are of course rather strict for political reality, and will be carefully relaxed to provide a modified but still rigorous economic model. The key theoretical problem for an explanation of group political strategies will then emerge clearly: to specify the relationship between the different organizational maintenance requirements facing group leaders and the different opportunities to satisfy those needs provided by the government.

A Modified Economic Model

The application of economic models to interest group behavior was originated by Mancur Olson in his 1965 classic, *The Logic of Collective Action.* Working with the simple assumption that individuals are motivated only by their economic self-interest, and analyzing their behavior according to standards of rational behavior, he fairly shattered the pluralist understanding of interest groups.[15] Olson notes perceptively that the political goals of interest groups are typically public goods and that, as a straightforward consequence, rational individuals will *not* join such groups. Economic self-interest dictates rather that they take a "free ride" when benefits are made available to them, with or without their contribution—joining only for selective benefits, such as group insurance rates, or under duress, as with the closed shop for labor unions. Exceptions occur if the individuals comprising a potential organization have substantial individual interests or are few in number.[16] Interest groups then form because one individual acts unilaterally to maintain a group, or because free-rider incentives lose force.

In general, and in its exceptions, the logic of collective action runs counter to pluralist theory. Interest groups seem far more likely to arise through the provision of selective private incentives than in response to aggrieved common interests. Further, those groups that do arise for primarily political reasons are more likely to represent large, concentrated interests such as those of big business. In sum, Olson argues that the constellation of active interest groups is unlikely to be representative of the plurality of interests in advanced industrial societies.

Olson's work has been challenged on a number of fronts. It pays little attention to the creative role of leadership. It makes unreasonable assumptions about the analytic capacity of individuals. It fails to entertain noneconomic motivations for political action, and it is rather inconsistent with the hordes of "public" and private interest groups that now cover Washington, D.C., like a blanket.[17] Indeed, if we entertain Olson's omissions theoretically we arrive at very different conclusions.[18] Collective action for political motives becomes more plausible, and the predicted arena of groups more pluralistic— and realistic. But none of the challenges to Olson advances a compelling case for abandoning the rational framework of analysis altogether. In fact, recent work by Terry Moe indicates that the criticisms of Olson can be accommodated within the rational framework, without forfeiting its considerable deductive power.[19]

The modified economic approach to interest group theory begins with the purely economic model advanced by Olson: it assumes that individuals are motivated by economic self-interest and pursue it rationally.* The economic model is then modified: first, by broadening the range of motivations to include noneconomic interests; and, second, by relaxing the standards of rationality to conform more closely with behavioral reality. The modified model retains a formal structure, enabling specific deductions of organizational performance. However, the model can be described and utilized in a nonmathematical form.[20] A simple graph, consisting of several marginal cost and marginal benefit curves, represents the *economic* costs and benefits to individuals of obtaining different amounts of some public good,† x, through organized action (Figure 2.2).[21] The curve MC represents the changing cost of providing additional increments of the good, i.e., marginal costs, and is the same for each prospective member. The curve MB expresses the marginal benefit accruing to the "group" of all N prospective members. Graphically, MB is intended to represent the sum of the marginal benefit curves, MB_1, that describe the incremental benefits derived by individual members. The curves MB_1 and MB_s indicate the levels of marginal benefits received by hypothetical members with large and small interests re-

---

*Rationality is construed as requiring simply that an individual's preferences over a set of alternatives are transitive, and that his choice among alternatives will be the first in rank.

†Public goods are a diverse lot, characterized by differing degrees of "excludability" and "jointness of supply"; however, only the former attribute is theoretically relevant to the organization of interests. Following convention in group theory, a public good is here defined as any good such that, once provided to one member of some nominal group, it cannot feasibly be withheld from any other member of that group.

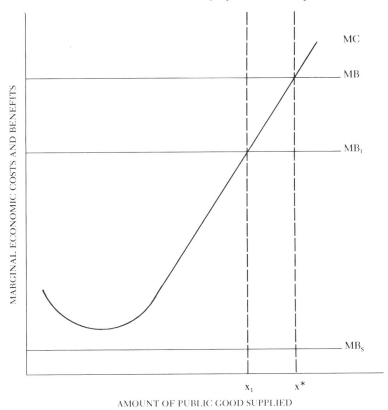

Fig. 2.2. An Economic Model of Interest Groups

spectively. The point on the x-axis labeled x* represents the optimal level of the good as determined by these marginal cost and benefit curves. It is optimal in the economic sense that the marginal cost of producing the public good is equal to the marginal benefit derived by the entire potential group if the good is provided. Amounts in excess of x* are not optimal because additional increments must be more costly to some individuals than they are materially worth. Amounts less than x* are suboptimal because net benefits for the group can still be realized through greater production. At x* the net benefits to the group are maximized.

This diagram, together with several assumptions besides rationality and economic self-interest, enables us to understand the implications of the pure economic model. The further assumptions are (1) that individuals are perfectly informed about the economic situation depicted in the figure; (2) that individuals decide the nature of their support for the group independently; and (3) that the marginal costs and benefits of public goods do generally follow the patterns described in the figure, i.e., increasing marginal costs beyond some point, and constant or decreasing marginal benefits.

The implications for collective action under these conditions are straightforward:

1. Interest groups will tend to be suboptimal in size. Small members, who are likely to dominate most interest arenas, will not join groups because the marginal cost (MC) of doing so far exceeds the marginal benefit (MB_s) at all levels of success. The size of the group, if it forms at all, is thus determined by the contribution of the largest potential member with individual incentive MB_1, and yields a suboptimal amount of the public good (x_1). If a group of larger size should form through a dues arrangement that creates economic incentives for small members, the free-rider incentive will eventually drive the group well below the optimal point.

2. Interest groups will be closer to optimality to the extent that they represent a small number of members who stand to receive substantial marginal benefits. Groups with potential membership of this sort have two ways out of the dilemma of collective action: they build on a base of individuals who have sufficient self-interest to invest heavily in collective efforts to secure public goods; and they face weaker free-rider incentives because members of small groups perceive the significance of their contribution for the provision of the public good, and suffer greater informal pressure from other members against desertion.

3. Numerically large interest groups are not likely to form or survive without selective benefits being provided to members. When marginal benefits are small and potential memberships are large, a rational, economically self-interested individual will not support a group unless his contribution provides benefits that are not associated with the public good; that is, his economic interest must be furthered selectively through material benefits that nonmembers do not receive.

These conclusions, first derived by Olson, indicate that collective political action is probably best viewed as a byproduct of nonpolitical organizing techniques. However, this strong conclusion is partly an artifact of narrowly economic assumptions. Within the same framework of public goods, rationality, and independent decision-making, very different conclusions are produced by more politically plausible assumptions:

1. Given imperfect information about the economic dimensions of collective action, rational individuals may be more likely to support interest groups. If individuals perceive the marginal benefits of collective action to be higher than is objectively the case and the marginal costs to be lower, they will be more likely to contribute to interest groups than the economic model predicts. Individuals could also misperceive these factors unfavorably, but the political efficacy of the American public suggests that net benefits will more often be overestimated and that imperfect information will increase economic incentives for membership.[22]

2. The non-economic selective benefits that individuals may derive from interest group membership increase the probability that groups will arise and prosper. In political organizations people are known to enjoy at least two broad classes of non-economic benefits: "solidary" benefits derived from the social interaction and conviviality of participation and "purposive" benefits derived from the satisfaction of good citizenship or support for a noble cause.[23] Both noneconomic benefits are selective because they can be derived only by group members, and both increase the likelihood of rational collective action for shared political goals.

3. A group leader or entrepreneur can and will increase the support for interest groups by manipulating and designing attractive packages of selective incentives. The pure economic model developed by Olson ignores the theoretical role of the organizational leader; however, the inclusion of such an individual improves the prospects of interest groups considerably. An entrepreneur can promote collective action by influencing perceptions of the efficacy of financial contributions, appealing to magnanimous instincts, establishing group activities that satisfy solidary desires, and producing material incentives at a profit to lure economically motivated members.

The modified economic model provides a formal, deductive framework, sufficiently flexible to accommodate political reality, but sufficiently constrained to permit specific predictions and explanations. Therein lies its strength: theoretical rigor without the sacrifice of political complexity. The model is not, however, without weakness, and therein begins our theoretical departure.

The rational approach has been developed primarily in order to understand the problems of organizational formation and maintenance. The implications of organizational problems for public policy and politics writ large have been drawn comparatively crudely. On issues of internal group politics theorists are careful to explore formally the consequences of information, incentives, and entrepreneurial strategies; however, on external political questions the economic models have yielded but a few broad generalizations. The pure economic approach indicates the probable upper-class bias of interest group politics, and the modified model explains the (lesser) performance of diffuse interest organizations such as environmentalists or public interest groups. By and large, however, economic theories of interest groups have been developed in a political vacuum.[24]

The political system has been conceptualized as an undifferentiated whole, and the effects of the system on interest organizations have gone largely unexplored. The consequences of varying political conditions for the political success of internally constrained groups have scarcely been considered. Economic theories try to explain the constraints without attending to the larger political factors on which these constraints often depend. For example, political entrepreneurs are constrained by the high marginal costs and low marginal benefits that individuals perceive in pursuing public goods, but this constraint undoubtedly varies in strength with the particular set of public goods being pursued and the target of political action. To describe this variation one must, of course, move outside the group to the political system. Similarly, a shrewd political entrepreneur may recognize the power of purposive incentives, but his most forceful and eloquent appeals can be muted by symbolic policies that rob an issue of its salience or by new problems that bump an issue off the public agenda.[25] Just as the political system is a major determinant of the costs and benefits of organized action, it is also a contributor to the utility of selective incentives.

The essential theoretical task is to identify probable and regular relationships between different political contexts and internal organizational constraints. Specifically, we must identify relationships between those variables that the economic model designates as theoretically significant and those characteristics of the executive bureaucracy that are likely to influence them.

Choosing Interest Group Strategies

In operational terms the political system affects interest group behavior by constraining the strategies available to group leaders who are trying both to secure public goods for their members and to maintain their organizations as politically viable. To understand the constellation of group initiatives toward the bureaucracy, we seek to understand the strategic choices of group leaders constrained by the needs of the government on the one hand and of their organizations on the other. Interest group leaders make these choices with a number of goals in mind. They want to maximize net economic benefits for their members by securing public goods. They want to maintain, if not expand, their organizations—which implies attention to non-economic and/or selective incentives. And they want to derive personal benefits—which may range from income, to power, to purposive satisfaction. To simplify our theoretical task attention is restricted here to the first two goals—producing public goods and maintaining the organization. Personal leadership goals are undoubtedly important for the formation of interest groups, but much less important to the survival and political entrenchment of interest groups—issues that are the primary concern of this study.[26]

To achieve the goals of public goods and organizational maintenance, an interest group leader has two general sets of tools to work with: external political tactics and internal membership incentives. Although this is a common distinction in organizational theory, it is not one that has generated significant political insights. In large part this occurs because the leader's choice of tools has not been viewed as being systematically constrained by the political system. Only the most general observations have therefore been drawn from the interaction of internal and external goals and tactics.[27] A reasonable case can be made, however, that the political system indeed affects leader choice in a systematic way. It clearly structures his alternative political strategies, and it limits his options among membership incentives. Ultimately it is a major determinant of interest group initiatives.

External Political Tactics

Because the goal of producing a public good is likely to determine the choice of tactics more directly than will the goal of organizational maintenance, we postulate: political strategies are chosen to provide public goods in an amount that maximizes the total net gain to the group, subject to budgetary constraints created by expenditures for organizational maintenance. How can a leader choose according to these criteria? Quite simply, he works to provide public goods as long as the marginal benefit to the group exceeds the marginal cost, or (more likely) until the organizational budget will permit no more political expenditures, whichever comes first. In other words, the leader assembles political tactics in order of decreasing net benefit until the group's political budget is exhausted. Because the monetary costs of interest group activity are substantial, and leaders are virtually compelled to weigh their options in economic terms, it is reasonable to assume that their calculations will approximate rational choice criteria such as these.[28]

The model enables us, then, to explain and predict the political strategies chosen by interest groups if we know the marginal benefits and costs associated with strategic options, and the budget constraint under which the leader must choose. *Generalizations* about the political behavior of interest groups vis-à-vis the bureaucracy or other strategic targets are possible if we can identify a general set of strategic options, complete with typical benefit and cost schedules, that interest groups regularly face. At this theoretical juncture the European corporatist perspective—i.e., viewing interest group politics from the vantage point of the government—becomes useful. The government determines many of the costs and benefits of interest group activity by structuring decision-making processes, establishing public policy, and selectively providing group access. A key, then, to predicting interest group initiatives lies in identifying regular variations in the costs and benefits of political options the government presents to groups. In the next chapter I will argue that the policy-making functions of the bureaucracy can be reduced to a few categories distinguished by their benefit-cost schedules, and that each encourages a different pattern of group initiatives. These predictions, in turn, enable the seeming morass of energy policy making to be understood in terms of several general patterns of group politics. It suffices here, however, to offer two general predictions to illustrate, and provide the basis for validating, the model.

Perhaps the most basic strategic choice faced by an interest group leader is how to allocate his political budget among major institutional targets. Should Congress be the primary focus of political activity? Or the White House? The executive bureaucracy? The courts? Public opinion? We hypothesize that the choice will depend, in any given situation, on the net policy benefits expected to result from the strategy. But how will institutional emphases vary in general? The economic theory enables a straightforward prediction of strategic differences at least between Congress and the executive branch of the federal government.

For general purposes the production of public goods can be conceptualized in terms of a linear policy-making process.[29] Before a public good can be consumed by society (and the groups that represent it), several productive phases must occur. The government must recognize the need for public action against a problem; that is, the problem must be placed on the policy agenda. A program must be formulated to ameliorate the problem. The proposal must be legitimated, or made legally binding on society, and the program must be implemented to ensure that intended outcomes actually occur. In practice this process often entails rather sharp shifts in institutional participation. The executive branch frequently dominates policy formulation and implementation, while the legislative branch controls legitimation.

At least hypothetically, the marginal costs and benefits of interest group involvement in the production of public goods vary systematically with the policy process (Figure 2.3). The marginal economic benefits of political action to an interest group are most likely to be single-peaked across the policy process. A group enjoys its first increments of benefits when a problem vexing it achieves agenda status. Because the marginal benefits of serious government attention to a problem are large relative to the status quo, the MB curve begins high.[30] Thereafter, the marginal benefits of political activity increase steadily. The formulation of a policy proposal and the legitimation of it provide benefits in increasingly larger increments. The rate of change continues to be positive until legislation—the single, most beneficial public good—is adopted. From that point the *total* benefits of group activity continue to increase, but the size of the increments decreases. The adoption of particular rules and the adjudication of specific disputes during implementation add increasingly smaller benefits to the aggregate already derived by the group.

Changes in the costs of group action essentially mirror the changes in the benefits. The costs of initial success tend to be very high because the government's behavior has to be changed qualitatively, from inaction to action. The marginal costs of effective group activity decline swiftly once the government becomes committed to seeking remedies for a problem. During the formulation of policy the costs are initially high, as groups face the obstacles of competing interests and experts in shaping the initial proposal, but as momentum is established, and the government begins seeking group cooperation, the marginal costs decline. They continue declining during

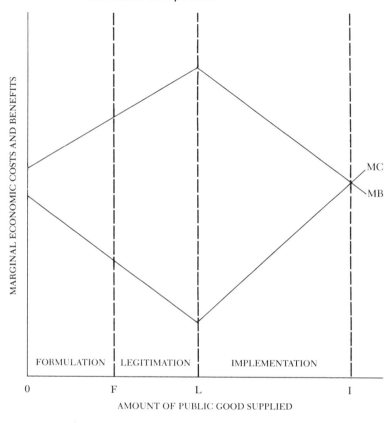

Fig. 2.3. Production Curves for the Policy Process

legitimation as group objectives shift from the construction of a detailed policy from scratch to lobbying for (or against) an established proposal. The nadir of marginal costs comes with the final enactment of legislation. During the subsequent implementation phase, marginal costs increase steadily. Each additional increment of benefits is more difficult to secure because bureaucratic policy processes are more complex; the number of crucial decisions increases; expertise becomes more important; and the possibility of protracted legal battles arises. The potential net benefits of implementation are nonetheless substantial. As marginal costs grow, however, and marginal benefits shrink, group participation grows less attractive. Ultimately some amount (L) of the public good is implemented, and efforts to secure more become suboptimal from a group perspective.

Policy making in reality does not adhere to a linear production model in which functional stages and institutional roles are neatly demarcated, but the hypothetical curves are surely reasonable as central tendencies. How, then, will an interest group leader choose his strategy for participation in the policy process? In strict economic terms, he would consider the prevailing level of supply—i.e., the amount of the public good likely to be supplied without his participation—then contribute up to the point that the group's political budget is exhausted, or the optimal amount (I) is produced. This economic calculation does not hold, however, in the political world. Because the policy process is cyclical and institutionally interactive, a leader cannot ignore formulation or legitimation processes that seem likely to be "supplied" by the efforts of others. The politically astute leaders would instead cultivate relationships with policy formulators and legislators, regardless of the prevailing level of supply. Without this complication the strategic calculation is straightforward. The leader maximizes the net benefits to his group by emphasizing participation first in formulation, then in legitimation, and finally, budget allowing, in implementation processes.

The allocation of group resources between congressional and executive liaison based on this model is plain. Congressional lobbying will be the first priority of most groups because Congress dominates the legitimation process, where net marginal benefits are maximized, and plays a consultative, if not creative, role in the formulation process. The executive bureaucracy will receive secondary attention because it shares formulation responsibilities with the White House and Congress, and its substantial implementation benefits must be sacrificed to group budgetary limits. Ironically, however, those groups that suffer less severe budgetary constraints will probably devote more resources to the Executive than to Congress. The total net benefits controlled by the bureaucracy (and associated in Figure 2.3 with the amounts L–I, and part of the amount O–F) exceed those controlled by Congress.

If the economical model is a valid representation of decision-making by group leaders, and if the marginal costs and benefits imputed to the policy process are reasonable, the following hypotheses ought to be supported empirically. First, the institutional emphasis of interest group demands ought to shift from Congress to the

TABLE 2.1
Institutional Emphasis of Group Strategies by Group Characteristic

Group characteristic	Congress		Congress and Executive equally		Executive (bureaucracy)		Total	
Resources								
Median annual								
budget ($000)	500	(21)	618	(16)	1,000	(12)	675	(49)
Median staff	15	(23)	17	(19)	22	(13)	15	(55)
Membership groups only	43%	(26)	31%	(19)	26%	(16)	100%	(61)
Membership incentives								
Primarily purposive	54%	(13)	21%	(5)	25%	(6)	100%	(24)
Substantial material	36%	(12)	24%	(8)	39%	(13)	99%	(33)

NOTE: Numbers in parentheses report sample sizes; totals are less than full sample because reliable data were sometimes unavailable.

bureaucracy as group resources increase. Second, given that a representative sample of groups ought to be dominated by "suboptimal" organizations, for most groups congressional lobbying will take priority over executive liaison. These hypotheses can be tested with data on group resources and institutional strategies provided by the membership organizations in the sample of energy-involved groups introduced in Chapter 1.

Table 2.1 reports the relationships between the institutional emphasis of group strategies—Congress, Congress and the Executive, and the Executive—and the median annual group budgets and Washington staffs. The resource data are imperfect indicators of political resources because budgets and staff are also used to provide selective membership services. They should, however, be valid indicators for this test because they are at least strongly correlated with political resources. The first hypothesis is unambiguously supported by the resource data. Groups that emphasized Executive liaison had, in the median, twice the financial resources ($1 million compared to $500,000) of groups that emphasized Congressional lobbying. Those that divided their time equally between the branches had, as expected, budgets (median $618,000) in between. Likewise, the median staff of a group that emphasized the Executive over Congress was twenty-two, but the staff of those that gave priority to Congress was only fifteen. Groups that covered both institutions equally had median staffs of seventeen. While these data do not say that group strategies are *actually* chosen according to benefit-cost considerations, they do indicate that decisions are made *as if* economic calculations are important.

The economic model is further supported by data showing that among membership groups 43 percent emphasized congressional lobbying and 31 percent concentrated equally on legislative and executive processes. In other words, 74 percent of all membership groups did not pursue their political goals optimally, through completion in the implementation process. The relationships in the table suggest that resource limitations hamper bureaucratic participation. Among all interest groups only 26 percent emphasized executive branch participation; they did indeed suffer the organizational difficulties predicted by economic models. Without resource constraints the executive bureaucracy would probably have received greater political attention.

The empirical support for these hypotheses indicates the potential of the model for understanding external group strategies in other political contexts. By studying the cost and benefit curves that are taken for granted in existing rational theories of interest groups, the strategic behavior of groups can be predicted, in large part, from government-imposed constraints. In the next chapter the model will serve to interpret the structure of group involvement in specific areas of policy making by the energy bureaucracy. Interest groups do, in fact, devote considerable resources to liaison with the energy bureaucracy. Of all the groups in this study, 51 percent reported increases in their coverage of the energy bureaucracy over the 1973-78 period and only 1 percent reported a decrease.[31] Moreover, lest the data in Table 2.1 be misconstrued, a full 57 percent of the membership groups concentrated more, or at least as much, on the energy bureaucracy as on Congress.

Internal Membership Incentives

When the external political strategies of interest groups are successful in providing public goods to group supporters, the group also furthers its goal of organizational maintenance. Membership is likely to be bolstered by the perception that contributions produce net economic gains, but political success can go only so far in sustaining an interest organization. Because political victories are rewarded with public goods, current and potential members are tempted to abandon the group and take a free ride. Group leaders must therefore supplement their political strategies with selective incentives to maintain group support. The political system directly affects the utility of certain selective incentives, however, and restricts the external strategies open to group leaders once a package of incentives has been installed.

From a systemic political perspective a sharp distinction must be drawn between material and solidary incentives on the one hand, and purposive incentives on the other. The use of the latter is likely to be constrained by political developments beyond the control of group leaders, while the use of the former is more independent of political limitations. Leaders can provide material incentives such as technical advice, publications, and group insurance as long as they can produce them profitably within the range of members and contributions they seek. The availability of solidary incentives such as conventions, local chapter meetings, and rallies is likewise limited mostly by a leader's management and business skills. The provision of selective purposive incentives is not, however, a matter of pure private business ability. The effectiveness of purposive incentives in motivating large numbers of people to support collective political action depends heavily on the political salience of the problems. For a political goal to be widely perceived as a worthy cause it must maintain visibility in the media, electoral campaigns, political debates, and social interaction. A leader can dramatize or publicize problems, as Ralph Nader did with automobile safety, but the reaction of the political system to the problem is the larger determinant of political salience.

The significance of this relationship emerges when we expand the time frame of political analysis. When we focus on the entrenchment of political interests and the long-term influence of groups, the durability of interest organizations becomes a key issue. Organizations that are unable, because of internal weaknesses, to offer sustained and substantial political support to the executive bureaucracy will be in weak, short-run bargaining positions. This is precisely the position in which groups dependent on purposive incentives are likely to find themselves. The objective stakes of interests such as environmentalists or consumers in energy issues are large and permanent, but the popularly perceived need for organized representatives of these interests is prone to vary with the visibility of energy problems on the government's policy agenda.[32] As new problems eclipse old ones in priority, or as the government satisfies popular

TABLE 2.2
Membership Incentives by Age of Groups

Date group established	Significant selective incentives			Totals[a]	Percent employing material or solidary
	Material	Solidary	Purposive		
1973–1978	9% (1)	18% (2)	100% (11)	11	27%
1963–1972	14% (2)	7% (1)	86% (12)	14	21%
1953–1962	75% (3)		25% (1)	4	75%
1943–1952	100% (5)			5	100%
1933–1942	100% (8)			8	100%
1923–1932				0	—
Before 1923	100% (19)			19	100%

N O T E : Corporations and nonmembership groups are excluded from these tabulations. Groups were coded as providing significant, selective incentives in one of three categories: (1) material, if they provided members with services, publications, or information that was valuable enough in and of itself to attract members; (2) solidary, if the cost of membership included conventions, forums, or local or chapter meetings that by themselves might attract members; (3) purposive, if the group did not provide significant material or solidary incentives, or if the group spokesman stressed the group's advocacy role as the major reason for members to join.

[a] Totals are for the number of groups in each longitudinal category. Some of the categories sum to more than the total figure because two types of incentives were judged as equally important in attracting members.

demands with symbolic policies, issues lose political salience and purposive incentives lose force. Groups that offer material or solidary incentives will be better able to survive spells of decreased political salience. In short, the probable dependence of purposive incentives on political salience ought to render organizations that rely on them less durable than those that offer other selective benefits.

This relationship is evidenced clearly in the membership organizations participating in this study. Table 2.2 classifies groups by their age and the type of selective incentives they most recently offered. A strong positive relationship exists between the age of an interest group and its propensity to provide selective material incentives. Of the thirty-six interest groups established earlier than 1963, only one does not offer significant material incentives. Among the twenty-five interest groups created since 1963, however, only three provide members with significant selective material benefits. Conversely, purposive incentives were the exclusive, or at least a very important, inducement for all of the most recently established groups, and for 86 percent of those formed between 1963 and 1972.

The availability of incentives is, of course, only an indirect indicator of member motivations, but the strength of the observed relationship is strong enough to dismiss serious questions of validity.

Without exception, old interest groups offered selective material incentives, and groups that did not offer material inducements were young. There can be little question that organizational longevity requires the provision of selective material benefits. We should expect, then, that the fledgling organizations active in energy politics will either weaken with time or begin producing nonpurposive incentives of their own. The potential political significance of this dependence will later become clear; 58 percent of the groups in this vulnerable category represent environmental, consumer, or conservation interests.

If systemic changes influence the effectiveness of membership incentives, they just as assuredly affect the choice of political strategies once an incentive system is in place. Again, the crucial distinction is between groups sustained by purposive contributions and those underpinned by material compensation. The leader of a group offering material incentives is hypothetically less constrained in choosing political strategies and issues than the leader of a purposive membership.[33] The leader of the former group knows that members will not automatically quit in response to strategic blunders, or over political disagreements, because material (or solidary) rewards are still available. He consequently worries less about the appeal of group strategies to the membership than does the leader of a purposive group. Members who derive primarily purposive satisfaction from supporting a group are likely to quit, the leaders know, for political reasons.

What effect does this constraint have on group strategies? Based on the view that purposive incentives depend upon political salience for their strength, groups that offer no material or solidary incentives will tend to pursue strategies that will promote the salience of their cause. They will choose tactics that will publicize issues and their participation in them. In institutional terms, this means they will be more prone to lobby in Congress than to try to participate in bureaucratic policy-making. Congress receives greater media attention than the bureaucracy. Congress also enables groups to involve their members in letter-writing campaigns and other grass roots activities that hold no sway with the bureaucracy. Groups that do not have to worry about maintaining visibility for their problems and organizations can become involved intimately with the executive bureaucracy without fear that members will lose interest.

This strategic hypothesis is supported by the behavior of the groups in this study (Table 2.1). Fifty-four percent of those that relied primarily on purposive membership incentives emphasized congressional lobbying, while only 36 percent of those that offered material incentives concentrated on Congress. Conversely, only 25 percent of the purposive groups emphasized the executive bureaucracy in their political strategies, but 39 percent of the materially-based groups did so. The relationship is not perfect, but it is strong. The congressional and bureaucratic arenas interact differently with purposive incentives, and therefore influence the strategic choices of interest group leaders.

As group leaders try to secure public goods and maintain their organizations, they are constrained, in their selection of political strategies and their use of internal incentives, by the structure of the political process in which they must participate. The specific effects of these constraints, we have seen, can be explained and predicted by incorporating them in a modified economic model of interest organization. In the chapters that follow we shall use this model to understand current, and anticipate future, interest group initiatives in several major areas of energy policy making. Preliminary to that, however, we must consider the other half of the public-private organizational nexus, i.e., the political strategies of the executive bureaucracy.

Bureaucratic Strategies

How do we explain variations in the strategies that different bureaucratic entities use to represent group interests? Under what conditions will a bureaucracy pursue corporatist, pluralist, or co-optive tactics toward interest groups? Why, for example, do some regulatory agencies cooperate with public interest representatives while others cooperate only with their regulated clientele? Answers to these specific questions lie in a general understanding of the behavior of the executive bureaucracy.

The hypotheses I shall offer to explain bureaucratic strategies toward interest groups are premised on the bureaucratic goals of survival or growth, and focus on external or environmental political constraints on strategies.[34] Internal bureaucratic causes of behavior toward interest groups are not explored systemically because they are likely to vary less than political environments across executive agencies. What effects different internal characteristics have on strategic interactions with interest groups will emerge inductively in the case studies. The research is designed to examine hypotheses that give causal priority to the political environment of the agency—where politically significant differences are potentially the greatest. The hypotheses are organized directly along major institutional lines. That is, the political environment of the agency affects the agency's mode of interaction with interest groups through congressional, presidential, and judicial constraints. Differences in these constraints ought to help explain why different executive agencies establish differing relationships with their interest group constituencies.

Congressional Constraints

If the bureaucracy is to accomplish its basic goals, it must be attentive to the wishes of Congress, which must appropriate funds for bureaucratic programs; approve authority to undertake new programs; confirm executive appointments and reappointments; and formally supervise policy implementation.[35] Whether the bureaucracy is formulating legislation or administering it, it must anticipate the congressional reaction. To do otherwise is to place its goals in serious risk of failure.

Any given department or agency comes to understand Congress in terms of the committee system. Since at least the early part of this century the committees of Congress have been the centers of effective legislative power.[36] A combination of factors—institutional rules, division of labor, and the weakness of political parties—have long limited the ability of Congress to operate through central direction, or to act as a unified political force. The situation became even more decentralized in the 1970s. Effective congressional power devolved, via rule changes and turnover, to a multiplicity of subcommittees.[37] Bureaucratic actors therefore interpret congressional constraints primarily through the structure and behavior of the subcommittees and committees to which they are accountable.

Bureaucratic attentiveness to congressional wishes should not imply, however, that the bureaucracy is powerless relative to legislative demands. For many reasons, not the least of which is congressional decentralization, the legislative branch has difficulty policing the executive branch. In fact, "oversight," the general term for legislative supervision of the bureaucracy, was long regarded as "Congress's neglected function."[38] Oversight did not offer congressmen the political payoffs of, say, working on major legislation or bargaining for district benefits. It had to compete for time on the tight schedules of Congress and its members. Moreover, Congress lacked the expertise and the staff to conduct oversight effectively when it chose to. Traditionally these factors combined to minimize the constraints placed by Congress on the behavior of the executive bureaucracy.

Today, however, the situation is changing. In the last decade Congress has equipped itself with the staff and analytical resources to evaluate independently the performance and proposals of the bureaucracy.[39] It has reorganized its budgetary process to allow for closer scrutiny of executive requests and to facilitate centralized analysis of national priorities. Provisions for "legislative veto," the congressional authority to reject administrative rules or decisions, are more common in legislation now than in the past. As Congress asserted its power relative to the Executive, it increased its annual enactments of legislative vetos from four or five per year around 1970 to about thirty in 1980.[40] Congressmen individually are also intervening in the bureaucracy with greater frequency. To build electoral support they appear to be playing a larger ombudsman role, untangling constituents from agency red tape.[41] Finally, to ensure that the bureaucracy never escapes evaluation, Congress is seriously considering several "sunset laws" that would automatically terminate programs unable to justify themselves after a specified period of time.[42]

The movement toward greater congressional supervision of the bureaucracy was well underway in the early 1970s. The number of House oversight hearings per congress quadrupled between 1968 and 1976, while the number in the Senate more than doubled.[43] By the end of the decade congressional reaction against administrative independence and the "imperial presidency" had become perhaps the defining quality of the institution. Before the 96th Congress convened in January 1979, it was being heralded as "the oversight Congress."[44] The conviction to reassert congressional power was reinforced by a wave of fiscal and political conservatism that began sweeping the nation in 1977, and seemingly reached fruition in the 1980 election. Multi-billion dollar federal budget deficits began to be blamed for persistent double-digit inflation, and congressional enthusiasm for new programs waned. Consistent with the trend of congressional assertiveness, bold plans for tough evaluations of existing programs emerged to fill the legislative vacuum.

How, though, do these developments affect the behavior of the executive bureaucracy? They have been expressly intended to increase congressional control over the bureaucracy. But do they? This is undoubtedly the major question raised by the changes. The question cannot be answered, however, with a simple yes or no. "Control" is a complex variable that can vary horizontally across congressional functions and vertically with levels of policy making. Control may be increasing, for example, in budgeting, but changing very little in implementation. Or, control may have strengthened at the subcommittee level, but weakened with respect to Congress as an institution.[45] The consequences of congressional efforts to control the executive bureaucracy must be analyzed, therefore, in more circumscribed terms.

Oversight may be broadly defined as any behavior by legislators or their staffs that is intended to have an impact or, regardless of intentions, has an impact on bureaucratic behavior.[46] Oversight therefore includes substantive oversight as practiced by authorization committees, fiscal oversight as conducted by budget and appropriations committees, and procedural oversight as usually handled by government operations (affairs) committees. Oversight is also a manifest as well as a latent process. It may occur through actual interchanges between Congress and the bureaucracy or it may operate through perceived threats.

How will oversight constrain bureaucratic strategies toward interest groups? I propose that congressional preferences regarding a particular bureaucratic activity are revealed through the *structure* and the *practice* of oversight. *Ceteris paribus*, the bureaucracy will attempt to accommodate those interests championed by Congress through its potential and actual oversight activities.

The structure of oversight is determined by the congressional committee system. Part of that structure is constant across all elements of the bureaucracy, and consequently cannot explain strategic variations. The administrative procedures of every executive agency are subject to oversight by the Senate Committee on Government Affairs and the House Committee on Government Operations. Similarly, every bureaucratic entity is subject to review, for budgetary purposes, by a specific subcommittee of the House and of the Senate Appropriations Committee. In the cases of both fiscal and procedural oversight the congressional structure is simple and unchanging.*

The major form of structural variation in oversight occurs in the substantive or authorizing committee system. Because of varying degrees of specificity in committee charters, single and multiple assignments of jurisdiction, differences in the substantive scope of agency missions, and assorted methods of committee decentralization, a bureaucratic agency may be subject to oversight by only one subcommittee in each house of Congress or by as many as a dozen or so subcommittees. Standing committees have also demonstrated differences in their enthusiasm for oversight responsibilities. Some encourage oversight by creating permanent subcommittees for investigations or oversight; others leave the chore to regular subcommittees.

Variations in the structure of oversight across agencies or across time ought hypothetically to affect bureaucratic relations with interest groups in several specific ways: (1) If an executive agency is subject to the authority of two or more standing committees and several subcommittees in each house of Congress, its strategy toward interest groups will tend to be *pluralistic*. (2) If, conversely, an agency falls within the exclusive jurisdiction of a single subcommittee in each house of Congress, its strategy toward interest groups will tend to be *co-optive* or *corporatist*, depending on the subcommittee composition. (3) If an agency falls within the jurisdiction of committees having special oversight subcommittees, its strategy toward interest groups will tend to be *pluralist*.

Together, these propositions express a more general hypothesis: the more heterogeneous the interests in the oversight structure, and the higher the probability that oversight will be carried out, the more likely that bureaucratic strategies will be pluralist. The logic is straightforward. If an agency recognizes that it is potentially subject to criticism from a variety of interested positions, its best defense, where interest groups are concerned, is to establish numerous and flexible relationships to provide support in different congressional contexts. This is not to say that congressional control is maximized when oversight is shared among subcommittees. To the contrary, a

---

*The individual composition of these committees and subcommittees may change and thereby encourage the bureaucracy to curry the favor of different interest groups. The effects of compositional changes are not apparent, however, in structural terms; they stem from changes in the practice of oversight and are best analyzed as such.

smart agency may be able to play the interests of one subcommittee off against the interests of another, and thereby avoid unwanted constraints.[47] But to maximize its bargaining strength an agency subject to multiple congressional sovereignty can be expected to pursue a pluralist strategy. If, on the other hand, its oversight is monopolized by a single subcommittee, an agency would be encouraged to accommodate the more homogeneous constituency likely to be represented by the subcommittee.

These hypothetical effects can be altered, of course, by the way in which oversight is actually carried out. Agencies acquire their most pertinent information about congressional interests from the practice of oversight. If, for example, oversight is confined to periodic reauthorization hearings, and is even then largely pro forma, the agency will learn that it need not be overly solicitous of the interests reflected in the oversight structure. Congressional oversight responsibilities are not carried out with uniform effort across committees. Investigations and oversight hearings consume substantial time and resources. Even in today's vigilant atmosphere, oversight is not likely to be vigorous unless a senator or congressman stands to reap some political benefit from it.

Differences in the quantity and quality of oversight make it important to look beyond structure to understand congressional constraints. Resource limitations restrict this study to the quantity issue; quality variations ought, however, to operate similarly.[48] Accordingly, I hypothesize that: (4) the more often an executive agency is subject to actual oversight activity, the more likely it is to pursue a *pluralist* strategy toward interest groups. While it is true that oversight hearings can be held to praise an agency, oversight in general, and frequent oversight in particular, is likely to be critical of bureaucratic behavior. Praise is usually reserved for appropriations or reauthorizations, or might be the essence of an occasional obligatory hearing. But when Congress becomes intensively involved in assessing the behavior of the bureaucracy, it is typically because it wants changes made in the administration or the performance of a policy. To the extent that oversight addresses the issue of interest representation, it is unlikely that agencies will be criticized for encouraging a pluralism of group inputs. The more frequent the oversight, then, the more likely it is to be critical, and the more likely the agency will be to pursue a pluralist strategy to buffer the criticism.

Together the structure and practice of oversight should constrain the relationships between bureaucracies and their constituents in these politically logical ways. Whether and how the constraints operate empirically will be evident in the case studies. The results are significant not only for what they reveal about energy policy making. They will also illuminate the general implications of the current surge of congressional enthusiasm for bringing the bureaucracy under control.

Presidential Constraints

Under the Constitution the president is charged to "take care that the laws be faithfully executed." To that end the president has been equipped with many formal powers over the executive bureaucracy. He has the authority to appoint and to remove political executives, today numbering several thousand. The annual budgetary requests of agencies must receive prior presidential approval, and final appropriations a presidential signature. The president is empowered to reorganize the bureaucracy (subject to legislative veto) to facilitate executive control. And the courts have given him almost complete discretion in directing the behavior of executive underlings, excepting only in those functions that are clearly "ministerial."[49]

The Constitution does not place the bureaucracy under the undivided control of the president. Through the "necessary and proper" clause Congress may make all laws deemed requisite for executing its enumerated powers or the powers vested in the federal government generally.[50] Consequently Congress can and does limit the formal control of the president over the bureaucracy. The Senate has the right to require its consent to executive officeholders and for the professional civil service. It can restrict executive discretion by specifying in detail how laws shall be administered and it holds powers at least equal to the president's in appropriating funds. It also has as much constitutional authority to intervene in policy implementation. Congress has used these powers, moreover, to create numerous "independent" regulatory commissions in which the president (and Congress) cannot intervene formally, which are not subject to presidential line authority, and which are not threatened by presidential removal power. In a legal sense the president's control over the executive bureaucracy is definitely shared with the Congress.[51]

The Constitution only sets the general parameters of national policy making. Within these parameters, which do provide important instruments for control of the bureaucracy, presidents may employ political methods to enhance their control. By varying their personal and institutional support for political executives in relationships with Congress, the courts, and the media, presidents can encourage cooperation. By providing or withholding effective access to the Oval Office, presidents can discipline high-level executives who hope to influence presidential decision-making. And through presidential leadership, an intangible quality stemming from personal charisma, office stature, and persuasion skills, presidents may inspire bureaucratic compliance.

Political influence has its limits, however. The federal bureaucracy is a huge organizational complex containing over one hundred major administrative entities and employing nearly three million people. Most of its policy decisions simply are of too little political consequence to command a president's attention. Presidents must allocate their time to the issues that hold substantial political significance for themselves or their party. On this point William L. Cary, an ex-chairman of the Securities and Exchange Commission, comments that "even excellent administration of the commissions will probably not help the President much politically. . . . [T]he White House is interested and involved in a regulatory matter only if there has been a scandal or wide newspaper publicity about the industry it regulates."[52]

Because of the bureaucracy's sheer size and the civil service regulations that rule it, presidential influence may have difficulty penetrating below the upper layer of presidential appointees. Formally, the president exercises control through a chain of command that extends (except in the case of independent commissions) into the bowels of the bureaucracy. But presidential power to direct even the upper echelon of employees governed by civil service rules (i.e., more than 6,000 persons holding "supergrade" and "executive schedule" positions) is substantially circumscribed. Prior to the Civil Service Reform Act of 1978 executive positions were rigidly classified as either career (about 90 percent of executive jobs) or noncareer (about 10 percent), limiting a president's ability to fill crucial jobs with cooperative personnel. Further, recalcitrant or inept career executives could not be reassigned, let alone dismissed, without extensive proceedings. And financial compensation could not be linked to job performance. Since the reforms were implemented in 1979 the president and his appointees have acquired greater formal control in these areas.[53] Those changes have failed to reverse the command problem that existed while this study was being conducted and that still persists. Central executive direction of bureaucratic behavior depends mostly on the political power and leadership of the president and his major appointees.

Relationships between the bureaucracy and interest groups are one important facet of bureaucratic behavior that a president hopes to influence. Besides issuing commands, the president can exploit the bureaucracy's need to build political support. If an agency believes it can acquire strong presidential backing, or at least avoid express rebuke, it may cooperate by accommodating groups that the president favors politically. At the same time, however, an agency prefers flexibility in choosing its interest group allies. The bureaucracy has goals and interests apart from, and more durable than, those of the president; interest group relationships are important for their achievement. In all likelihood, any trade-offs between allegiance to and independence from the president will be settled in favor of the latter unless the president takes a strong and active political interest in the bureaucratic function. Presidential wishes transmitted only through the formal authority of the presidency are unlikely to constrain bureaucratic behavior. Unless the president has a substantial stake in agency decisions and exerts political pressure on behalf of his interests, an agency's preference for unconstrained relationships with its constituency will probably prevail.

This aspect of presidential influence could be observed, if it is true, in the behavior of agencies that differ in priority on a president's policy agenda. Higher priority agencies would appear more constrained than lower priority agencies. In the case of energy, however, this cannot be observed, or tested, because the behavior of the energy agencies has been a major concern of every president since the oil embargo of 1973. Hypothetically, presidential interests were a potentially important constraint on the behavior of the energy bureaucracy throughout the last decade. But this does not mean that the influence of presidents upon the strategies of the bureaucracy cannot be gauged and understood. Presidential constraints are not simply dichotomous or nominal in their effects. We are not concerned purely with whether an agency is constrained or unconstrained. Rather, we are interested in how the composition of accommodated interests is shaped by presidential interests.

To this end we "control" for the degree of presidential political effort in a sphere of bureaucratic policy making, and concentrate on the various effects of presidential constraints. The following effects, derived from the preceding generalizations about presidential influence, should be observable in the energy bureaucracy where presidential attention has been strong.

1. Bureaucratic strategies toward interest groups should be less constrained by the president, the lower the level of the bureaucratic hierarchy at which they are pursued. This effect should manifest itself in two ways. First, when the presidency changes hands, bureaucratic relationships with interest groups should show more rapid and more substantial change at the top of the bureaucracy than at lower levels of executive decision making. Second, the cumulative effect should entail a *pluralist* strategy among political executives and a *co-optive* or *corporatist* strategy among subordinate and career executives.

2. The correlation between presidential interests and the interests accommodated by the bureaucracy should weaken at successively lower levels of the bureaucracy. This hypothesis is a substantive corollary of the first. The probable fluidity of upper-level relationships will encourage cooperation with interests favored by the president, while the probable entrenchment of lower-level relationships ought to sustain cooperation whether favored by the president or not.

3. "Independent" agencies should appear less constrained in their behavior toward interest groups than agencies under presidential line authority. If the formal independence of agencies such as the Nuclear Regulatory Commission has political significance, it ought to buffer the agencies against presidential preferences regarding the treatment of particular interests.

These hypotheses are fairly straightforward extensions of conventional wisdom about presidential influence to the issue of interest group politics, but their validity is far from certain. Empirical research into presidential control of the bureaucracy is sparse and unsystematic; research into the limited area of executive cooperation with groups is spottier still.[54] The tests conducted in this study are empirically reliable and systematic, but they are limited to the energy bureaucracy. The results cannot be interpreted, therefore, as a general indication of the workings of presidential control; they are nonetheless important for offering valid measures of the sensitivity of organizational influences in energy policy to presidential leadership.

Judicial Constraints

When the bureaucracy implements public policy it establishes law. By promulgating general rules and adjudicating specific cases the bureaucracy gradually fills in an area of legal rights and obligations with standards, criteria, and precedents. Not all implementation actions—e.g., persuasion, guidance, and threats—constitute law, but the durable structure of a policy is determined by countless and various decisions that are legally binding and, as such, are always subject in principle to judicial review. Moreover, since the initiative for judicial review usually comes from the bureaucratic constituency, the bureaucracy is potentially constrained by the courts in its relationships with interest groups. Agencies typically do not benefit politically from frequent court battles over their decisions. Supporters of the private party may object loudly in Congress, in the media, or even in mass demonstrations. Less partial observers may denounce the agency for the high litigation costs it imposes on the treasury. A politically prudent agency recognizes the avenues of appeal open to its constituents, and is therefore constrained by the judiciary in its relations with them.

The courts generally affect administrative behavior by reviewing agency decisions on grounds of procedural and substantive due process. If the agency hopes to avoid litigation (and provide justice) it must bring its decision-making processes and statutory interpretations into line with the views of the federal courts. In anticipation of, or as a result of, judicial decisions in favor of the procedural or substantive claims of particular interests, an agency may be more accommodating to those interests. This does not mean, however, that every interest with the financial means to litigate (including most of the groups in this study) will be accommodated by the agency. The courts do not look with equal favor on the claims of every interest affected by an agency. Those interests favored by the courts are more likely to be accommodated by the agency than those interests not so favored.

A priori, judicial constraints appear to operate through three types of court decisions: (1) determinations of "standing," (2) rulings on "reviewability," and (3) decisions on the merits of a case.[55] Each of these decisions hypothetically constrains administrative agencies in their relationships with interest groups.

1. The more liberal the rules of standing established by the courts,

the more interests are eligible (by definition) to sue an agency and, consequently, the more likely it is that an agency will pursue a *pluralist* strategy. In most statutes eligibility to sue an agency over an implementation decision is not unambiguous. When courts rule on standing they indicate which interests have a legitimate stake in an issue and, similarly, which interests an agency must consider a threat to litigate. To reduce the probability of litigation, an agency has incentive to accommodate groups with standing to sue.

2. The more likely the courts are to accept responsibility for judicial review of agency decisions, the more likely the agency is to pursue a *pluralist* strategy. Not all legally binding decisions of administrative agencies are subject to judicial review. On matters of substantive interpretation, in fact, the courts are inclined to accept an agency's exercise of discretion.[56] Unless Congress specifies clear rules and standards for implementation, the agency has considerable, legitimate latitude in choosing courses of action. Courts are more likely to review administrative actions on grounds of procedural impropriety. The Administrative Procedures Act establishes mandatory procedures for formal and informal rule-making and adjudication. If interest groups (or individuals) can raise doubts whether appropriate processes were followed, judicial review may be granted. Evidence of the operation of this constraint should be found in agencies bound by different procedural rules or endowed with different degrees of discretion. The frequency of accepted court appeals should vary across these agencies, as should the pluralism of bureaucratic strategies.

3. The more numerous the judicial decisions in favor of different interests, the more likely the agency is to pursue a *pluralist* strategy. To minimize judicial interference with policy administration, an agency is likely to try to accommodate groups that have successfully challenged its decisions in the courts. An antagonistic or exclusionary posture toward groups will prove unacceptable in political terms if those groups are able to battle the agency successfully in the courts. Eventually agencies will find greater political benefit in establishing a working relationship with groups effective at litigation.

Summary

This chapter was built on the premise that political influence can be understood best by studying the relationships between the major organized representatives of public and private sector interests. To that end a theoretical framework has been developed for conceptualizing and explaining the relationships that evolve between executive bureaucracies and interest groups. Included in it are a two-dimensional typology of relationships determined by interactions between interest group initiatives and bureaucratic strategies, and two sets of hypotheses to explain variations along these dimensions. The hypotheses indicate the considerable potential effect that the government has on the structure of its relationships with interest groups. Indeed, the resulting explanation of these relationships amounts to a virtually complete turn of the prevailing theoretical table on these matters.

To test this theoretical approach I have derived or identified specific hypotheses concerning the probable effects of government-controlled variables. Several of the hypotheses were supported by the general political behavior of the interest groups in the study. In the next chapter I will integrate the theoretical framework and its hypotheses with the energy policy-making system, and demonstrate how the course of energy policy can potentially be explained and anticipated. The validity of the individual hypotheses, and the utility of the organizational approach generally, will be evaluated in the empirical cases. Let us return, then, to the problem of understanding political influence in the complex arena of energy policy.

3

ORGANIZATIONAL CHANGE
AND ENERGY POLICY

Why does the organizational theory of political influence provide an especially promising means for understanding national energy policy? It does so, quite simply, because it focuses on the behavior of large corporations, executive agencies, and interest groups—organizations that have long been prominent in U.S. energy policy—and proposes general explanations of their contributions to public policy. The purpose of this chapter is to demonstrate precisely how the theory may aid explanation in the energy field.

The demonstration proceeds chronologically. First, the historical roles of interest groups and the bureaucracy in energy policy are examined. A brief overview of past major programs will show that the goals and actions of organizations are necessary components of any explanation of historical energy policy. Second, the American response to the 1973 oil embargo and its aftermath is studied for evidence of significant organizational contributions. The highlights of this recent period will reveal that, indeed, several processes of organizational change—including bureaucratic and congressional reorganization, and interest group proliferation—were among the most important developments in energy politics during the 1970s and warrant a central place in explanations of current energy policy. Finally, the immediate future of national energy policy is considered. That is, how will energy policy already enacted be carried out, and what major policy initiatives are likely to emerge from the policy-making system now in place? The organizational theory of political influence will be used to generate substantive propositions responsive to these questions. Although the propositions will not be tested in this chapter, they will plainly illustrate the promise of the organizational approach to energy politics.

Energy Policy Past

In the fall of 1973 the Arab OPEC nations imposed an embargo on oil exports to the United States and other nations supporting Israel in the Yom Kippur War. Although the cutoff reduced normal American energy supplies by only 5 percent, its effects were calamitous. The immediate hardships included 25 percent higher fuel prices and lengthy lines at filling stations. The aftermath was worse yet; it brought inflationary and recessionary side-effects unprecedented in the post-World War II era.[1]

How could the United States have left itself so vulnerable to a temporary and relatively small supply interruption? A partial answer is provided by the element of surprise. American policy makers did not fully anticipate the readiness or ability of the Arab cartel to use oil exports for political leverage against Israel.[2] But faulty forecasting, however genuine a difficulty, cannot nearly explain the susceptibility of the United States to energy-based problems.

In retrospect it is clear that the original energy crisis was not a simple matter of being caught off guard. American energy vulnerability has deep and tenacious roots. The federal government had known as early as the mid-1960s that domestic oil and gas production were at or near their peaks.[3] By the mid-1970s the limits were confirmed and the unreliability of foreign supplies also demonstrated. By the late 1970s ample time had surely passed to manage any problems truly rooted in an unfortunate surprise. Yet, a severe gasoline shortage rocked the country in 1979, and OPEC price increases helped saddle the economy with chronic double-digit inflation that endures in the 1980s.* The persistence and intensification of these symptoms of vulnerability underscore the depth of the problem, and indicate the need to consider causes in the more distant past. As history reveals, the recent failure of U.S. energy policy to offer foresight, comprehension, and change has considerable precedent.

Prior to the oil embargo of 1973 the United States lacked an express, national energy policy. A durable set of priorities was never articulated. A single energy authority was never established in the executive or legislative branches. Issues of obvious relevance to a

---

*The 1979 crisis demonstrates the seriousness of American vulnerability better than the 1973 crisis because surprise played less of a role and the economic repercussions were more severe. The Iranian revolutionary upheaval behind the 1979 shortage provided far more notice than the Yom Kippur War, and the resulting price increases were more than twice as large in absolute terms in 1979.

national policy, such as demand management and emergency pre-paredness, were all but ignored. Many federal policies, to be sure, affected energy supply and demand, but these policies were tradi-tionally designed and implemented in relative isolation from one another. For instance, the major policies governing fossil fuels—i.e., oil, natural gas, coal, and nuclear power—were enacted and admin-istered without any explicit attention to the relationships between them.[4]

Despite the absence of a central policy or apparatus *per se*, the United States did possess at least the semblance of a national energy policy. A number of prominent federal programs had similar effects on the energy situation and therefore gave the appearance of a coordinated policy. Import quotas, prorationing, and tax incentives such as the depletion allowance and the foreign royalty deduction subsidized the oil industry.[5] Federal research and development, ra-dioactive fuel processing, and liability protection encouraged nucle-ar power development.[6] A number of programs promoted cheap prices and high demand for energy. Interstate natural gas rates were regulated below market levels (though not until the 1960s), thereby stimulating the profligate use of gas as a heating fuel.[7] The burning of copious amounts of oil for transportation and power generation, and the extensive use of electricity in homes and industry were similarly encouraged; oil prices were moderated by foreign policies that maximized production abroad, and electricity costs were de-pressed, especially for large users, by federal subsidies and promo-tional rates.[8] These assorted programs gave the overall appearance of a national policy, consistently attempting to stimulate energy production and consumption.

Justification for such a policy was not lacking. For years it was possible to subsidize energy producers without overburdening ener-gy users, and to generate rapid economic growth in the process.[9] Because economic growth could be so widely enjoyed, the govern-ment possessed a unifying goal around which a national policy could be built. The appearance of such a policy, however, is deceiving. Inconsistencies were in fact rampant in historical energy programs, and national goals were not paramount in the creation of those programs consistent with economic growth.

In the 1960s and 1970s the Federal Power Commission (FPC) encouraged the consumption of natural gas in interstate markets such as the Northeast, but encouraged its production only for intra-

state markets such as Texas and Louisiana. The source of this inconsistency, which produced several winter gas shortages, was not national policy. Rather, wellhead price regulation began in 1954 when
the Supreme Court required it, pursuant to the 1938 Natural Gas
Act, and continued until 1979 largely through the political pressure
of Northern consuming interests.[10] Bureau of Land Management
administration of federal lands was inefficient in exploiting coal and
oil resources. Permissive leasing policies effectively delegated control over the rate of development to private companies.[11] The Army
Corps of Engineers and generations of Western congressmen established the country's hydroelectric power without regard for national
energy goals. Logrolling and classic "porkbarrel" politics account
best for the development of that energy source.[12] Nuclear electrical
generation does not owe its swift progress to its superior potential as
an energy source. Generous nuclear subsidies are more consistent
with the political autonomy of the promoters of nuclear power—the
Joint Committee on Atomic Energy and the Atomic Energy Commission—than with national energy goals. Indeed, most federal programs that affected energy supply and demand—like important
others such as rural electrification, public power marketing, and
environmental and safety regulation—originated and survived without substantial influence from national energy goals.

Extensive as the support for this negative conclusion surely is, it
does not immediately suggest a positive alternative. Of course, a
general explanation for past energy policies is unlikely, or at least
unlikely to be parsimonious, given the diverse historical circumstances in which they emerged. Nonetheless, several political factors
can be identified that are common to their development and are also
particularly striking in the unfolding of oil policy. As an illustration
of general political patterns, and equally important for background
on the governance of America's major energy source, the history of
oil policy merits closer attention.

The Reasons for Past Policy: Evidence in Oil

Major government involvement in the production and consumption of oil began during World War I.[13] Because of oil's crucial role
in the war effort, President Woodrow Wilson sought the cooperation
of the leaders of the industry to allocate oil supplies between domestic and military needs. Organized as the National Petroleum War

Services Committee, oil executives assisted the United States Fuel Administration in its efforts to ensure adequate petroleum supplies for America and British war vessels and for ground transportation. This was accomplished through company pooling agreements that coordinated production, distribution, and, in the process, prices. The Federal Trade Commission criticized this method as a restraint of trade, but the arrangement continued through the war years. The corporate members of the War Services Committee evidently enjoyed the stability and predictability of cooperative self-management, and tried to persuade Wilson to maintain the committee in peacetime.[14] When Wilson chose instead to disband the Fuel Administration and the Committee shortly after the war, the industry quickly reconstituted the committee as its private trade association, the American Petroleum Institute (API). For its first president it installed Mark Requa, the former leader of the Fuel Administration. This early episode is significant for two reasons. First, it reveals the oil industry's longstanding objective of stability through limited competition.[15] Second, it illustrates the cooperation that has frequently characterized the relationships between the government and the oil industry.

After the Teapot Dome scandal of 1922, cooperative relations between the industry and the executive branch temporarily broke down. The oil industry did not cease benefiting, however, from public policy. In 1926 it gained one of its largest government subsidies. Widespread fears of a shortage prompted Congress to legislate a 27½ percent depletion allowance against corporate taxes to encourage oil production. The policy was truly generous; it offered drilling incentives on top of already lucrative "expensing" write-offs in the tax laws.[16]

Industry cooperation with the executive branch resumed during the New Deal. The National Industrial Recovery Act (NIRA) of 1933 offered major oil companies a welcome opportunity to use government authority in their latest bout with excessive competition. The tax incentives of the 1920s had interacted with record East Texas oil discoveries at the end of that decade to stimulate almost frantic oil production by companies of all sizes. As supplies rose and the Depression reduced demand, oil prices plummeted to a low of ten cents a barrel. To combat these developments the major companies pursued a two-pronged strategy that began with demands on the governments of oil states and culminated with negotiations with the Roosevelt administration.

The state governments were natural, initial targets because they shared with major oil an interest in slower development than the existing reserve ownership laws were encouraging. Oil and gas ownership in the United States was premised on the "rule of capture," and entitled landowners to all the oil they could pump from reserves lying beneath their properties.[17] When an oil reserve lies beneath the property of several landholders, each owner has the incentive to produce as much oil as quickly as possible to prevent neighboring owners from "capturing" it. This incentive benefits consumers in the short run with low prices. In the longer run, however, rapid exploitation is arguably inconsistent with social interests. Oil is definitely not recovered to the extent that is physically possible, and unmarketable oil is frequently dumped. In broad view, these practices are not efficient uses of capital and labor. Apart from major oil's concern with profitability, then, state governments had reason to advocate a general interest in conservation.

Beginning in 1916 the large companies tried to persuade Oklahoma and Texas to adopt policies to limit production competition. At first the majors advocated "field unitization" laws that would force all owners of land over a new oil reserve to pool their resources and develop the field cooperatively. This plan was opposed by independent drillers and was never passed. Until the Depression and record discoveries coincided to underscore the wasteful consequences of existing law, the states were unable to act. Finally, in the ostensible interest of conservation, major oil-producing states adopted policies of market prorationing. In essence, these policies regulated competition by limiting the daily production of oil wells to a fraction of the maximum efficient rate. States determined the proration fraction by estimating monthly state demand and calculating the supplies necessary to bring a just profit and maximize the long-run output of the field.[18]

Prorationing did not solve the industry's problems, though, because it encountered compliance problems. In the late 1920s independent producers in Oklahoma succeeded in having the law declared unconstitutional. A federal court soon reversed the decision, but not until violence among competing drillers broke out in the oil fields and martial law was declared. Similar events attended the Texas Railroad Commission's efforts to implement prorationing; federal troops had to occupy the East Texas field until the Supreme Court upheld that state's right to sustain a higher price through regulation. Judicial support was not sufficient, however, to make the system work. Without coordinated proration fractions across all producing states, interstate competition with unregulated states would drive the price down and effectively undermine the system. The prorationing states therefore sought federal enforcement and coordination of prorationing.

The National Industrial Recovery Administration (NIRA) was the first source of hope for the management of competition through prorationing. Under the National Recovery Act Roosevelt delegated responsibility for developing a federal solution to an NIRA board dominated by the American Petroleum Institute. Because of company differences, however, API members could not agree on whether the federal government should set mandatory production quotas. They agreed instead to ask the (pro-major oil) Department of Interior to enforce NIRA prohibitions against the interstate shipment of "hot oil"—i.e., oil produced in excess of state fractions. The request was granted, but soon became a moot point; the NIRA was declared unconstitutional in 1935.

The end of the NRA caused a good deal of concern in the API. Its demise meant an end to major oil's legitimate incorporation in the administrative decision-making processes that enforced quotas and thereby fixed prices. The API feared that the cooperative arrangement might be replaced by strict federal regulation, which would in turn minimize their discretion over production and prices. To avert this possibility the API supported a plan, advanced by the state of Oklahoma, to create an Interstate Compact to Conserve Oil or Gas. The treaty, which included all the major oil-producing states, was approved by Congress in 1936 and finally made the regulation of supply and price effective. It reinforced the Connally Hot Oil Act, enacted the previous year at the industry's urging, which prohibited interstate hot oil shipments. The API preferred this plan to federal regulation because it vested prorationing power in the state governments where sympathy for the industry's stability and profitability goals was greatest.

Until but a year before the 1973 oil crisis, the Compact held proration fractions below 100 percent, and thereby controlled prices at a higher level than would have existed under free market conditions. For nearly four decades, then, oil regulation worked to transfer income from consumers to the petroleum industry.[19] American consumers may now be enjoying some delayed benefit from those oil policies, but current and diffuse rewards cannot explain the choice of policies a half-century in the past. The pattern of political pressure that brought the oil regulations into being, and the concentration of immediate regulatory benefits on the oil industry, indicate that the prosperity of the established oil companies was the central purpose of early oil policy. Conservation of natural resources was but a convenient justification.

The oil industry's close relationship with government continued unperturbed until at least the early 1970s. During World War II major oil representatives were incorporated into the government's fuel-supply planning body, and anti-trust policies were suspended to permit a pooled industry effort. After the war, President Truman reorganized the Interior Department, taking petroleum responsibilities away from the Bureau of Mines and vesting them in an independent Oil and Gas Division. To assist the new office, Truman also created the National Petroleum Council (NPC), an advisory committee composed of the presidents of the major oil companies, representatives of petroleum trade associations, and some independent petroleum refiners and producers. In effect it institutionalized the channels of communication and patterns of cooperation that had existed formally during the wars and in the NRA, and informally at other times.

The significance of the relationship and the political value of the independent Office of Oil and Gas became particularly evident with the creation of the Mandatory Oil Import Program (MOIP) in 1959. By 1947 the United States had become a net importer of oil, with foreign sources providing 10 percent of the national supply by 1953. Because the foreign crude was cheaper than domestic, it was undercutting the prices fixed by state prorationing. Naturally, producers feared the loss of markets for domestic crude; the large Northeastern refiners could readily accept imported crude.* Producers took their complaint to President Eisenhower who, after several years of hesitation, imposed the MOIP. The program limited imports east of the Rocky Mountains to 12.2 percent of refinery throughput, and thereby protected nearly 88 percent of the market from foreign price competition.

Eisenhower instituted the MOIP under the guise of national secu-

---

*This argument is complicated by the vertical integration of many large oil companies. Revenue lost in domestic production can be recovered in refining if a company has access to low-priced foreign crude oil.

rity, arguing that it was necessary to avoid supply vulnerability. The justification, however, strains credibility. East Coast supplies remained vulnerable to seizure on the high seas as they were transported by tankers from Texas.[20] Until the late 1960s, moreover, most imports were coming from politically secure sources in the Caribbean and Canada.[21] In addition, recoverable domestic resources were adequate until 1970 to pick up the slack should a supply interruption have occurred. The MOIP can best be explained as a government effort to protect the prices and markets of American oil producers, most of whom were major companies. The conclusion was stated unambiguously years ago by Nobel Laureate Milton Friedman: "The political power of the oil industry, not national security, is the reason for the present subsidies to the industry. International disturbances simply offer a convenient excuse."[22]

Although the program was costing consumers four to seven billion dollars annually, the political benefits it offered apparently outweighed those substantial sums. The program was structured so that politicians and bureaucrats, as well as the oil industry, could prosper from its operation. Permission to import oil was controlled by the Department of Interior's Office of Oil and Gas through the issuance of licenses. Because refiners were anxious to acquire as much low-priced foreign crude as possible, they were willing to "pay" dearly for the right to import. "Payments" took the form of escalating campaign contributions to politicians in positions—e.g., on the House and Senate Interior Committees—to influence the Office of Oil and Gas.[23] Major integrated companies regarded the contributions as more than a fair price for import protection. Politicians could support the program because of its diffuse impact on consumers and could encourage licensing as an arguable benefit to consumers. The agency, for its cooperation, could expect a more favorable political environment. The MOIP was thus perpetuated by a three-way agreement amongst a bureaucratic agency, a major interest group, and a few congressional committees.

The history of oil policy is not an uninterrupted story of domination by classic "subgovernments" or "iron triangles." * To acquire its

---

*The most popular names for the relatively autonomous, cooperative, and invisible policy-making arrangements, involving a major interest group, a congressional committee, and an executive agency, that dominate many policy areas. The terms were originated respectively by Freeman (*Political Process*) and Cater (*Power in Washington*).

policy benefits the oil industry had to work with state governments as well as numerous parts of the federal government, and to weather plenty of political storms. Throughout, however, important factors remained fairly constant. The policy issues always focused on the prosperity of the oil industry, and the executive branch of the national government continually cooperated with the representatives of major oil.

Despite the fact that historical oil policies and other energy programs had diverse causes and consequences, common denominators should now be clear. First, the issues from which they emerged were sufficiently circumscribed to restrict political conflict to a limited, usually single industry, producing interest, and a limited—either consuming, labor, or spillover—opposing interest. Second, the benefits that these programs conferred upon specific interests seem to have been related more strongly to the relative political resources and support of a producing interest and its opponent at particular points in history than to any overriding energy goals. Finally, the programs were maintained by political partnerships between administrative agencies, major interest groups, and, at times, congressional committees, that were able to limit the scope of issues and thereby minimize political conflict over the continuation of the programs. This familiar pattern of policy subsystems was made possible by the relative abundance of energy supplies that permitted most organized interests—especially producers, but occasionally their opponents—to be promoted piecemeal without imposing high costs on each other.

The lack of coordination, comprehension, and foresight characteristic of energy policy in the 1970s is thus rooted in historical policy making dominated by producer organizations and cooperative bureaucratic and political patrons. It would be folly to investigate contemporary energy politics without addressing the current role of these traditionally powerful organizational relationships. How this study will do that is the issue to which we now turn.

Energy Policy Present: Organizational Flux

When domestic energy supplies were effectively abundant, policy makers could overlook the interdependence between the production of those supplies and other important social values. In the early 1970s, when domestic oil production peaked and the marginal price of oil came under OPEC's control, the relationships between energy production and other values could no longer be avoided. Oil production could not be encouraged without raising the specter of damaged coastal ecosystems, or allowing shocking price hikes. Coal, the most abundant domestic fossil fuel, could not be returned to heavy use without jeopardizing air quality or western landscapes. Nuclear development could not be accelerated without facing the long-postponed issue of permanent waste disposal. Synthetic fuels could not be advanced beyond the demonstration stage without accepting forty-dollar-per-barrel prices and confronting a host of negative land, water, and waste spillovers. The scarcity of domestic oil and gas in the 1970s, in essence, imposed a new set of problems on the political system: the traditional equation of energy supply and demand complicated by new tradeoffs in economic growth, environmental quality, income distribution, price stability, employment, public safety and international relations.

Much of the political response to the energy problems of the 1970s involved organizational change. Bureaucratic agencies were frequently restructured, congressional committee jurisdictions redrawn and the interest arena regrouped. The rapid pace at which the federal government reorganized itself for the new problems was indeed a stark contrast to the sluggish rate at which it produced substantive policy. So numerous were these organizational changes that traditional patterns of energy politics and policymaking have to be questioned. Whatever the policy consequences of this organizational flux, it is a much reorganized system, and not the obviously fragmented, producer-dominated system of the abundant energy era, that must be understood to explain energy policy in the 1970s and beyond.

Bureaucratic Change

The days when the Washington representative of a major oil company could visit the Office of Oil and Gas to find relief for his company's problems are over. Gone too is the opportunity for utilities or representatives of the nuclear industry to assist the Atomic Energy Commission quietly in the development of nuclear policy. The federal government responded to the energy crisis of 1973 with many potentially important organizational changes. Significantly, for it reflects the reluctance of congressmen to relinquish spheres of influence in committees, the preponderance of organizational changes has occurred in the executive branch.

TABLE 3.1
Bureaucratic Change and the 1973 Energy Crisis

New agencies

Energy Research and Development Administration (ERDA)
Federal Energy Administration (FEA) (replacing temporary Federal Energy
   Office [FEO])
Nuclear Regulatory Commission (NRC)

Agencies losing functions

Atomic Energy Commission (AEC): R&D to ERDA; regulation to NRC
Cost of Living Council: energy division to FEA
Environmental Protection Agency (EPA): coal research, fossil fuels to ERDA
Department of Interior: coal research, fossil fuels to ERDA; energy conserva-
   tion, energy data and analysis, oil and gas, petroleum allocation to FEA
National Science Foundation: geothermal and solar to ERDA

In response to the fuel oil shortages of the winter of 1972–73, the gasoline shortages of the summer of 1973, and the crude oil shortage caused by the oil embargo of late 1973, President Nixon created the Federal Energy Office (FEO) in December 1973 to prepare for fuel shortages and manage supplies in the event of one.[24] The office also planted the seeds for centralized executive management of energy policy, and offered an important symbol of the comprehensive approach to energy many deemed necessary.* The government's apparent change in policy perspective was reflected clearly in the office's first major task—preparation of the Project Independence Report, a broad-based assessment of the nation's long-run energy supply capacity and demand requirements, and its prospects for eliminating dependence on imported petroleum by the end of the decade.

On May 7, 1974, Congress took Nixon's organizational consolidation initiative a step further by creating the Federal Energy Administration (FEA). The FEA incorporated (Table 3.1) the staff of the FEO, and several offices of the Interior Department and the Cost of Living Council. This organizational step should not be interpreted, however, as a decided break with the traditional policy system. The

*Prior to the creation of the FEO the same functions were performed by two ad hoc groups in the White House and by part of the Cost of Living Council. Nonetheless, the reorganization of these functions into the FEO had great significance. First, by transferring the Cost of Living Council's responsibility for petroleum price regulation to the FEO, Nixon emphasized that petroleum regulation was energy policy, not economic policy. Second, the FEO symbolized the need for comprehensive solutions to energy problems—a view not widely appreciated prior to that time.

FEA represented a less ambitious reorganization than the Department of Energy and Natural Resources President Nixon had proposed. The FEA's ambitious research and planning responsibilities notwithstanding, Congress provided adequate funding for only the petroleum regulation program. Congress further restricted the FEA by providing that it should cease to exist on June 30, 1976. The swift passage of the FEA Act should not be viewed therefore as a capitulation by independent spheres of influence to the need for reorganized policy making. Rather, it should be understood as an incremental change, necessitated by the supply crisis and conceded by major oil producers and their government allies in exchange for limitations on the FEA's tenure and discretion.

The substantive significance of another 1974 reorganization, the Energy Research and Development Administration (ERDA) Act, should also be interpreted cautiously. Although the creation of ERDA was a top legislative priority of the new Ford administration, the act really promised less than the ambitious, wide-ranging, innovative research and development program ERDA symbolized.[25] It was largely an answer to several years of criticism of the intermingling of promotional and regulatory responsibilities at the Atomic Energy Commission, and was not a response to the energy crisis; it split the AEC into ERDA and an independent Nuclear Regulatory Commission. ERDA also received several offices from the Department of Interior, the National Science Foundation, and the Environmental Protection Agency. While the act may be viewed as a significant victory for nuclear safety advocates, it cannot be interpreted, in and of itself, as a substantial change in the direction or management of energy R&D. Ninety percent of ERDA's original appropriations were carried over from the AEC; no changes were made in the heavy financial emphasis on nuclear technology. Amendments to strike a new balance were repeatedly defeated in House and Senate committees.[26] ERDA's organizational structure did little to alter extant fragmentation; it simply provided an umbrella organization to house, but not integrate, six R&D areas distinguished by fuel sources. The act further reinforced the image of central policy making by creating an Energy Resources Council in the White House to coordinate the remaining fragments of the energy bureaucracy. Without adequate staff or clear purpose, however, the council also provided more a symbolic than a substantive change.

In the first year following the 1973 crisis Congress was essentially torn between its urge to reorganize policy making—a time-honored way of responding to problems by delegating responsibility for them—and its incentive to maintain established policy subsystems. While the products of this cross-pressure were circumscribed bureaucratic reorganizations, they were not exclusively of symbolic value. The creation of the FEA and ERDA broke important ground for the subsequent, structurally substantial reorganizations embodied in the Department of Energy and new congressional committees.

On March 1, 1977, President Carter submitted to Congress a proposal to create a Department of Energy (DOE) by consolidating FEA, ERDA, the Federal Power Commission, and programs from five other federal agencies (Table 3.2). The proposal was less ambitious than President Nixon's earlier proposals to consolidate the Department of Interior as well; yet, it did pull together a variety of programs that might otherwise work at cross-purposes, and provided the organizational resources and Cabinet-level status necessary for strong policy initiative. In contrast to Nixon's proposals, which never got out of committee, Carter's proposal sailed smoothly through both houses.[27] The only significant revision was the creation of an independent Federal Energy Regulatory Commission within the department with price-setting authority over natural gas and elec-

TABLE 3.2
The Department of Energy (DOE) Reorganization, 1977

New agencies

    Economic Regulatory Administration (ERA)
    Energy Information Administration (EIA)
    Federal Energy Regulatory Commission (FERC)

Agencies eliminated

    Energy Research and Development Administration (ERDA)
    Federal Energy Administration (FEA)
    Federal Power Commission (FPC)

Agencies losing functions

    Department of Commerce: industrial energy conservation
    Department of Defense: naval oil and shale reserves, naval reactors
    Department of Housing and Urban Development: energy conservation standards
        for buildings
    Department of Interior: lease terms, mining data and research, power marketing
    Department of Transportation: part of authority for auto fuel efficiency, van- and
        car-pooling
    Interstate Commerce Commission (ICC): oil pipelines

tricity; Carter had proposed vesting pricing authority in the secretary. By late July the conference committee filed its report, and on August 2, 1977, the bill cleared the House 353 to 57, and the Senate 76 to 14, to be signed by the president two days later.

Unlike the nominal reorganizations that cleared the way for the new department, the structural changes wrought in the DOE significantly altered established private constituencies and at least promised to redirect substantive policy. The changes illustrate the potential significance of the reorganization. Research and development policy is no longer segregated by fuel source. Separate Offices of Energy Research, Energy Technology, and Resource Applications now oversee an assortment of supplies as they mature from basic research concepts, to technological possibilities, to demonstration projects, to commercialization programs; alternative energy sources are theoretically in competition with each other. The new department also houses an Energy Information Administration that reduces the dependence of energy policy development on the potentially self-serving data bases of independent agencies. Economic regulatory policy and research and development policy may now be coordinated to ensure that new technologies are introduced into appropriate competitive environments. Finally, the department is mandated to develop comprehensive five- and ten-year energy plans and, equally important, is supplied the resources to do so. No other peacetime energy bureaucracy was ever granted comparable powers of coordination and integration.

Congressional Reorganization

Shortly after the opening of the 95th Congress in January 1977 the Senate adopted the most sweeping overhaul of its committee system since the Legislative Reorganization Act of 1946. Although the reorganization resolution fell short of the recommended reduction of committees from thirty-one to fifteen, it did pare the number back to twenty-one and instituted several significant restrictions on the number of committees and subcommittees a senator could sit on or chair. The central objective of the plan proposed by Senator Adlai Stevenson's Select Committee to Study the Senate Committee System was to realign committee jurisdictions to follow more closely the boundaries of perceived policy problems of the 1970s. The plan was aimed, in short, at consolidating the components of interdependent policy areas that were fragmented by a committee structure designed to handle problems of an earlier era.[28] Among the many consolidations finally agreed to, energy was probably the most comprehensive.

The Senate's reform resolution established a single committee, Energy and Natural Resources, with jurisdiction over virtually all issues of energy conservation, regulation, supply production, and research and development, as well as public lands and water resources. The committee was formed by renaming the Interior and Insular Affairs Committee and transferring powers from other committees; hence, the membership of the committee was identical to that previously comprising Interior. The many jurisdictional fragments transferred to it included the naval petroleum and Alaskan oil shale reserves from the Armed Services Committee, water power from Public Works, nonmilitary development of nuclear energy from the Joint Committee on Atomic Energy, and previously undefined responsibilities such as solar energy systems, outer continental shelf energy reserves, coal production and distribution, and energy regulation and research and development generally. Relevant subject matter excluded from the Energy Committee's jurisdiction included environmental pollution and nuclear regulation, which were given to the old Public Works Committee (now renamed Environment and Public Works); pipeline regulation and coastal zone management, retained by the renamed Committee on Commerce, Science, and Transportation; rural electrification, left to the renamed Agriculture, Nutrition, and Forestry Committee; and energy taxes, tariffs, and import quotas, retained by the Finance Committee. Within the Committee on Energy and Natural Resources four new subcommittees with energy jurisdiction were created: Energy Conservation and Regulation, Energy Production and Supply, Energy Research and Development, and Public Lands and Resources. The new jurisdictions represent a substantial structural integration of many of the energy subsystems that had long functioned independently.

The most dramatic change embodied in the reform is surely the abolition of the Joint Committee on Atomic Energy, which had had its way for years in promoting the growth of nuclear power. Its demise followed quickly on the heels of a number of setbacks suffered by the Joint Committee during 1976. A Committee authorization of ERDA funds and the appointment of a veteran Committee staff member to the NRC were blocked by the Senate; at the same

T A B L E 3.3
Year Washington Office Established

Period	Environmental groups	Consumer and PIGs	Petroleum and gas industry	Electric power	Conservation and renewable energy	Labor unions	Commercial users	Financial institutions	Totals
1973–1978	11% (1)	56% (5)	19% (3)	22% (2)	58% (4)		31% (4)		26% (19)
1963–1972	78% (7)	33% (3)	25% (4)		14% (1)		8% (1)		22% (16)
1953–1962			19% (3)			12% (1)			5% (4)
1943–1952		11% (1)	25% (4)	22% (2)	14% (1)	12% (1)	15% (2)	50% (1)	12% (9)
1933–1942				22% (2)		50% (4)			12% (9)
1923–1932									0% (0)
Pre-1923	11% (1)		12% (2)	33% (3)	14% (1)	25% (2)	46% (6)	50% (1)	22% (16)
Pre-1973 groups with energy staffs prior to 1973	88% (7)	0% (0)	100% (14)	100% (7)	0% (0)	25% (2)	33% (3)	0% (0)	45% (33)

time other House and Senate committees were beginning to infringe on the Joint Committee's jurisdiction. Its fall was engineered primarily in the House and was accepted by the House Democratic Caucus in December 1976 after the nuclear industry had resigned itself to the swelling tide of change.[29]

The House did not, however, follow the Senate's lead and restructure its committee system. It had done its comprehensive reorganization bit in 1974 and rejected the Select Committee on Committees' recommendation that a standing Committee on Energy and Environment be created. The House reorganization plan encountered stiff opposition because it proposed a radical reduction in the power of committee chairmen as well as several dramatic realignments of committee jurisdictions. The compromise ultimately accepted weakened the power of committee chairmen considerably, but left committee jurisdictions largely unchanged. At least ten House committees (including Appropriations) continue to claim jurisdiction over important components of the energy system.[30] In contrast to the Senate committee structure that has become less fragmented, the House committees remain multiple and often in jurisdictional conflict.

Regrouping in the Interest Arena

The group environment of national energy policy has changed unmistakably since the basic problem was redefined in 1973. The most noticeable change is simply the sharp increase in the number of organized groups active in the area. More groups are expending more effort to convince the government to protect their respective interests now that energy scarcity precludes the simultaneous satisfaction of all of them. The change is reflected clearly in the data on the seventy-three interest groups included in this study.

The group environment was larger and more functionally complex by the late 1970s than ever before. Table 3.3 provides a longitudinal view of the development of the group environment. Over a quarter of the groups in the sample either were created, or opened governmental relations offices in Washington, D.C., after the oil embargo of 1973. Nearly half (48 percent) of them did not exist or operate in the nation's capital in 1963. Moreover, many of the groups with longer histories did not get involved with energy issues or have energy staffs until the embargo. As the bottom line of the table indicates, the group environment prior to 1973 fits well with the limited scope of historical energy policy issues and traditional institutional structures. Only 45 percent of the recent group environment was involved with national energy policy in any way prior to 1973. Three functional interests—consumers, conservation and renewable energy, and finance—had no regular advocates on energy issues until 1973.[31] Only one-fourth and one-third respectively of the labor and commercial user constituencies attempted to play any role in energy policy prior to the early 1970s. Labor's past interest was confined to the wage and safety issues of energy production, and thus involved only the Oil, Chemical, and Atomic Workers Union, and the United Mine Workers. Although three commercial user groups played minor roles in the field before 1973, two were concerned with the transportation of fuels, and the third merely anticipated the impending need for organized user representation, and established itself in 1972.[32] By and large, the functional role of commercial energy users was not perceived nor activated until the embargo raised the specter of supply scarcity.

The historical group environment of energy policy was monopolized by the energy-producing industries and utilities on the one hand, and environmentalists, who organized en masse in the decade preceding the embargo, on the other. All but five of the twenty-five groups representing petroleum, natural gas, and electricity production were at work in Washington before energy became a national issue. Before the undesirable environmental side-effects of energy production became an issue in the mid-1960s, the producing industries had little continuous, organized opposition in their relations with the government. Energy supplies were abundant, prices were relatively low, and energy policy could be developed and implemented without imposing sufficient costs on excluded interests to generate organized opposition.

As traditional energy supplies grew scarce, however, energy production began to tap sources such as surface coal, offshore oil, and nuclear power that entailed substantial environmental costs. Shortly thereafter, large price increases and the prospect of shortages brought about by the nation's growing dependence on cartel-controlled oil imports imposed another set of costs—this time on the broad constituencies of individual and commercial consumers. These same factors underscored the relationship between energy supply, prices, and jobs; organized labor accordingly took an interest. The prospect of future crises gave economic impetus as well to the development of alternative energy technology and to conservation. Financial institutions then developed new interests in energy development and conservation investments.

As the data on group formation make clear, organizations responded in kind to these disturbances in established relationships between the functional interests in energy. Five of the nine consumer groups in this sample formed after 1973, and four of those in direct response to the new issues in the energy field. The petroleum and natural gas industry added three groups in that time, and the Washington staffs of Chevron, Gulf, Shell, and Sun oil companies increased two- to threefold. Moreover, the American Gas Association, in existence since 1918, moved its entire organization from New York to Washington in 1970 "to be closer to the regulators." The post-embargo years also witnessed the addition of two nuclear industry associations to the Washington scene. The Atomic Industrial Forum, the major association of nuclear interests since its formation in 1958, moved its whole operation to Washington in 1975 as it became necessary "to engage in more advocacy" to further its members' interests. In 1975 the American Nuclear Energy Council joined the fray in order to perform the public and governmental relations functions the industry had long neglected. A spokesman for the council explained that "the industry's governmental relations effort traditionally had been too technical and scientific . . . appropriate for an issue handled by a small specialized network composed of the Joint Committee on Atomic Energy and the Atomic Energy Commission, but inappropriate for the hot arena that exists today."[33]

The increased number and functional diversity of interest groups actively concerned with national energy policy reinforces the trends of organizational change observed in the bureaucracy and Congress since 1973. The onset of scarcity in domestic oil and gas thrust previously quiescent and nonconflicting interests into competition for government protection or promotion. The government reacted to the new demands by consolidating many of the fragments of the traditional energy bureaucracy and, at least in the Senate, aggregating responsibility into fewer committees. The proliferation of interest groups and the centralization of the policy-making apparatus together suggest that the traditional energy policies of limited participation and independent policy subsystems may have been superseded. This is precisely the conclusion of a prominent student of executive policy making, who observes a general trend away from subgovernments and toward fluid, pluralistic, and expert "issue networks" at the national level.[34]

That conclusion, however, may be premature. The expansion of the group arena does not necessarily put challenging interests on competitive political footing with established producer interests. The bureaucratic reorganization is incomplete; the Department of Energy lacks control over such crucial functions as nuclear regulation, mineral lands leasing, and environmental protection. The House committee structure remains largely consistent with traditional subgovernmental politics, and the Senate energy committees are far from fully centralized. The key organizational relationships between interest groups and the bureaucracy simply remain major question marks.

The time that has passed since the oil embargo is brief in comparison to the many decades during which traditional political alliances developed. As we are painfully aware, energy problems are not solved overnight. Policies must be implemented, monitored, and reformulated. Organizations, both public and private, are the lifeblood of that lengthy process. It is plainly prudent not to allow the pluralism of contemporary energy policy debates to divert attention from the causes and consequences of those durable political relationships that inevitably develop in any policy arena. When the dust of organization-building settles, the complex activity of the construction period will undoubtedly be less evident. To understand the politics and policies these organizational changes bring, the theory of political influence already developed will prove most useful.

Applying the Organizational Theory

How shall we characterize the politics of energy in this new era of scarcity? History, both distant and recent, indicates that the relationship between the energy bureaucracy and energy interest groups will be most influential. Granting that, however, the political structure and policy impacts of those relationships remain major uncertainties. The organizational changes of the 1970s challenged the traditional politics of fragmented, producer-dominated subsystems but have not provided a clear replacement.

The organizational theory predicts that the political relationship between the bureaucracy and interest groups will vary with the policy costs and benefits distributed by the bureaucracy, and with the institutional context surrounding the bureaucracy. The political relationships that characterize national energy policy making should, then, be identifiable and explainable with reference to these two sets of factors. Although innumerable combinations of the factors are theoretically possible, a limited number of combinations, and through them several modal types of relationships, are likely to prevail. The subsequent analysis is built around three types that *a priori* are the most prevalent and generic.

Distinct organizational relationships are logically associated with each of three basic policy functions performed by a bureaucracy: *allocation*, *regulation*, and *planning*. At a general level of analysis these functions distinguish the major tools available to governments to effect social and economic change. This particular set of categories, as opposed to similar others that have gained prominence,[35] delineates different contextual influences on bureaucracies. Further, these functions are all clearly represented in national energy policy. Most of this nation's energy policy can, in fact, be subsumed by these categories of government activity. This does not mean that they supersede the rich political variations postulated in the organizational theory. The categories are rather a simplifying device that aids in understanding the theory's policy relevance and in selecting for empirical analysis cases with enough variation to validate the theory.

Of the three methods that governments use to bring about change in society and in the economy, the first provides the means or incentives to individuals, firms, or local agencies to change their activities in a manner consistent with national goals. In other words, government resources are either entrusted to recipients for their good faith pursuit of public goals or awarded after a demonstration of progress toward those goals. These stimulus and incentive programs can be implemented in many ways; tax incentives, grants, contracts, loan guarantees, and research and development projects are among the most common. Whatever the particular approach, the policies are predicated on a common theory: the *allocation* of public resources to target groups can encourage desired social change. The purest examples of allocation policy in the energy field are programs for research, development, and demonstration. By conducting these economically risky activities directly, or subsidizing them in the private sector, the government hopes to encourage commercial production of greater and alternative energy supplies. The now defunct

Energy Research and Development Administration and the Synthetic Fuels Corporation are primarily allocation agencies.

The second method governments commonly employ to effect change is *regulation*. Specific adjustments are required of target groups by law, and sanctions are imposed for failure to comply. In contrast to allocation policies, the subjects of regulation are given little discretion over how and whether to alter their activities. Changes are legally mandated with detailed instructions. Regulation can be implemented in various ways, including price- and rate-setting, market entry licensing, dispute adjudication, and remedial market failure rule-making. The common theory behind these policies is that publicly prescribed change is necessary when either the mechanisms for incentive approaches are unavailable (e.g., imperfect markets) or the goal is too important to be left to private discretion (e.g., nuclear safety regulation). Natural gas rate-setting, domestic oil pricing, nuclear reactor licensing and environmental protection illustrate the substantial role of regulation in the energy field.

The other general method by which governments pursue public ends is *planning*. The American variety of this instrument is typically less coercive and comprehensive than the familiar socialist approach; nonetheless, planning is a significant bureaucratic function in the United States. In essence, it occurs when several interrelated tasks are performed by an appropriate agency: the establishment of long-range (5–10 years) goals of real consequence for policy making, the formulation and coordination of a set of programs to pursue those goals efficiently, and, finally, the monitoring of and adjustment to progress toward those goals. Planning differs in important ways from allocation and regulation. It is concerned explicitly with the choice of policy objectives and entails greater bureaucratic discretion in policy formulation. Indeed, planning agencies construct policies from the gamut of allocation and regulation instruments. Planning, which is broader in substantive scope than the other functions, is employed when a multidimensional problem demands the coordination of numerous disparate programs.

Planning, at least in the strict sense used here, is less common than allocation or regulation, for characteristically American reasons: an independent Congress, a formally weak presidency, a disorganized interest group system, and an ideological aversion. Planning has been tried, however, in the energy field since the 1973 embargo.

The long-term and wide-reaching nature of the problem seems to demand the foresight and comprehensiveness promised by planning. It was legally institutionalized with the creation of the Department of Energy, which must submit biennially to Congress five- and ten-year plans, complete with priorities and policy proposals.

The value of these distinctions among bureaucratic functions is twofold. First, because each of the functions creates different participation incentives for interest groups, and imposes different institutional pressures on bureaucratic strategies, each ought to be characterized by a distinct and predictable organizational relationship. Identification of the differences allows the theory to be readily tested by comparing the organizational relationships actually observed in the bureaucratic activities. The second benefit accrues to energy politics. If organizational politics differ systematically across bureaucratic functions, the complex politics of energy can be simplified and interpreted in terms of allocation, regulation, and planning components.

Table 3.4 summarizes the politics that the organizational theory predicts will be associated with each bureaucratic function. The pertinence of the functions to the theory is plain. Each one is associated with one of the three types of predicted relationships: allocation activities by corporatism, regulation by capture, and planning by

TABLE 3.4
*Predicted Organizational Relationships for Three
Generic Policy Instruments*

Organizational variable	Policy instrument		
	Allocation	Regulation	Planning
Policy costs	diffuse	concentrated	uncertain
Policy benefits	concentrated	diffuse	uncertain
Interest group initiatives	Monopsonistic	Monopolistic	Competitive
Congressional constraints	strong	weak	moderate
Presidential constraints	weak	weak	strong
Judicial constraints	weak	moderate	weak
Bureaucratic strategies	Corporatist	Cooptive	Pluralist
Organizational relationship	*Corporatism*	*Capture*	*Pluralism*

pluralism. The functions represent, then, all of the equilibrium relationships contained in the main diagonal (see Figure 2.1) of the organizational typology.

It must be emphasized, however, that the predictions are not themselves intended to constitute a typology. The policy instruments are but convenient labels for extreme patterns among the independent variables of the theory. The predicted relationships will only occur to the extent that bureaucracies actually create these specific incentives for group participation and are actually subjected to the specified contextual pressures. The predictions are not meant to suggest that all policy making usually thought of as allocation or regulation or planning will be characterized by the designated relationships, e.g., that regulatory agencies will be captured or that planning agencies will be highly representative. Only if all of the independent conditions, i.e., the economic incentives and institutional constraints, are met would these predictions be made. In reality, the three disparate combinations of conditions are rarely satisfied to perfection. Bureaucracies often employ a combination of policy instruments to accomplish their goals, and are surely pressured by their political sovereigns in ways other than those posited here. Such variations are, of course, the very point of the organizational theory. It proposes that political relationships and policy outcomes different from the conventional predictions of the table can be explained with reference to particular patterns of interest group incentives and institutional constraints associated with a given bureaucracy. The predicted relationships may well be modal types for policy arenas in which the respective instruments predominate; however, the purpose of generating the predictions is to organize the empirical analysis around cases that ought *a priori* to exhibit important political differences.

The predictions follow directly from the theory and propositions advanced in the last chapter. Consider first the variety of expected interest group initiatives. Group participation in policy processes is dependent on leader calculations of net group gains, subject to the constraints of organizational maintenance. This calculus is based, it may be recalled, on (1) the expected group benefits of participation, (2) the expected group costs (including opportunity costs) of participation, (3) the group's political resources and budget, and (4) the effects of selective membership incentives. Leaders hope to maximize net group gain, given by the difference between factors (1) and (2), but are constrained in doing so by the group's membership, through factors (3) and (4).

All of these factors are affected by the policy instruments employed by the government. Bureaucratic agencies establish the stakes of participation and the costs of competing for them. They also affect the incentives for individuals and firms to support groups, and thereby affect group resources. Finally, bureaucracies affect the utility of selective incentives through their methods of decision making. At this juncture it suffices to consider only the most basic influence: the strong effect of policy instruments on the incentives of constituents to contribute to collective action aimed at influencing the use of those instruments.

Consider in turn the contribution incentives established by each instrument. Allocation instruments encourage monopsonistic patterns of interest group initiatives; i.e., beneficiaries predominate and cost-bearers are scarce. Allocation programs distribute public resources in relatively concentrated amounts to target groups but disperse the costs of the program much more widely; policy benefits are concentrated and policy costs are diffuse.[36] The average beneficiary therefore has far greater incentive to contribute to collective action than the cost-bearer. As benefits become extremely concentrated (e.g., the corporate beneficiaries of the Synthetic Fuels Corporation) and the costs completely diffused (e.g., among all taxpayers), interest group initiatives should approximate monopsony.

Precisely the opposite pattern is generated with the regulatory instrument. Because regulations usually proscribe or prescribe the behavior of some limited target group for the benefit of society generally or for some other large social aggregate, the incentives for organized action are concentrated for cost-bearers but diffuse for beneficiaries. In the extreme, group initiatives are dominated by a single cost-bearing interest—a condition of monopoly. Planning instruments encourage a more competitive constellation of group participants because the impacts of the activity are less certain. The goals of policy are rather up for grabs during planning. More interests will therefore perceive expected net benefits in participation. This is not to say that a host of interests will be equally well represented through planning incentives; free-rider problems will still plague some interests more than others. The prediction simply indicates the probable tendency toward greater group competition when the prospects of policy gains are relatively dispersed through uncertainty.

It is these basic relationships between policy incentives and group initiatives that are summarized in the upper portion of Table 3.4. Exceptions to these simple expectations can readily occur. The purpose of the full theory, which is not represented in these predictions, is of course to explain deviations from the benchmarks specified in the table.

The predictions of bureaucratic strategies in the table are likewise based on a simplified and stylized version of the theory, suggesting that the environmental pressures on the bureaucracy are likely to reinforce the group initiatives. Bureaucracies engaged in allocation are likely to feel keen and continuous pressure from Congress, but relatively little from the president or the courts. Congressional interest will focus on the geographic distribution of benefits—a matter of substantial electoral concern.[37] This beneficiary support may be counteracted by the president through budgetary pressure for cost containment; however, presidents rarely take sufficient interest in matters of implementation to constrain bureaucratic strategies. The courts are also an ordinarily weak influence; allocation policies are seldom governed by strict rules of process that provide the most common basis for legal appeal. The sum of these influences is a contextual incentive for allocation agencies to establish supportive relations with their best organized beneficiaries, i.e., to pursue corporatist strategies.

The major contextual influence on regulatory agencies, by contrast, is that of the courts. Congress historically created regulatory agencies, in part at least, to avoid difficult decisions; it is therefore disinclined to intervene in regulatory policy making. Although this reluctance may be giving way to enthusiasm for oversight and constituent service,[38] the most reasonable prediction of congressional constraints is a weak influence of indeterminate direction. The president likewise imposes typically little constraint on regulatory behavior.[39] Only under unusual circumstances will he stand to reap sufficient benefit to justify intervening. The courts are likely to impose pressure on regulatory bureaucracies because regulation is inherently legalistic, but the influence is unlikely to be more than moderate. Being an adversarial arena, the judiciary will usually not apply pressure in the consistent interest of either cost-bearers or beneficiaries. Together, the institutional constraints on regulators will tend not to be strong. The agency will then be relatively free to pursue the preferred co-optive strategy of accommodating well-organized cost-bearers.

Yet another bureaucratic strategy is likely to emerge in planning bureaucracies. The formulation of long-term goals and appropriate policies is an activity of considerable interest to Congress and the president. Because the activity occurs within the executive branch, the pressure of an interested president will tend to be substantial. The constraints of Congress, which must ultimately enact any plan, will be significant but indirect. To win the support of the president, with his national constituency, and of the Congress, with its multiple constituencies, a planning bureaucracy will probably attempt to accommodate a pluralism of groups.

As with predictions of interest group initiative, these predicted strategies are merely benchmarks derived from an assessment of modal conditions. Bureaucratic strategies will in reality deviate from these simple expectations because institutional contexts need not conform to those specified. Further, the theory predicts many more subtle institutional influences than those predicted from the general "strength" of contextual pressure. The predictions do, however, provide a useful baseline for explaining actual organizational behavior, and for selecting promising and interesting energy cases for empirical analysis.

PART II

THE ORGANIZATIONAL POLITICS OF ENERGY

4

NUCLEAR REGULATION

"The only way to get a different Commission would be to change the political support for the Commission, and reward commissioners on a basis unrelated to their services to the carriers. Until the basic logic of political life is developed, reformers will be ill-equipped to use the state for their reforms, and victims of the state's support of special groups will be helpless to protect themselves. Economists should quickly establish the license to practice on the rational theory of political behavior."[1]

With this rather ironic entreaty, renowned Chicago economist George Stigler concluded his seminal "Theory of Economic Regulation." The analyses of regulatory policy making in this chapter and the next are premised on this very conclusion. To understand the performance of regulation we must understand the sources of its political support. This is a huge task in the energy field because regulation is the policy instrument most extensively employed in federal energy policy. By one estimate over forty regulatory programs directly affect energy supply and demand.[2] Although all the programs are valuable for a thorough understanding of policy, an exhaustive empirical study is beyond the scope of this book. The development of a "theory of political behavior" relevant to regulation generally is therefore most important. Numerous attempts at such a theory precede and enhance the organizational approach explicated in Part I.[3] If the organizational theory of political influence can be validated, it will help explain the politics and performance of the varied regulatory programs that comprise national energy policy.

Historical Perspective

Until the mid-1970s, nuclear power was being widely and confidently touted as the major long-term source of energy in the United States. How nuclear power achieved that exalted status is largely a story of policy making by a promotional subgovernment closed to competing values and demands. Indeed, the "regulation" of nuclear power more nearly epitomized the corporatist mode of policy making: an exclusive relationship between the Atomic Energy Commission (AEC) and the beneficiaries of its subsidies, with the encouragement of a singular congressional sovereign, enabled nuclear power to be promoted without significant concern for economic, environmental, or other costs.

The source of the supportive organizational politics of nuclear power can be traced back to the military purposes for which atomic energy was first used[4]—purposes that justified the unique, institutional structure governing nuclear power. In the wake of the atomic explosions over Hiroshima and Nagasaki, policy making for peacetime became preoccupied with the role of atomic energy in national security. The overriding security concern dictated that the federal government assume complete responsibility for the awesome, new energy source; the sophisticated and sensitive nature of the technology recommended that jurisdiction be granted to a limited and autonomous group of officials. The Atomic Energy Act of 1946 implemented these imperatives by establishing an independent AEC and a unified congressional overseer, the Joint Committee on Atomic Energy (JCAE).

In the first postwar years of nuclear energy development the AEC was the dominant organization. Many of the scientists associated with the wartime Manhattan Project were reconstituted as the AEC's influential General Advisory Committee, and directed the commission toward further military applications.[5] In the early 1950s, however, the AEC began to feel the constraints of Congress. At the urging of the JCAE, it undertook to explore the possibilities of nuclear electrical generation and in 1951 created an Industrial Participation Program, thereby initiating the involvement of the private sector in nuclear policy making. Although the outreach represented a break with the strict government monopoly the AEC had maintained to that point, national security continued to demand government control of nuclear power throughout its fuel cycle—

from the mining of uranium ore to the disposal of reactor waste. Although the controls predictably discouraged private power companies with interests in commercial nuclear power, many of the objections were satisfied with a new Atomic Energy Act in 1954. At the urging of President Eisenhower and a rare Republican majority in Congress, the right of private nuclear power development was granted.[6] The government retained patent rights, fuel ownership, safety responsibility, and interstate electricity pricing.

The AEC was now mandated to oversee the private development of nuclear power through the issuance of licenses, either experimental or commercial, for the construction and operation of generating plants. Experimental licenses regulated demonstration plants and typically received AEC subsidies. Commercial licenses were awarded to plants capable of generating electricity at competitive rates; however, none of these were issued until 1964. The slow pace of commercial power development stimulated another political conflict between the cautious AEC and the enthusiastic JCAE. The battle concluded with an agreement in 1959 to achieve competitive nuclear power within ten years.[7] This was the last serious conflict within the emerging subsystem until the 1970s. Throughout the 1960s a cooperative and autonomous subgovernment composed of the AEC, the JCAE, and private vendors and power companies promoted the rapid growth of nuclear power. By the early 1970s, the subsystem's direct and indirect subsidies, such as basic research, technological demonstrations, cheap fuel, waste disposal, insurance underwriting, and expeditious licensing, had made nuclear power a far greater reality and prospect than its inherent competitiveness justified.

Organizational Politics in the Final Days of the AEC

Shortly before the oil embargo of 1973 a political scientist, Steven Ebbin, and a physicist, Raphael Kasper, completed an intensive, year-long study of AEC decision making and the influence of numerous interest groups upon it.[8] Their findings provide an immensely useful baseline for identifying changes in organizational politics over the ensuing decade, and for assessing the causal significance of changes in institutional constraints and participation incentives. Review of their conclusions provides a useful introduction to the policy-making processes of central concern in this analysis.

Ebbin and Kasper's ultimate assessment of organizational politics in nuclear power during the early 1970s was stark: environmental and citizen interest groups exerted no influence over the AEC, but electrical utilities and nuclear vendors saw their interests favored consistently. Why was the AEC an apparently captured agency? Two general types of causes emerged.

First were the numerous resource advantages enjoyed by utilities and vendors, who benefited from complete command of the technological and scientific information relevant to the licensing proceedings. "Intervenor" groups, meanwhile, made do with the advice of graduate students or the fortuitous contributions of a handful of concerned scientists. Even when citizen groups possessed the resources to hire sufficient expertise, they found it difficult to locate knowledgeable individuals who did not have ties to the nuclear industry or the AEC. The lawyers retained by intervenor groups proved competent at insuring procedural due process at licensing and rule-making hearings, but their usual lack of technical expertise made them ineffective adversaries of the expert industry witnesses. Such imbalances, coupled with the lack of permanent, national organizational support for the isolated opposition of ad hoc citizen groups, gave the industrial constituency a distinct advantage before the AEC.

Disparities between the resources of the beneficiaries and cost-bearers of regulation are, of course, problems for most regulatory programs. The imbalance is ostensibly corrected by the regulators, who are not supposed to act simply as impartial arbiters of the issues argued before them; they are mandated guardians of the public interest, empowered to fill the advocacy void inevitably disadvantaging the intended beneficiaries of regulation. The negligence of AEC regulators in fulfilling this responsibility is symptomatic of a second set of causes of regulatory failure cited by Ebbin and Kasper—factors that the organizational theory labels contextual or institutional constraints. Because a regulatory agency has significant discretion in satisfying its mandate, its decision calculus may include variables other than those having direct substantive bearing on the issue at hand: in particular, the external political needs of the agency. In 1972 the AEC was still within the exclusive jurisdiction of the promotion-oriented JCAE. Historically the JCAE had been *the* significant institutional constraint on the agency, and an ardent supporter of nuclear development. Presidentially appointed commissioners had long been public promoters of nuclear power rather than neutral arbiters of nuclear controversies. Further, the agency was formally accountable for the conflicting objectives of nuclear development and regulation. In the view of Ebbin and Kasper, the AEC resolved its goal conflict in favor of the promotional cues dominating its political environment.[9]

The decision-making processes adopted by the AEC to discharge its regulatory duties reflected this mutuality of interests. The commission implemented its vague regulatory mandate by requiring individual power plants to be licensed prior to construction and operation, and by promulgating general health and safety standards.[10] To the benefit of producing interests, however, the licensing process was not designed to incorporate input from nonproducing interests effectively. Further, the generic rule-making process, in which groups can participate more cheaply and with wider impact than in licensing, was seldom employed. The licensing process, Ebbin and Kasper concluded, was "geared to the promotion of nuclear power plants."[11] The only opportunities for nonproducer interests to make input were the public hearings held before the issuance of construction permits and operating licenses. For long periods of time—often several years—prior to the hearings the AEC regulatory staff would have worked closely with the applicant and the vendor to work out the details of construction.

The regulatory process began when a utility initiated informal contacts with the AEC, presumably to acquire licensing information and discuss the prospective application.[12] Subsequently the utility made formal application for all licenses needed to build and operate a nuclear power plant and filed a preliminary safety report in support of a construction permit. The report was reviewed by the staff of the Office of Regulatory Activities, and any shortcomings were corrected through informal conferences between the AEC staff, the utility, and the nuclear vendor.[13] The staff report was then reviewed by the independent Advisory Committee on Reactor Safety (ACRS)—a process that usually included one or more informal meetings (until March 8, 1973, closed to public attendance[14]) with the AEC staff and the applicant. After the ACRS made its determination of the probable risks to public health and safety, the AEC scheduled a public hearing, the first opportunity for input by nonproducer interests, who had to file petitions to intervene. Only after intervenor status was granted did their representatives have access to the documents and information that the applicant, vendor, and AEC staff had considered for months or even years. Intervenors then had between thirty and sixty days to detect specific problems in a highly technical set of plans.

A separate pre-hearing process, only marginally more open to diverse input, was employed to evaluate the environmental impact of proposed plants. Interested groups, individuals, and state or local governments could submit written comments on the adequacy of the applicant's initial environmental report. After review the AEC staff prepared a "Final Detailed Statement on the Environmental Considerations," which set the parameters for debate in the subsequent licensing hearings.

By the time the public hearing was held to rule on the issuance of a construction permit, the decision was a foregone conclusion. The burden of proof for raising issues and demonstrating potential health, safety, or environmental problems lay with the intervenors. The agency was satisfied with the plans; challenges were therefore opposed not only by the applicant but by the AEC staff as well. Ebbin and Kasper concluded that the public hearings (both at this stage and at the subsequent operating license stage) provided no meaningful opportunity for public input nor an effective means of establishing a factual base or of resolving technical issues. They found, indeed, that all parties to the public proceedings regarded them as charades[15]—essentially public relations efforts that often produced delays through procedural and legal wrangling but rarely permitted substantive issues to be thoroughly examined or resolved.[16] While it could not be denied that the AEC scrupulously guarded procedural due process, it made little apparent effort to provide substantive due process.[17]

AEC decision making tended to preclude opposing input in yet another way. Basically, administrative agencies have available two ways to interpret and implement laws: a case-by-case procedure, evaluating the merits of a proposal on the basis of the peculiar circumstances of the case, or the establishment of general rules, rates, or standards to be followed by all subjects within their jurisdiction. Generally speaking, the latter procedure is preferred by public interest groups and other financially deficient interests because a single proceeding produces a decision of wide impact. While regulated interests appreciate the certainty of general rules, they are less disadvantaged by an adjudicatory approach that of-

fers the hope of more flexible regulatory interpretations and greatly increases the participatory burden upon their opponents.

This is not to say that generic rule making clearly places opponents on equal footing with regulatees. The Administrative Procedures Act permits rule making to be conducted on an informal
basis, without an "on the record," adjudicatory format. Informal
rule making, which was employed by the AEC and is the norm for
energy regulatory agencies, adheres to a legislative model of decision making.[18] Decisions are based on staff analysis and outside comments submitted in writing or in public hearing, and are not governed by quasi-judicial rules of evidence, procedure, ex parte communication, and the like. Without legal guidelines, informal rule
making is more vulnerable to direct bureaucratic lobbying—a tactic
that regulatees are generally more capable of employing. In view of
the late stage in the licensing process at which formal hearings
occur, informal "lobbying" also plays a prominent early role in case
adjudication. On balance, though, the rule-making approach to regulation, by virtue of its broader impact, provides a higher long-run
probability of effective input by the beneficiaries of regulation.

The AEC did not begin to use rule making to resolve major,
generic, licensing issues until 1971.[19] This practice meant that recur-
ring points of contention—the adequacy of emergency core cooling
systems, permissible levels of radioactivity in effluents, and environmental effects associated with the transportation of nuclear fuel and
waste—were dealt with in an ad hoc fashion time and time again.
Ebbin and Kasper had a close look at the AEC's first major, contested rule making, the 1972 Emergency Core Cooling System (ECCS)
Hearings. The AEC employed an experimental, quasi-judicial hearing format, later known as a "hybrid procedure," which proved far
from successful in resolving this technical issue. Over one hundred
days were consumed by the experimental hearings—much of that
time devoted to expensive, legal wrangling over the scope of the
proceedings and the qualifications of participants.[20] The rules finally
adopted were more conservative than those originally proposed;
however, the cause of the reversal was more probably the critical
testimony of several national laboratory scientists than the citizen
intervention.[21] Though they concluded their study with the recommendation that generic rule-making be employed more frequently,
they were thoroughly convinced that the AEC rule-making hear-

ings, as much so as licensing hearings, offered nonproducing interests only the opportunity for very circumscribed participation.

The "Changing Context" of Nuclear Regulation

In the years since Ebbin and Kasper completed their study a great
deal has changed and a great deal has remained the same. There
have been a number of organizational changes. The AEC was abolished and its regulatory and promotional programs transferred respectively to the Nuclear Regulatory Commission and the Energy
Research and Development Administration. When the JCAE was
disbanded in 1977 its oversight responsibility for nuclear regulation
was vested in the House Interior and Senate Energy and Environment committees. These structural changes diluted the traditional
political support for nuclear growth that had been so closely associated with nuclear regulation for a generation.

At the same time the nuclear industry began to fall on economic
hard times. As a result of the energy crisis of 1973–74, electricity
consumption experienced no growth in 1974 and 1975. Dramatically higher oil prices put a severe financial burden on oil-burning
utilities that, coupled with the standstill in electricity demand, led
many utilities to cancel expansion plans. The retrenchments hit the
nuclear industry particularly hard since it had been the greatest
beneficiary of most recent expansions in electric generating capacity. From mid-1974 to the spring of 1976 utilities cancelled orders for
23 nuclear plants and deferred plans for 143 more.[22] In 1976 and
1977 demand for electricity resumed its upward course, growing by
over 10 percent; yet, in those years eight more plant orders were
cancelled and another fifty deferred. New reactor orders—only
twelve from 1975 through 1977—did not come close to balancing
the decline. The short-term reactor building-rate projected in 1978
was only around five per year; yet, industry spokesmen regarded a
twenty-per-year pace as the minimum necessary for a healthy industry. Since the data for this study were collected in 1978 and 1979,
the downward trend has continued. The Three Mile Island radiation
leakage accident near Harrisburg, Pennsylvania, in March 1979 led
the NRC to impose a one-year moratorium on operating licenses.
What is more, a moratorium on construction licenses remains in
effect even three years after the accident.

The nuclear industry lays some of the blame for its ailing condition on the regulatory process that it feels imposes unwarranted delays.[23] For example, mid-construction rule changes can force expensive and time-consuming plant alterations; intervenor participation in licensing hearings causes delays without constructive contributions; and the uncertainties of the lengthy process increase regulatory costs by discouraging investors. Although recent studies indicate there is good reason to doubt industry claims that NRC regulation is a significant cause of nuclear power's overall decline, there can be no doubt that licensing has unwarranted dilatory consequences for plant construction.[24] The problem is widely recognized, but there is little consensus as to how it should be remedied. The Carter administration proposed, but failed to get enacted, a licensing reform bill in 1978. The Reagan administration supports reform in principle but has yet to offer a feasible alternative.

In important respects, then, the context of nuclear regulation has changed little since the completion of Ebbin and Kasper's study. That is, the regulatory process follows much the same course in the NRC as it did in the AEC. The procedures for securing a license are identical. Generic rule-makings, while receiving more frequent use, have not resolved enough issues to provide even a nearly standardized set of plant standards. The NRC estimates that between one and two hundred generic nuclear safety issues presently remain unresolved.[25] Just as the NRC adopted virtually all of the AEC's rules and procedures, it also carried over almost the entire AEC regulatory staff.[26] The only things the NRC did not continue were the AEC's research and development responsibilities, which by statute were transferred to ERDA. It is against this background of change and stasis that current NRC relations with its constituency must be interpreted.

Organizational Politics in the Late 1970s

Interest Group Initiatives

In the early 1970s four types of interests attempted to play a role in nuclear regulation: electric utilities, nuclear reactor vendors, environmental groups, and ad hoc local citizen groups.[27] Since that time many more interests have developed significant concerns with nuclear power development and begun advocating them in one political forum or another. These newly activated interests are well represented by the groups in this study.

Consumer-oriented interest groups have joined the nuclear fray because of the rapidly escalating costs of nuclear power. Groups such as Congress Watch, Energy Action, and the National Taxpayers Union actively oppose additional government subsidization of nuclear power, given the availability of cheaper alternatives. Other public interest groups such as New Directions base their political involvement on the increasingly salient "nonproliferation" issue. They accept the interim use of light water fission reactors, but oppose the next stage in nuclear development—breeder reactors—fearing the threat of weapons-grade plutonium produced as breeder waste. The oil industry has also staked a major claim in nuclear power. Several companies, Kerr-McGee and Gulf Oil being most involved, have acquired substantial uranium holdings and, accordingly, promote swift nuclear development.[28] Organized labor is yet another interest now drawn into nuclear debates. Although unions are disturbed by the rising cost and prospective subsidies of nuclear power, they tend to favor nuclear development, counting on reactor construction to provide employment.[29] Commercial energy users are also obviously concerned with the availability and price of electricity, and have organized the Electricity Consumers Resource Council to represent them. In fact, all of the sectors in this study, from environmentalists to financial institutions, now claim significant interests in nuclear power development and recognize the salience of regulatory issues.

Espousing an interest and acting on it, however, are two very different things. In the American political system it is not uncommon for a number of government entities to have authority over an issue or some aspect of it. It should not be surprising, then, that interest group activities do not converge on one decision-making point, but fan out into a number of arenas. Such is the case with much of energy policy making. Table 4.1 provides a summary picture of interest group initiatives toward the NRC from 1974 through 1978. The indicator, "frequency of group interaction," summarizes a variety of methods of group participation: formal and informal, written and oral, direct and indirect. Taken together, these types of participation form natural clusters of activities that provide important distinctions among regulatory constituents. What the table indicates most clearly is that the active group constituency of the NRC five years after the energy crisis of 1973 was not much different from that of the AEC during its final days, even though the nuclear

TABLE 4.1
Frequency of Group Interaction with the NRC, 1974–78

Interest groups[a]	Constant[b]	Frequent[c]	Sporadic[d]	Infrequent[e]	None[f]	Sporadic or more frequent
Environmental groups		38% (3)	38% (3)		25% (2)	75%
Consumer and PIGs				11% (1)	89% (8)	0%
Petroleum and gas industry					100% (16)	0%
Electric power	11% (1)	11% (1)	11% (1)	33% (3)	33% (3)	33%
Conservation and renewable energy					100% (7)	0%
Labor unions			12% (1)	12% (1)	75% (6)	12%
Commercial users				8% (1)	92% (12)	0%
Financial institutions					100% (2)	0%

[a] One group is missing from this tabulation because interview time did not permit discussion of the NRC.

[b] At minimum: daily monitoring of agency business; exhaustive, formal participation in rule making; and establishment of effective two-way, informal substantive communication between agency and group.

[c] At minimum: close, if not daily, monitoring of agency business; formal participation in all rule makings of acknowledged major importance to membership or constituency; and some substantive, informal communication, some of which is agency-initiated.

[d] At minimum: no close monitoring of agency business; formal participation in no more than one rule making and one adjudication proceeding (or two of either) per year; and little informal, substantive communication, almost none of which is agency-initiated.

[e] At minimum: less monitoring, or formal or informal participation, than above categories. E.g., joining a joint petition or intervention, or submitting written comments on a proposed rule perhaps once or twice over a four-year period.

[f] At minimum: no communication with or participation in agency.

debate expanded to include many previously quiescent interests. Of the eight sectors sampled in the study only three—environmental groups, electric power, and labor unions—had sporadic or more contact with the agency. Differences in participation within these three sectors, moreover, describe a still narrower constituency.

Labor for the most part refrained from involvement with nuclear regulatory issues despite their impact on the rate and cost of power development. The only union with even sporadic contact with the NRC—the Oil, Chemical, and Atomic Workers Union—confined its interactions to matters of worker safety. This long-standing concern provided the union informal access to NRC commissioners and staff whenever it was necessary, but the relationship was not cultivated for other energy issues. The only other labor participant was the

United Mine Workers Union (UMW), a recent and infrequent presence in NRC policy making. It began joining licensing interventions in opposition to power plants proposed in areas with substantial coal supplies. The union adopted the strategy in response to the new economic vulnerability of nuclear power, and hopes to employ it more frequently in the future.[30]

The labor situation contrasts sharply with the role of the electric power sector, where two-thirds of the groups interviewed maintained some relationship with the NRC. Three of those groups, however, enjoyed only infrequent interactions with the agency. The American Public Power Association, which represents small, municipally-owned utilities; the National Association of Regulatory Utility Commissioners, which represents state and consumer power interests; and the American Nuclear Energy Council, which specializes in congressional lobbying for the nuclear industry, were not regular forces in NRC policy making. Only three industry groups played prominent parts as NRC constituents: the Atomic Industrial Forum, the Edison Electric Institute, and the National Rural Electric Cooperative Association. Representation of the electric power sector was thus dominated by the major developers, owners, and operators of nuclear power plants.[31]

The other interest that maintained significant visibility before the NRC was environmental protection. Six of the eight environmental groups had at least sporadic interaction with the commission. Four of them—Friends of the Earth, the Natural Resources Defense Council (NRDC), the Sierra Club, and the Union of Concerned Scientists (UCS)—played roles of varying importance in Ebbin and Kasper's study; however, two groups subsequently joined those core participants and began to fill serious gaps in the environmental opposition: poor coordination across licensing interventions and woeful shortages of scientific and technical expertise. Progress in both areas was made through the efforts of two Ralph Nader organizations. Critical Mass, one of the independent satellites of Nader's mass membership group, Public Citizen, was created in 1974 to facilitate the interventions of citizen groups throughout the country by providing them technical support, procedural advice, and close monitoring of NRC activities. The Public Interest Research Group (PIRG), which is essentially Nader's personal research staff, was formed in 1970 but only later came to concentrate on technical and procedural issues of nuclear regulation.[32] PIRG made its research reports available to licensing intervenors and on occasion presented its positions in rule makings on generic issues.

The expertise of the environmental opposition was improved as well by the growth and experience of interest groups such as the NRDC and the UCS that, though prominent in the early 1970s, were really only fledgling operations. The NRDC was by 1978 a $2.5 million operation, with a staff of sixty-five. Because it was involved with a great number of environmental issues, only about 15 percent of its resources were devoted to NRC matters, but, significantly, it did assign three scientists primarily to nuclear regulatory issues. The UCS, a more modest operation, had a 1978 budget of approximately $675,000 and a total staff of twelve. It was nonetheless an important source of expertise and, like the NRDC, a more competent operation in the late 1970s than in 1972. The UCS supplemented its in-house resources with the donated assistance of numerous sympathetic scientists and managed to increase its budget fourfold from 1975 to 1978.[33] In sum, the environmental constituency of the NRC was more competent technically and better coordinated and staffed than the close-knit, marginally informed opposition that confronted the AEC in the early 1970s.

The significance of these strides by the intended beneficiaries of nuclear regulation should not, however, be overestimated. In the context of the cost-bearing constituency with which they had to compete, the beneficiaries' progress was small. Table 4.2 offers indicators of the competitive balance between beneficiary and cost-bearing interests. The annual expenditures and staff sizes of the Washington offices of environmental and electric power interests indicate at least indirectly and relatively their capacities for governmental relations.[34] The table reveals a striking difference in financial and human resources available to the two sectors that figure most prominently in the NRC constituency: namely, that the typical interest group in the electric power sector had seven times the financial resources and over five times the human resources of the typical environmental interest group.

Of course, inferences from these figures can be drawn in only the most general terms. Trade association representatives are often reluctant to release expenditure information for fear of misinterpretation, and are invariably quick to stress that a Washington-office budget is not a direct indicator of political effort expended. Substantial resources, they emphasize, are channeled into research and non-

TABLE 4.2
Washington Offices of NRC Constituents

Amount	Environmental groups[a]	Electric power
Annual expenditures		
Over $5 million		25% (2)
$1–$5 million	11% (1)	38% (3)
$500,000–$1,000,000	22% (2)	12% (1)
$250,000–$500,000	22% (2)	12% (1)
$100,000–$250,000	22% (2)	
$0–$100,000	11% (1)	
Not ascertained	11% (1)	
Median budget	$318,000	$3,500,000
Total resources of five wealthiest groups	$4,810,000	$34,750,000
Size of staff[b]		
200 and over		12% (1)
150–199		12% (1)
100–149		12% (1)
50–99	11% (1)	25% (2)
25–49		12% (1)
10–24	56% (5)	25% (2)
0–9	33% (3)	
Median staff size	12	64
Total staff of five largest groups	126	659

[a] In the Natural Resources Defense Council and the Union of Concerned Scientists, the Washington office was so thoroughly integrated into the headquarters operation that separate Washington budgets and staff sizes could not be estimated. Appropriately, the total organizational resources for these groups are reported.

[b] Paid, full-time employees.

political member services, while governmental relations expenditures are divided among a plethora of issues and agencies. While these qualifications are all legitimate, they do not vitiate the usefulness of resource measures for *comparative* purposes with groups similarly burdened. Environmental interest groups *are* similarly burdened. While only three of them provided members with significant material incentives, organizational resources can still become thoroughly diluted. The cultivation of membership, usually through direct mail solicitation, is a large drain on public interest group resources. Nader's Public Citizen, for example, must rechannel 35 percent of its contributions back into mailing.[35] Further, environmental groups deal with many issues besides nuclear power. Even the groups most concerned may devote only a small fraction of their resources to it. Friends of the Earth, for example, allocated about 5 percent of its financial and human resources to nuclear regulation, the Sierra Club approximately 10 percent, and the NRDC, the leader in this area, about one-sixth of its resources. It is true, at least for this sample, that environmental interest groups do not expend nearly as large a percentage of their resources for research as do trade associations; however, research expenditures are not without benefit for governmental relations. Research produces expertise, and expertise is a potentially important component of any strategy of influence. There are other variables that make resource comparisons between private and "public" interest groups problematic. Volunteer workers, cheap office space, and spartan office accommodations may squeeze more influential activity out of each public interest group dollar; yet trade associations enjoy an offsetting advantage from the expertise contributed by their corporate members. On balance, then, simple comparisons of organizational resources are not politically misleading.

No matter how you view the NRC constituency, the gains of environmental groups in the 1970s left that sector handicapped in bureaucratic politics. The meagerness of environmental group resources is striking in the median; at the sectoral level, where political competition is more appropriately assessed, the resources appear even less adequate. Sectoral-level data are more valid measures of group capabilities than are individual organizational resources because the former capture the common strategy of cooperative lobbying.

Table 4.3 provides a picture of political cooperation for the entire group sample. Respondents were asked whether they cooperated regularly with other interest groups in pursuing energy policy objectives, and if so with whom. The question elicited mentions of 199 dyads of cooperation, or an average of about three cooperating partners per group. The diagonal entries indicate the great extent to which cooperation was intrasectoral. The average group devoted 45 percent of its cooperative efforts to groups in the same sector, and every sector except labor cooperated more with groups in the sector than with groups outside the sector. The predominance and extensiveness of intrasectoral cooperation lends additional validity to the boundaries of these functional categories, and to the analysis of sectoral resources. The electric power and environmental sectors, moreover, were leaders in cooperative lobbying, which occurred in

TABLE 4.3
Cooperative Lobbying

Frequency with which column groups mention row groups[a]	Environmental groups	Consumer and PIGs	Petroleum and gas industry	Electric power	Conservation and renewable energy	Labor unions	Commercial users	Financial institutions
Environmental groups	65% (24)	38% (12)			27% (3)	6% (1)	4% (1)	
Consumer and PIGs	22% (8)	38% (12)		6% (2)	9% (1)	50% (8)	4% (1)	
Petroleum and gas industry			70% (32)		9% (1)		15% (4)	
Electric power			15% (7)	65% (20)	9% (1)		19% (5)	
Conservation and renewable energy	11% (4)				36% (4)	12% (2)		
Labor unions	3% (1)	19% (6)	2% (1)	10% (3)	9% (1)		4% (1)	
Commercial users			13% (6)	19% (6)		31% (5)	54% (14)	
Financial institutions								
TOTALS[b]	101% (37)	101% (32)	100% (46)	100% (31)	99% (11)	99% (16)	100% (26)	100% (0)

[a] The upper right and lower left triangles of the table are not mirror images of each other because groups did not always corroborate mentions of cooperation.
[b] Included in this table are 25 mentions of groups not in the sample. That amounts to only 12.5% of the total of 199 mentions made of cooperating groups.

more than average amounts—a mean of four mentions per group—and was 65 percent intrasectoral.

When group resources are pooled, strategies coordinated, and work allocated to avoid duplications of political effort, the disparity between the electric power and environmental sectors is magnified. Table 4.2 records the disparity in its bottom lines where the budgets and staffs of the five largest groups in each sector are totalled. Over $30 million and 500 personnel separated the capacities of environmental and electric power interests to advocate their respective positions. For the smaller number of groups comprising the "active" NRC constituency, the differences are equally dramatic. The six groups at least sporadically involved had total annual expenditures of $3.7 million and a combined staff of 109, while the three trade associations with at least sporadic NRC interactions had aggregate resources of $29.25 million and 531 staff.[36] What is more, this comparison ignores the Washington offices of nuclear vendors, such as General Electric and Westinghouse, and major investor-owned utilities. Their presumed prominence in the NRC constituency tilts the already formidable imbalance of sectoral resources well beyond the point of ambiguity. Environmental interest groups, despite considerable strides during the 1970s, were far from prepared to compete in nuclear regulatory politics. In the language of the organizational theory, the interest group initiatives associated with the NRC tended toward monopoly; they were dominated by a few representatives of the interests intended to bear the costs of nuclear regulation.

Bureaucratic Strategies

The initiatives of interest groups, it is important to remember, tell only half the story of the relationship between an executive agency and its constituency. Bureaucracies possess the substantive discretion and the political incentive to structure their group relations in advantageous ways, independent of the pressures that groups otherwise apply—by manipulating the costs and benefits of group participation, and by directly courting or spurning group relations through informal channels. This behavior is particularly in need of study in the NRC's case because its putative causes, external institutional constraints, changed markedly during the 1970s.

To clarify the strategies of the NRC toward its constituency it is helpful to distinguish two channels through which organizational relationships develop: the one, formal, includes written and oral exchanges in licensing and rule-making proceedings. Relationships through these channels will be influenced most by formally established benefits and costs of group participation. The other, informal, includes traditional forms of involvement such as direct lobbying or "informing" of agency staff and commissioners, indirect interactions through overseers in Congress or the White House, and distant relations through mass protests and other publicity stunts. Relationships through these channels will be influenced chiefly by the institutional constraints on the agency.

Administrative agencies have substantial discretion both in choosing and structuring procedures for policy making and in weighing the multiple values and alternatives that inevitably arise.[37] For licensing reactors the NRC relies heavily on the ad hoc approach of the formal adjudicatory process. It also employs generic rule making, though less often than most observers regard as desirable, and employs hybrid or informal legislative procedures for that purpose.[38] Both processes are subject to influence through informal as well as formal channels, though the licensing procedures are better insulated from informal pleading.

The six environmental and three electric power groups most involved with the NRC agreed almost completely on the relative importance of the channels in establishing agency policy. Exchanges between the agency and interest groups through formal channels were more likely to be translated into policy than were interactions conducted informally. Group representatives repeatedly stressed that the NRC maintained high standards of procedural integrity and, particularly during licensing proceedings, scrupulously avoided ex parte communications. These informal contacts, occurring outside of ongoing or completed formal proceedings with the intention of informing or influencing decision makers, occupy something of a gray area in administrative law. That is, what types of outside contacts are illegal and at what point during formal proceedings they become illegal are to some extent within an agency's discretion.[39] The NRC chose a strict definition of ex parte communication and based its policies largely on the formal record. Groups in the active NRC constituency agreed that licensing and even generic rule making were not substantially influenced by informal lobbying. Environmental groups continued to express dissatisfaction with the licensing procedures because they build a presumption against intervenor positions in advance of hearing; however, none of the groups felt disadvantaged by informal relationships between the agency and the industry once proceedings began. In generic rule makings, where all of the environmental groups except the NRDC had great-er experience, satisfaction with decisional processes was generally high. Several recent proceedings that produced rules acceptable to environmentalists led them to agree that technically and legally competent group participation in formal proceedings definitely in-fluenced NRC policy making.[40]

These assessments belie in part the recognized importance of in-formal channels. Groups cited several important functions for policy influence. At the formative stages informal relationships with the staff were a crucial source of information on rules, interpretations, and policies. Staff contacts also provided advance notice of pending proceedings, thereby allowing more time for the groups to prepare formal input. Informal ties to staff or commissioners also provided opportunity for the groups to contribute to the agenda of future issues. Unlike formal channels, however, these avenues were not open equally to all groups with sufficient resources to participate. Informal relationships differed in quality from one group to the next, largely because of the behavior of the NRC. Each group that attempted to participate seriously in formal proceedings contacted the NRC staff frequently for information, interpretations, clarifica-tions, and routine assistance. No group reported difficulty in dealing with the NRC staff on that level. These contacts do not, however, constitute a relationship; it exists only when NRC staff members contact the group for assistance or support, not when the initiative lies with the group. A representative of the EEI explained that they gauge the success of their liaison efforts with the question: "Will they call you?" He explained further, "That's when you know you've made it and you've entered the fraternity . . . when they call and ask: what would the utilities think of this?"

Agencies attempt to establish such relationships in order to have credible sounding boards for proposals and to gain the political support of key interests. Both industry and environmental groups emphasized that expert credibility was important for the establish-ment of a working relationship with the NRC staff. The staff is involved with policy at the creative stages, and does not want to risk embarrassment in public forums by recommendations that have disastrous, unforeseen consequences. As a precaution it is not un-common for the regulatory staff to seek sounding boards among outside groups. The potential benefits should be obvious: early access provides the opportunity, no matter how well-intentioned the staff's effort, for outside groups to fix the parameters of subsequent debate at the public hearing stage. Generally speaking, the staff's primary concern in seeking sounding boards is to eliminate technical inaccuracies or misperceptions, and not to mitigate subsequent political (valuative) conflict. The staff can be expected, therefore, to seek the aid of technically competent groups. This, of course, resurrects group resources as a gatekeeper to organizational relationships. All things being equal, resources provide expertise, and expertise provides the possibility of privileged access.

This causal logic was supported empirically. The only two groups that maintained "working relationships" with the staff of the NRC were the AIF and the EEI. The AIF maintained "daily contact" with the NRC staff, which initiated "fifty percent" of their communications. The AIF spokesman explained that it had "credibility in the eyes of the NRC," which therefore "relied heavily on [the AIF] as a conduit with the industry." The basic disposition of the staff toward the AIF was said to be "sympathetic." In the opinion of the EEI its relationship of mutual trust with the NRC staff could be attributed to its own expertise and experience. In contrast, the Sierra Club and Friends of the Earth attributed their less useful relationships with the staff to the shortage of group resources that prevented them from developing technical credibility.

While the staff's behavior toward the constituency was influenced by technical concerns, the commissioners themselves worked in a more political environment, ostensibly affected by the changing institutional constraints of recent years. A closer look at the relationships of environmental groups with the NRC suggests that these changes did not go unnoticed by its politically sensitive members. Three environmental groups—the Sierra Club, Friends of the Earth, and Critical Mass—reported enjoying two types of agency initiatives. The Sierra Club and Critical Mass were routinely notified by the NRC staff of impending proceedings and informed of decisions before the news was released for public consumption. Also, the Sierra Club and Friends of the Earth had sporadic policy level discussions with, and exclusively at the request of, the NRC commissioners. What is especially interesting is that both types of initiatives occurred only after 1977—the year in which President Carter was inaugurated and the JCAE disbanded. Because the NRC staff did not undergo any abrupt turnover at that juncture, one can only infer that both the staff overtures and the policy level initiatives were responses to contextual political considerations.

None of the groups, however, thought to connect directly their new relationships with the contextual changes. Critical Mass presumed that "the staff was beginning to realize which way the wind is blowing." Friends of the Earth suspected that the NRC "knew they were being sold a bill of goods by industry . . . and wanted relief from industry bombardment." The Sierra Club suggested that "they do these things because they have a public image problem. They are trying to court support, and feel public interest group participation is good for their reputation." Friends of the Earth agreed that "they are trying to build support by providing access."

The significance of the recent overtures by the NRC should not be underestimated. None of the environmental groups viewed the changes in their informal relationships as merely symbolic or disingenuous agency overtures, i.e., as providing minimally meaningful access in order to defuse opposition. The initiatives of the commissioners, in particular, were regarded as sincere efforts to establish working relationships. On the other hand, the initiatives of the staff were regarded as more reluctant—a problem environmentalists attributed to the staff's extensive roots in the AEC and its antagonistic predisposition toward safety and environmental values. This view contrasts with the AIF's appraisal of the staff as "sympathetic." The tenuous nature of staff-outreach efforts is reflected in the fact that contacts were meant to inform rather than to solicit feedback—the latter being the essential feature of the electric sector's relationship. Nonetheless, environmental groups clearly valued the new effort of NRC staff to keep them informed, and felt that greater resources might enable them to cultivate better relationships.

The bureaucratic strategy employed by the NRC to manage its constituency is clear. The agency established elaborate formal procedures for policy making and, within them, for interest representation. It strove to base and justify its decisions on the record thus established. Until approximately 1977 informal NRC overtures toward its constituency were essentially "co-optive." That is, the agency sought to build support by accommodating its cost-bearing interests. In the late 1970s, however, the agency's strategy began to become more "pluralistic" through significant efforts by NRC commissioners and noticeable efforts by NRC staff to involve environmental groups in policy making. Why the agency altered its strategy toward greater pluralism and why it made its other strategic choices are matters to which we shall turn shortly. Let us consider first, though, the causes of the other half of organizational relationships: the initiatives of interest groups.

Theories and Explanations

Interest Group Initiatives

Although nuclear power today raises issues that prompt concern from a wide range of interests, the active, national-level constituency of the NRC is limited now, as in the past, to several environmental groups with slender resources and a few major associations of nuclear vendors and electric utilities. The reasons for the limited nature of their operations seem to lie with the problems of organized political action and the structure of incentives for action as established by the NRC. On the one hand group initiatives are constrained by the rigors of maintaining an interest organization, and on the other hand by the net benefits or costs of participation options established by the government. The effects of the constraints are plain in the NRC's active constituency.

Nuclear regulation is a classic, social regulatory policy.[41] Because nuclear power production also causes negative externalities and "public bads" such as environmental damage and hazards to human life and health, government policy is the only means of ensuring that the side-effects are reduced to society's satisfaction. Inasmuch as market incentives will obviously not represent society's demand for the reduction of nuclear byproducts, the NRC must be responsible for determining how much byproduct is acceptable. Essentially, then, it is weighing the interests of nuclear equipment vendors, electric utilities, and their customers and stockholders in nuclear power against the interests of society at large in health, safety, and environmental quality.[42]

The incentives for interest organization in social regulation are clear and familiar. At the micro level of individuals and firms where the impacts of regulation are felt, the consequences of NRC decisions are either concentrated upon a relatively small number of producers or diffused among millions of nonproducer citizens. Although the collective policy impacts are approximately equal (and often opposite) for producer and nonproducer interests, it is the producers who are more likely to organize to promote favored policies. For them the marginal benefits of collective action are simply much larger, and the free-rider incentives much weaker, than for the typical nonproducer.

The effects of organizational incentives are much as predicted in the last chapter (Table 3.4). Nonproducer interests have indeed organized important groups such as the NRDC and the UCS to advocate environmental, health, and safety values in nuclear regulation; but their material resources pale in comparison to those of producer groups such as the AIF and the EEI. The sectoral level resource discrepancy (see Table 4.2) between cost-bearing and beneficiary groups is strong confirmation of the differential rigors that beset them. The dilemma of collective action does not appear to prevent interests from becoming nominally organized, but it impedes considerably their development to a collectively optimal size.

The impediment is greatest for the most diffuse interests—in this case the intended beneficiaries of nuclear regulation, whose limited resources handicap their efforts to influence the NRC. A lawyer for the Environmental Policy Center summed up their problem rather bluntly: "You can't be successful at a regulatory agency unless you have the financial resources to sue their asses off." A spokesman for the Sierra Club observed that close liaison with agency staff and policy makers was essential for influencing the NRC, but complained that they were inadequately equipped to be so involved. "If the Sierra Club had the same resources as the [producer groups]," he added, "we would be more effective."

The gaping disparities that exist are the fundamental consequences of political competition between concentrated and diffuse interests for public goods, but they do not make inevitable the emergence of monopolistic group initiatives. Many of the national environmental groups in this study have sufficient financial resources to participate significantly in NRC policy making. Why then do group initiatives tend toward monopoly? They do so, the organizational theory indicates, when the incentives and disincentives for group involvement established by the agency are also discouraging.

Once an interest group is established, group leaders are hypothetically concerned with maximizing the public goods produced for group supporters and doing whatever else is necessary to maximize support for the organization. Accordingly, leaders can be expected to decide when and how to participate in politics, based on (1) the expected value of public goods produced through alternative strategies and (2) any other effects of participation on support for the group. Over a span of time, such as a one-year plan, the leader will cumulate strategies, beginning with those that promise the greatest return on the two objectives, until the budget limit is reached.

The government directly affects the strategic choices by determining the costs and benefits of participation. In the case of the NRC, incentives manipulated by the agency tend both to discourage participation by national interest groups of all points of view, and to promote a participation disparity favoring cost-bearers over beneficiaries. The first consequence stems from the NRC's reliance on ad hoc licensing proceedings rather than generic rule makings to establish regulatory "policy," and its adherence to formal or hybrid judicial procedures to receive group input. The incremental development of policy through reactor licensing minimizes the benefit that any national organization derives from successful participation in an agency decision. The approval, disapproval, or modification of a reactor is but a small component of a nuclear policy. At the same time, the judicial formats of licensing and generic rule making at the NRC make effective involvement expensive. Relative to other participation options such as congressional or presidential lobbying for public goods, the agency option promises less benefit, more cost, and a lower expected value. After groups exhaust more profitable options and confront their resource limitations, participation at the NRC on a regular basis is left to a select set of groups. Out of a sample of seventy-three interest groups, most of which have nuclear interests, only one maintained a "constant" presence (see Table 4.1) and only four participated "frequently."

The decision-making routines of the NRC also foster unequal participation by cost-bearers and beneficiaries. This occurs for two reasons. The low expected value of regulatory participation encourages groups to pursue other political strategies first; hence, only groups with relatively large budgets will have sufficient resources to cultivate the NRC directly. Unequal resources ultimately effect unequal bureaucratic participation because that strategy must usually be justified at the margin of organizational budgets. Resource limitations are probably only slight deterrents in the implementation of the most profitable strategies, but in less promising, secondary arenas they seem to impose harsh and disparate ceilings.

Nuclear regulatory decision making further exacerbates unequal participation by its effects on the maintenance of interest groups. Interest groups that generate technical analysis—on which NRC policy making must rely heavily—for their members have an advantage over groups that do not produce it as a matter of course. Firms and scientists value the technical information provided by the AIF and the EEI, and support the associations in part to receive these selective rewards. Individuals that support groups such as the National Resources Defense Council derive purposive and/or solidary satisfaction from membership and give no organizational reason for the group to produce extensive technical information. Associations of cost-bearers therefore find NRC decision-making procedures consistent with their goals of organizational maintenance, while groups of beneficiaries find them inimical. Cost-bearers can offer technical support to the NRC as a byproduct of their organizing efforts. Beneficiaries, who must expend extra resources to produce that expertise, prefer to rely on media events or mass protests that reinforce the salience of the group's purpose or provide members with solidary benefits.

In sum, the major consequences of NRC participation incentives are that (1) a national mediation of interests in nuclear power is discouraged; (2) the resolution of issues by the NRC is subjected to an imbalanced presentation of views, favoring producing interests; and (3) group participation is often left to parochial, local utility interests and local concerned citizens.

Bureaucratic Strategies

Bureaucratic agencies need not behave as passive and impartial recipients of the inputs and pressures of their interest group constituency. They can favor or disfavor interest groups through informal communication and policy discretion as they choose, and they can affect the initiatives of interest groups by the incentives they establish for participation. Why, then, does the NRC favor formality and adjudication, and why did it broaden its outreach in the late 1970s to include several beneficiary groups? The answers, as proposed in the organizational theory, lie in the cues and constraints emanating from its sovereign political environment. Let us consider, then, the effects of Congress, the president, and the courts on NRC behavior toward its constituency.

Congressional Constraints. Bureaucratic agencies do not relate to Congress as an institution; they understand Congress in terms of the committees that oversee them. If the conventional wisdom is true, and if the wishes of committees affect agency behavior toward interest groups, the NRC's overtures to interest groups should have changed during the 1970s. Until the opening of the 95th Congress in January 1977, the NRC had the simplest oversight structure and probably the clearest congressional cues of any agency of the federal government. The Joint Committee on Atomic Energy monopolized control over it and expressed vigorous support for the rapid development of commercial nuclear power. The JCAE's monopoly began to weaken, however, as the environmental movement of the late 1960s and early 1970s, and the energy crisis of the mid-1970s, expanded the political arena. In 1977 the JCAE was dissolved, and primary congressional jurisdiction over the NRC was assigned to the Environment Committee in the Senate and to both the Interior and Commerce committees in the House. The reorganization drastically altered the interests of the NRC's overseers. The agency's legislative sovereign was restructured from a centralized single-interest committee of twenty to a decentralized, multi-interest, set of committees composed of fifteen senators and eighty-seven congressmen with virtually no jurisdiction over promotional policy such as nuclear research and development programs. Furthermore, of the eighteen members of the 1974 JCAE (see Table 4.4) only three—Senator Howard Baker, and Representatives Teno Roncalio and Manuel Lujan (both House Interior)—sat on NRC oversight committees in 1977–78. Finally, the House Interior Committee was chaired by Morris Udall of Arizona, a long-time proponent of environmental values. By 1977, then, whatever institutional or individual support for permissive regulation the NRC might have accumulated had been thoroughly eroded.

The reorganization produced (or was associated with) several changes that hypothetically condition bureaucratic behavior (see Chapter 2). First, and obviously, the interests represented in the NRC's oversight structure were multiplied. Primary committee responsibility increased from one to at least three, with two of the new overseers—the House Interior and the Senate Environment Committees—explicitly representing environmental concerns. Even granting the possibility of heterogeneous interests among individual members of the joint committee, the new system provided stronger representation for regulatory (as opposed to promotional) interests by institutionalizing their connection with the NRC. Second, the

TABLE 4.4
The Last Joint Committees on Atomic Energy, 1974 and 1976

Year	Senate		House	
	Democrats	Republicans	Democrats	Republicans
1974	Pastore (V-Chr.)	Aiken	Price (Chr.)	Hosmer
	Jackson[a]	Bennett	Holifield	Anderson
	Symington	Dominick	Young	Hansen
	Bible	Baker[b]	Roncalio[c]	Lujan[c]
	Montoya		McCormack	
1976	Pastore (Chr.)	Baker[b]	Price (V-Chr.)	Anderson
	Jackson[a]	Case	Young	Lujan[c]
	Symington	Pearson	Roncalio[c]	Horton
	Montoya	Buckley	McCormack	Hinshaw
	Tunney		Moss[d]	

[a] Member Senate Committee on Energy and Natural Resources, 1978 (no NRC oversight).
[b] Member Senate Committee on Environment and Public Works, 1978.
[c] Member House Committee on Interior and Insular Affairs, 1978.
[d] Member House Committee on Interstate and Foreign Commerce, 1978.

new structure formalized the congressional job of investigation and oversight of administrative action. The House Interior Committee employs a subcommittee on special investigations, and the House Interstate Commerce Committee a subcommittee on oversight and investigations. The latter, moreover, was chaired in 1977 and 1978 by John Moss of California, a long-time advocate of consumer and environmental concerns. The JCAE had no subcommittee charged only with oversight.

The structural changes seemed to influence the effort that Congress put into the oversight of nuclear regulation. Prior to the demise of the JCAE, the NRC had been one of the least frequently scrutinized federal regulatory agencies. During the 93rd and 94th Congresses it ranked fourteenth out of seventeen in hearing frequency (Table 4.5), and from 1973 to 1976 it was the subject of only 21 hearings, while the average regulatory agency was subjected to 61.6 hearings. In further comparison, the EPA, which pursues objectives similar to those of the NRC, received ten times as much attention. Relative to other congressional overseers the JCAE was simply not very busy.[43] After the new committees assumed jurisdiction over nuclear regulation, the volume of congressional activity increased sharply. From an average of only 12 hearings per congress[44] during the 93rd and 94th, the frequency of NRC oversight more than doubled to 28 hearings during the 95th Congress.

TABLE 4.5
Congressional Hearings on Regulatory Agencies:
93rd and 94th Congresses Through June 30, 1976

Regulatory agency	Number of hearings
Environmental Protection Agency	208
Federal Energy Administration	120
Federal Trade Commission	114
Federal Power Commission	90
Food and Drug Administration	80
Federal Reserve Board	77
Interstate Commerce Commission	70
Securities and Exchange Commission	65
Civil Aeronautics Board	55
National Transportation Safety Board	33
Federal Maritime Commission	26
Consumer Product Safety Commission	25
National Highway Traffic Safety Administration	25
Nuclear Regulatory Commission	21
Occupational Safety and Health Administration	20
National Labor Relations Board	13
Commodity Futures Trading Commission	5
TOTAL	1,047
	(mean = 61.6)

SOURCE: James P. McGrath, "Hearings on Selected Regulatory Agencies: 93rd and 94th Congresses, thru June 30, 1976," Congressional Research Service, September 22, 1976, p. iii. Rank ordering and mean calculation are mine.

If oversight influences bureaucratic strategies toward interest groups as we have hypothesized, the structure and practice of NRC oversight ought to have unambiguous impacts: all of the congressional constraints point in the same direction. Prior to 1977 they were all conducive to co-optive bureaucratic strategies. A single congressional sovereign with promotional interests, no oversight subcommittee, and a low level of oversight activity allows, and indeed encourages, a regulatory agency to accommodate its cost-bearing constituency. After 1977, however, the congressional constraints all encouraged a more pluralistic strategy. The joint influence of multiple overseers, oversight subcommittees, and increased oversight activity ought to promote agency cooperation with beneficiaries and cost-bearers alike.

The behavior of the NRC toward its interest group constituency over the period of this study is essentially consistent with the influence of Congress as hypothesized. This is especially true of NRC efforts to interact with groups through informal channels. Before the

Joint Committee was disbanded, NRC overtures were directed almost exclusively toward the national representatives of electric and
nuclear power producers. After 1977 the agency extended "insider"
status to several environmental groups. Even though they lacked the
rapport their opponents enjoyed with the NRC staff and were precluded by scant resources from establishing a regular working relationship, they benefited from the agency's sincere effort to broaden
participation in nuclear regulation, and presumably to expand its
political base.

Important aspects of the formal NRC decision-making routines
are also mostly in line with the cues the agency has received from
Congress. The emphasis on ad hoc policy making through licensing
proceedings and on quasi-judicial procedures were not mandated by
law,[45] but were developed by the AEC while the Joint Committee
was in power, and inherited by the NRC. The elaborate licensing
procedures, tailor-made for accommodating the needs of individual
applicants and for defending reactor and disposal plans against subsequent attack in hearings and litigation,[46] did not change substantially during the late 1970s. Congress tried unsuccessfully, however,
to reform them with generic standards—an important nonproducer
goal.

Whether the behavior of the NRC toward its constituents was
substantially caused by the cues from Congress or was simply coinci-
dent with them cannot be determined with confidence until alternative explanations are entertained. The relationship is plain, but the
degree of causality depends on the contribution of other factors, in
particular presidential and judicial constraints.

Presidential Constraints. Although the size, expertise, and political support of the bureaucracy make it difficult to control, presidents have sufficient resources of their own that they can reasonably
expect to influence even the independent agencies of the government's "fourth branch." The NRC is an independent agency; it is
not, like the Department of Energy, under the president's direct
control. Nevertheless, even a one-term president can influence the
agency in several ways. The chairman of the NRC is selected by the
president from the five commissioners, and serves at the president's
pleasure.[47] The commissioners, who serve staggered five-year terms,
are appointed by the president. The president also possesses the
familiar leverage of recommending the agency's budget and bargaining with its congressional overseers. Presidents Ford and Carter,

who were strongly interested in nuclear power, employed all of these channels.

President Ford was a strong supporter of nuclear power development. His commitment included not only the expansion of domestic generating capacity but also the increased use of nuclear power by oil-poor nations abroad. In his February 26, 1976, message to Congress he emphasized that "greater utilization must be made of nuclear energy. . . . It is likewise vital that we continue our world leadership as a reliable supplier of nuclear technology."[48] While decontrol of oil and natural gas prices and adaptation by the free market were the cornerstones of his energy policy, Ford nevertheless demonstrated strong and continuous support for enhanced nuclear power development. His administration annually endorsed the requests by ERDA for its liquid metal fast breeder reactor program, even though the costs were already triple original expectations. In 1976, for example, it approved an annual increase of 33 percent in the program's budget, largely to cover the unexpected costs of the controversial Clinch River demonstration project. Ford also proposed to Congress in 1976 the Nuclear Fuel Assurance Act, which would have expanded the nuclear fuel supply by opening the uranium enrichment industry to private firms, ending thirty years of government monopoly. The bill eventually succumbed to congressional concern about the administration's desire to assume the liabilities and assets of failed private ventures and to a crowded late-session Senate docket, but the attempt underlined Ford's support for nuclear power.[49]

The Ford administration also demonstrated its developmental enthusiasm through its choice of NRC commissioners. During the final years of the promotion-oriented AEC, President Nixon attempted to instill environmental sensitivity in the panel through its leadership. His appointments of James Schlesinger in 1972 and Dixie Lee Ray in 1973 as chairs were calculated to accommodate environmental criticism of the agency.[50] Ford reversed the practice with his choice of William Anders, a past commissioner of the maligned AEC and an ex-astronaut, as the first chairman of the NRC. When Anders resigned in 1976, Ford nominated George Murphy, the ex-director of the JCAE, but the Senate rejected him as too much of the old establishment. Ford persisted in recycling the establishment, however, by appointing Marcus A. Rowden, the final General Counsel of the AEC, as NRC chairman for 1976.

President Carter's position on nuclear power development was nearly opposite that of Ford and expressly more intense. During his 1976 presidential campaign Carter repeatedly stressed that he viewed nuclear power "as a last resort." His opposition derived primarily from his concern about the spread of nuclear material around the globe and, concomitantly, the proliferation of nuclear weapons. Particularly alarming was the plutonium breeder reactor, the latest generation in nuclear power, under demonstration in Europe and construction at Clinch River, Tennessee. The breeder is potentially the answer to the inefficient consumption of scarce and nonrenewable uranium by conventional light-water reactors because it produces as waste more plutonium than it consumes. The danger is that the higher radioactive content of breeder waste makes it a deadlier toxin, and a readier fuel for nuclear weapons. The plutonium waste from conventional reactors must be reprocessed in expensive plants to achieve a much higher radioactive concentration before it can be used for atomic weapons.* President Carter therefore ardently opposed plutonium breeders, but tolerated as immediate necessities conventional light-water reactors.

The president's position was articulated frequently and forcefully, and could not have been lost on the NRC. In his 1977 National Energy Plan and throughout his administration Carter recommended termination of the Clinch River breeder demonstration project even though Congress annually rebuked the request. European countries were often urged by Carter to forsake development of plutonium breeders and to rely on conventional reactors until a nonplutonium breeder was developed. In 1977 he even offered the United States as a site for the disposal of conventional reactor waste that other countries could not handle.[51] Finally, he postponed indefinitely the nuclear industry's proposal for reprocessing reactor waste to recover hazardous plutonium. The proposal would have alleviated long-term storage problems but exacerbated weapon proliferation dangers.

Despite his intense concern about nuclear weapons, Carter realized the importance of conventional reactors in the near term, and in 1978 introduced a bill, welcomed by the nuclear industry and denounced by the environmental community, to expedite reactor

---

*Even conventional reactors in the wrong hands are feared. Iraq's research reactor was not a breeder, yet Israel found it sufficiently threatening to destroy it in June 1981.

licensing. It promised to cut the licensing period roughly in half. The cues from the White House were not, however, ambiguous; the president also insisted that the safety and inspection standards for reactors be strengthened.[52] His appointments to the NRC further clarified his cautious approach to nuclear power development. His first three selections—Joseph Hendrie as chairman, Peter Bradford, and John Ahearne—were all cleared with national environmental groups before going to the Senate for successful confirmation.[53]

The behavior of the NRC toward its constituency tended toward congruence with the disparate interests of Presidents Ford and Carter. Under President Ford the cues were consistently promotional; hence, the new NRC had no executive incentives to deviate from the patterns of interest group relations that had long prevailed at the AEC. Under Carter the road to presidential approval was newly constrained. The NRC undoubtedly recognized that any environmental or beneficiary groups spurned by the agency would be sympathetically received at the White House. The repercussions for even an independent agency could be unpleasant. Given the obvious concern that President Carter expressed about the byproducts of nuclear power, it is reasonable to attribute the more pluralistic strategy of the NRC in the late 1970s to presidential influence.

This conclusion raises the obvious question of the relative importance of presidential and congressional constraints on bureaucratic behavior. In the case of the NRC the presidential constraints appear to have had greater force as evidenced in the different behavior of NRC policy makers and staff toward attentive interest groups. The major change in agency-group relations in 1977 was effected by the upper echelon in the NRC, when the commissioners took the initiative and cooperated sincerely with beneficiaries who had previously been excluded. The staff only reluctantly began extending routine informational courtesies. In general, because presidential influence filters down through the bureaucratic hierarchy, it should manifest itself in precisely this way. Congressional influence, by contrast, is exercised through committees, subcommittees, and their staffs, which have political and professional ties to the permanent bureaucracy. The fact that the significant changes in NRC strategies did not seriously involve the permanent regulatory staff suggests that the congressional reorganization was not yet carrying much weight. It is, of course, only prudent to conclude that the unambiguous shift of both external influences in 1977 toward environmental values produced the shift in bureaucratic strategy. It is nonetheless worth keeping in mind as we try to understand the organizational politics of energy that the influence of presidential turnover was, in this instance, greater than that of congressional reorganization.

Judicial Constraints. The 1960s and 1970s were decades of judicial activism in the realm of administrative policy making. The courts became vigorous overseers of policy implementation; indeed, in fields such as education, civil rights, consumer protection, and environmental quality they probably became the dominant oversight institution. The general thrust of this activism has been to expand the rights of interests that had traditionally been underprotected in the administration of the law. Environmental and other nonproducing interests in nuclear regulation have benefited, or stand to benefit, from judicial decisions in at least four areas: the doctrine of standing, application of the National Environmental Policy Act (NEPA), the awarding of legal fees, and administrative procedure.

Before an interest can influence an agency with a lawsuit, the interest must have legal standing. Until the early 1970s the courts employed a doctrine that tended to make the diffuse beneficiaries of regulatory laws ineligible to bring suit against a regulated industry. Traditionally a party was granted standing only if it could satisfy the "legal wrong" test. That is, it must have suffered an injury against which it was afforded protection explicitly by common law or statute.[54] The doctrine prevented suits by interests harmed by administrative action but not explicitly designated for protection in the law. In a 1970 Supreme Court decision the test was mostly supplanted by a more liberal "zone of interests" test, requiring that the interest seeking to sue be "arguably within the zone of interests to be protected or regulated by the statute or constitutional guarantee in question."[55] Qualified interests are then entitled to seek review of agency actions under Section 10(a) of the APA. The essence of the new doctrine was to shift standing determinations from a legalistic to a substantive basis; if the courts construed an interest to be *intended* for protection by a law, the interest was entitled to sue.[56] The practical effect was to increase the number of agency constituents who could influence the agency through lawsuits.

Standing has also been liberalized with respect to the type of interest or value that can claim injury. Traditionally it required a claim of "injury in fact"—operationally, economic or direct physical damage.[57] Since 1966 a series of decisions has granted standing for injuries to intangible and noneconomic values. Of relevance to nuclear regulation were the 1965 decision, *Scenic Hudson Preservation Conference v. FPC*, which recognized injuries to conservationist and aesthetic values, and the 1972 decision, *Sierra Club v. Morton*, which acknowledged the standing of environmental and recreational values.[58] Although interest groups must still contrive an injury to a concrete individual on whose behalf a suit is brought, the liberalized rules of standing now effectively provide access to judicial review for all of the interests affected by nuclear regulation.[59]

Another area of potential judicial impact is the court's interpretation of the applicability of the National Environmental Policy Act that took effect January 1, 1970. In the first two years of its operation, over 150 suits were filed in federal court to determine which public actions had to be assessed for environmental impacts, and how the assessments had to be carried out. In 1971 an environmental group was granted standing to sue the AEC in defense of water-quality interests. Although the fact that the suit was allowed was, at the time, a significant challenge to AEC discretion, its success affected far more than the agency's concern about judicial review. In *Calvert Cliffs Coordinating Committee v. AEC* the court found that the agency's decision to permit nuclear plant construction while environmental impacts were being assessed was in violation of the NEPA.[60] Nuclear licensing has subsequently required prior assessments of all environmental impacts and evaluations of those impacts relative to interests in power production and reasonable cost.

A third area of potential judicial impact is the issue of legal fees. Beneficiaries of nuclear regulation suffer, as we have seen, a gross disadvantage, relative to regulatory cost-bearers (producers and plant applicants) because they have been unable to accumulate the resources required for successful participation. To compensate partially for their own resource inadequacies intervenors must request extra time for preparing each phase of their case, but this produces a further undesirable outcome—lengthy licensing delays. The unequal representation, and perhaps even the delays, could be avoided if legitimate intervenors were compensated for the costs of legal counsel and expert witnesses. Although such a policy raises difficult issues of qualifications and fairness, legal precedent for it has developed since the mid-1960s.

Groups such as environmentalists are acting in effect as "private attorney generals" when their administrative interventions and judicial appeals attempt to secure compliance with broad laws. Because their participation serves this important function and goes unrewarded by financial settlements, it is arguably worthy of public support. The courts generally reject requests for compensation unless provided for by statute; however, precedents for more generous criteria exist.[61] A. U.S. District Court, for example, used its "equitable powers" to award legal and expert witness fees to a group that brought suit under an environmental law that did not provide for compensation.[62] Congress has shown sympathy for the concept and, in fact, excluded nuclear intervenor compensation from the 1974 Reorganization Act only in a last minute conference committee compromise.[63] Notwithstanding such legislative and judicial support, and the additional precedent of paid participation in other federal agencies, the NRC continues to resist the innovation.[64] A statutory requirement for nuclear intervenor compensation is unlikely to be enacted by the conservative government of the early 1980s, but further judicial support could succeed in encouraging its adoption by the NRC itself.

Although the thrust of future judicial constraints can only be guessed, a major 1978 Supreme Court decision provides strong clues to demands that will be made of NRC administrative procedures by the courts. The decision, *Vermont Yankee Nuclear Power Corporation v. Natural Resources Defense Council, Inc.*, represents a clear, though not complete, break with the trend of expanding beneficiary rights in regulation. At issue in the decision were the NRC's rule-making procedures to determine, on a general basis, the environmental hazards of nuclear waste disposal and fuel recycling. The NRC had followed the notice and comment procedures for rule making under Section 553 of the Administrative Procedures Act: participation was allowed through written submissions and oral statements, but formal procedures such as cross-examination were eschewed. The case facing the Supreme Court was an appeal of a Federal Court of Appeals decision that the procedures failed to provide a "thorough exploration" of the waste disposal issue or to afford a "meaningful opportunity" for environmental group participation, and that the NRC employ one or more suggested devices in "creating a genuine dialogue." The Supreme Court unanimously overturned the lower court ruling and, more significantly, "announced the broad, novel and important principle that federal courts may not, absent extraordinary circumstances, require federal agencies to employ procedural formalities beyond those specified in the Administrative Procedures Act."[65]

The *Vermont Yankee* decision reversed nearly a decade of efforts by lower courts and federal agencies to develop "hybrid" rule-making procedures that would provide an adequate record for administrative action and judicial review on the merits of generic issues. It does not, however, guarantee that the courts will be helpless overseers as agencies practice greater rule making. It also recognizes that agencies must provide evidentiary records even in informal rule making and authorizes courts to remand administrative records to the agency for elaboration even though the agency has complied with APA requirements. In effect the Supreme Court is giving regulatory agencies two conflicting signals. The courts may not impose novel procedures such as hybrid rule making on informal administrative policy making, but they reserve the right to reject decisions on the merits until satisfactorily substantiated. With regard to group participation, the signals are less mixed. The agency need not establish improved participation opportunities unless its own research and that submitted spontaneously by interested parties are inadequate to justify a decision.

Despite this profusion of judicial oversight of regulation generally, and of nuclear regulation particularly, the NRC was not led to modify its relationship with interest groups. To be sure, lawsuits by environmental groups have forced it to assess carefully the environmental impacts of nuclear power plants and to reconsider its decisions in numerous cases. But neither the successful appeals nor the steady expansion of the rights of all regulatory beneficiaries altered appreciably the efforts of the NRC to cooperate with its constituency. Its licensing and rule-making procedures stood firm throughout the 1970s against the many judicial pressures to make them more accessible. Its informal overtures toward interest groups, though more pluralistic in later years, seem similarly unperturbed by judicial influence. What improvements environmental groups enjoyed in their political relationship with the NRC did not coincide with their major legal victories. Overall, the courts have aided the substantive cause of nonproducer interests in nuclear power, but they have not significantly improved the important informal and political relationships between those interests and the agency.

Conclusion

In the late 1970s the organizational relationships of nuclear regulation were evidencing movement away from the basically "captured" form of the old AEC, and toward a more "pluralistic" config-uration. The movement was not, however, great. The initiatives of interest groups still tended toward a monopoly of major producer associations with poor environmental competition. The cause of this, we can at least tentatively conclude, was in large part the incentive (or disincentive) structure for organized participation established by the NRC. Without change in these incentives, group initiatives will continue to be characterized by monopoly.

Some limited movement toward broader interest representation in nuclear regulation resulted from changes in informal efforts by the agency to cultivate wider political support. These changes appear to have been encouraged primarily by the turnover in presidential leadership from Ford to Carter, and secondarily by the reorganiza-tion of congressional oversight. Although the hypotheses concerning the effects of presidential and congressional constraints were basical-ly supported while those governing judicial constraints were not, conclusions regarding the absolute and relative strength of these hypotheses must await the evidence of additional cases. At this junc-ture it is equally remarkable that, despite the external incentives for the NRC to pluralize its interest group support, its efforts to do so were meager indeed. With the change of presidential administration in 1980 back to pro-nuclear leadership, it is only reasonable to ex-pect the organizational relationships underpinning nuclear regula-tion to return quickly and easily to their tenacious, captured form.

5

OIL REGULATION

When President Reagan decontrolled domestic oil prices in January 1981, he terminated one of the most controversial programs ever operated by the federal government. Critics of the program indeed blamed oil regulation for many of the energy and economic problems of the 1970s. Supporters, by contrast, regarded it as a necessary defense against cartelization of the world oil market and "windfall" profiteering by major oil companies. The charges against regulation described utter failure: creating gasoline shortages, subsidizing oil imports, discouraging conservation and domestic production, and undermining the dollar. The case in its defense approached nobility: protecting American business and consumers against extortionate OPEC prices, preserving competition in the oil industry, and mitigating the energy hardships suffered by the poor. The extent to which oil regulation actually produced these costs and benefits is a matter of dispute—and a contributor to the controversy. The key to the controversy, however, is not the magnitude of the program's successes and failures but the sheer number and diversity of interests that it directly affected.

This aspect of oil regulation in particular provides an instructive case for understanding modern energy politics. The entire oil industry, the gamut of industrial and commercial energy users, and individual consumers of gasoline and home heating oil had major stakes in the program. Also experiencing sizable impacts were conservation interests, alternative energy sources, labor, and finance. Interest was widespread because oil regulation addressed matters of fundamental concern: the price and availability of the major modern energy source. For nearly a decade the now-terminated program exposed the political consequences of government efforts to manage basic problems of both energy production and consumption—problems and politics that will be with us for some time to come—and, in that role, provides a valuable area for research of more than historical significance.

Incrementalism and the Creation of Oil Regulation

If one understands nothing else about the oil regulatory program of the 1970s, it should be this: oil regulation was not the product of a thorough and reasoned effort to address fundamental issues of the national energy problem; rather, it was the accumulated product of many efforts to handle essentially short-term problems incrementally. This fact alone helps to explain many of the program's important aspects. The immense complexity, counterproductive consequences, eroding political support, and swift demise of oil regulation can all be traced to the program's incremental development.

The latest regime of oil regulation—not to be confused with earlier prorationing and import restrictions—had its inception with President Nixon's general wage-price freeze of August 1971. From that date until 1973 oil prices were regulated by the Cost of Living Council in the same fashion as prices for other domestic goods and services. That is, after several months of frozen prices during Phase I of Nixon's program, oil prices rose by administrative determination. Phase II of administered prices lasted until January 1973, when Phase III of voluntary price restraint was instituted. In the summer of 1973, however, rapid price increases in heating oil and gasoline began drawing special attention to oil. The result was a special Phase IV of controls for domestic crude oil and its products.

The controls imposed in August 1973 established the basic framework for the regulations that subsequently became part of American energy policy. A two-tiered system of pricing was developed as a compromise between general interests in stable, noninflationary prices and industry interests in profits and production incentives. The price of domestic crude from properties that were producing in 1972 was fixed at May 15, 1973, prices plus $1.35/barrel, for volumes up to 1972 levels. This production was termed "old" oil. To encourage production of "new" oil—defined as (1) from properties not producing in 1972, or (2) in excess of 1972 levels from properties already producing then—it was not subjected to price controls. The prices of refined products were controlled by rules governing the passthrough of refining, transportation, and distribution costs.

The basic trade-off between lower prices and increased domestic production was exacerbated and complicated that fall by the OPEC embargo on oil exports to the United States, and the following spring by rapid increases in OPEC oil prices. The immediate concern raised by the embargo was the prospect of severe product shortages that not only inconvenienced and burdened consumers but also threatened the existence of many independent refiners and marketers who were unable to purchase crude oil and refined products. Congress responded to the crisis by passing the Emergency Petroleum Allocation Act (EPAA) in November 1973.[1] The terms were vague and left a great deal of discretion to President Nixon and the Federal Energy Office (FEO) he created to implement the act. In essence the act instructed the administration to promulgate mandatory price and allocation regulations that would (1) protect consumers against price gouging, (2) distribute resources fairly and with minimal harm to the economy, and (3) preserve competition in the petroleum industry by protecting the market share of independents. It placed the FEO in the business of not only setting prices at every level of the complex petroleum industry, but also allocating crude oil and products among its hundreds of thousands of small and large firms.[2] The act also complicated the regulatory constituency. The FEO's supporters included consumers, commercial users (particularly in transportation and agriculture), independent marketers of refined products, wholesale and resell distributors of refined products, and independent refiners. Opposition to the regulations came from major integrated oil corporations and independent producers.

In May 1974 the temporary FEO was replaced by Congress with the permanent Federal Energy Administration (FEA). Although ostensibly the center of national energy policy development, the FEA was mainly occupied with the implementation of oil price and allocation controls. From this point forward oil regulation shed its crisis mode of operation and settled into a routine much like other regulatory agencies. Over the ensuing three-and-a-half years of the FEA's existence petroleum regulation was to evolve in incremental fashion; general rules were frequently adjusted, and specially burdened firms were granted exemptions.

The FEA made two decisions, however, that were notable for

their political impact. First, it established the "entitlements" program to equalize crude costs throughout the industry and thereby correct the artificial competitive advantages created by a two-tiered system. Refiners with large supplies of domestic crude had by law to subsidize refiners who relied on greater than average amounts of foreign crude. Another important decision responded to concerns that were far more parochial than the national energy problem. A "small refiner bias" was included in the program to bolster the competitive position of firms producing less than 100,000 barrels per day—and to win the support of 150 small refiners across the nation.

Congress also made several significant changes in the regulatory program. When the 94th Congress convened in January 1975, the country was in the throes of a veritable economic crisis; unemployment was at its highest level since the Great Depression, and inflation was raging at an annualized rate of 12.2 percent. No small part of the blame was being heaped on energy prices, which had soared 33.5 percent in 1974, and on oil imports, which had doubled over the same period.[3] To much of the Congress the energy problem seemed to be essentially one of exorbitant price. This was not the view of the Ford administration, which regarded high prices as a bitter but necessary antidote for wasteful consumption and sluggish domestic production of energy. After a year of acrimonious bargaining, however, Ford reluctantly signed into law on December 22, 1975, the Energy Policy and Conservation Act (EPCA).[4] It pursued conservation through regulation: automobile manufacturers were required to satisfy a progressive scale of fuel efficiency standards, and appliance manufacturers to label their products with energy efficiency information. Most of the law, however, addressed the immediate problem of energy prices.

The EPCA's answer to inflation and the balance of payments deficit was an extension of the EPAA oil regulatory program until September 30, 1981 (with presidential authority to terminate the program after May 1979). It also made multi-tier oil prices statutory and established an average domestic price for crude oil of $7.66 per barrel, which amounted to a price rollback of $1.09 per barrel.[5] The FEA was given discretion to increase the average price up to 10 percent per year—or more, with congressional approval. It implemented the average price by limiting old oil—which it now labeled "lower tier"—to $5.25 per barrel and controlling previously uncontrolled "upper-tier" oil at $11.28 per barrel. *All* domestic crude oil

TABLE 5.1

Positions on Petroleum Regulation, by Sector

Sector	Percent of groups taking position	Dominant position(s)	Reasons for absence of positions[a]
Environmental groups	22% (2)	Deregulate prices (regulate profits)	Divides organization; causes conflict with consumer PIGs (7)
Consumer and PIGs	33% (3)	Continue all regulation	Divides organization (6)
Petroleum and gas industry	88% (14)	Total deregulation; product decontrol (1); continue regulation (1)	Both natural gas associations avoid conflicts with oil industry (2)
Electric power	12% (1)	Deregulation	Divides organization; deference to oil industry (7)
Conservation and renewable energy	29% (2)	Deregulation (1); continue regulation (1)	Divides organization (5)
Labor unions	88% (7)	Continue all regulation	Divides organization (1)
Commercial users	62% (8)	Deregulation of new crude; continue regulation (1)	Impact too indirect (5)
Financial institutions	(0)		Impact too indirect (2)
TOTALS	51% (37)		49% (35)

[a] Number of groups not taking positions given in parentheses.

was thus regulated below world levels.[6] The FEA also received discretionary authority over the decontrol of product prices (subject to congressional veto) and resources to assess compliance and demand refunds. These were the last substantive statutory changes that affected oil regulation over the period of this study. President Carter's decision to begin gradual decontrol of domestic crude oil prices in May 1979, and the imposition of the Windfall Profits Tax on the proceeds of decontrol in 1980, did not affect the results of this analysis.

The Regulatory Constituency

To establish the outer boundaries of the constituency concerned with oil regulation, each group was asked if it held a formal position on the program. If the answer was affirmative, the position was ascertained; if negative, an explanation was sought. The results, summarized by interest sector in Table 5.1, show that slightly more than half of the interest groups took a formal position. Although the large number of petroleum groups in the sample undoubtedly makes this figure an overestimate of the level of interest among the complete group population, the issue does appear to have attracted serious consideration from a broad range of interests, including groups in every sector except finance.[7]

Environmental groups generally avoided taking positions on petroleum regulation, in part because it was not an issue on which environmentalists were in consensus. On the one hand, higher oil prices through deregulation might promote conservation and renewable (e.g., solar) energy, both of which environmentalists favor. On the other hand, environmentalists are perpetual opponents of major oil corporations and are reluctant, to say the least, to advocate the industry's position. Their reticence on the issue is also in part strategic: they would risk the loss of consumer groups as future political allies if they opposed those groups on this issue. As a consequence only the Sierra Club and the Natural Resources Defense Council took positions—favoring deregulation for its incentives for conservation and renewable energy, but insisting that immediate corporate profits be taxed or otherwise limited.

Among general public interest groups, only those that profess exclusively consumer interests took positions on oil regulation. These three—the Energy Policy Task Force of the CFA, Energy Action, and the Citizen-Labor Energy Coalition—adamantly opposed deregulation of oil prices. They rejected the argument that the oil industry required higher prices as incentives to increase supplies, and believed that current prices provided generous returns on investment. They argued further that a free market does not exist in petroleum and that American consumers should not be asked to pay OPEC-determined prices. Finally, they claimed that demand for petroleum products such as gasoline and home heating oil is price-inelastic and therefore unlikely to be reduced substantially by higher petroleum prices. Higher prices in their view would only be inflationary. The remainder of the public interest groups accepted many of these arguments, but were forced into silence by the competing prospects of price conservation and alternative energy stimuli.

Though only three or four national public interest groups represented the consumer interest in continued oil regulation, the position was not without substantial group backing. Organized labor lent nearly unanimous support to the cause, with seven of the eight unions in this study, including the AFL-CIO, standing firmly behind the regulations.[8] Like consumer groups they were persuaded that a free market does not exist in petroleum and therefore that deregulation would not necessarily stimulate supplies. Though they recognized that supply curtailment can cost jobs, they believed their members would suffer harsher consequences from the inflation that oil deregulation could produce. Joining labor and the public interest advocates of regulation was an organization of agricultural users, the National Farmers Union, and a public interest group specializing in decentralized, renewable, energy delivery systems, the Institute for Local Self-Reliance.

The greatest support for deregulation of oil came from the petroleum industry and commercial users of petroleum. The American Petroleum Institute (API) and the major integrated oil firms were unequivocal, and their position had multiple justifications: the inherent incentives for vigorous exploration and production; the conservation promoted by higher prices; the absence of the shortages that brought the regulations into existence; the public and private resources "wasted" on administrative costs and onerous reporting requirements; and the increased oil investment that would result if the uncertainties of regulation were eliminated. Somewhat less adamant was the position of the Council of Active Independent Oil and Gas Producers, the National Oil Jobbers Council (NOJC), and the partially integrated, large refiners such as Ashland Oil. The National Petroleum Refiners Association (NPRA), which represents both the smallest independent refiners and the largest integrated refiners, did not take a position on crude price regulation but did advocate product decontrol.

The only industry opposition came from the American Petroleum Refiners Association (APRA), which represents small refiners, and the Society of Independent Gasoline Marketers of America (SIGMA), which represents nonbranded, independent marketers of gasoline. The APRA was internally divided on crude pricing but favored the retention of crude oil allocation and the small refiner entitlement bias. SIGMA favored continued product allocation but was uncommitted on the issue of crude price controls. Both groups took positions only on the portion of the regulatory issue that affected them most directly; they did not wish to cause unnecessary friction with the industry on secondary issues. Similarly, the American Gas Association (AGA) and the Natural Gas Supply Committee had an understanding with the API, of which they are members, that they would not become involved on issues of central importance to the other's industry.[9]

Support for deregulation was rounded out with a number of commercial users. The Business Roundtable, the Chamber of Commerce, the American Trucking Associations (ATA), and the Motor Vehicle Manufacturers Association, among others, favored deregulation because it served their primary interest in adequate supplies, albeit at higher prices. Being commercial users, they can often pass higher costs on to consumers and are therefore not internally divided by the conflicting interests of more supplies and lower prices.

What relationship did this sizable population of concerned groups have with the relevant energy bureaucracy? Table 5.2 summarizes the relationship by reporting the "frequency of interaction" between the bureaucracy and each group, by sector. The indicator subsumes a range of political contacts including monitoring, informal lobbying, and formal participation. Although it does not measure the effectiveness of the relationships or distinguish the source of their development, it provides a valid "first-cut" at describing the organizational relationships. That is, groups not engaged in these conventional interactions will not emerge as important relations of the agency, and the quality of the relationships will not be disproportional to the frequency of interactions.

Only those groups that engaged in "constant" or "frequent" inter-

TABLE 5.2

Frequency of Group Interaction with Petroleum Regulatory Agencies (FEA and ERA)

Interest groups	Constant	Frequent	Sporadic	Infrequent	None	Percent with sporadic or more contact
Environmental groups			11% (1)	22% (2)	67% (6)	11% (1)
Consumer and PIGs			11% (1)	22% (2)	67% (6)	11% (1)
Petroleum and gas industry	69% (11)	12% (2)	6% (1)		12% (2)	81% (14)
Electric power				22% (2)	78% (7)	0%
Conservation and renewable energy					100% (7)	0%
Labor unions				12% (1)	88% (7)	0%
Commercial users		8% (1)	31% (4)	38% (5)	23% (3)	38% (5)
Financial institutions				50% (1)	50% (1)	0%

NOTE: For definitions of "frequency of group participation," see Table 4.1.

action are plausible candidates for mutually supportive political relationships with the regulatory agency. They are the ones that participated in all formal proceedings of importance, lobbied the agency informally and regularly, monitored agency agenda-building and
decision-making closely, and received numerous requests from the
agency for assistance. The "sporadic" participants were involved in
at most only a few formal proceedings, and pursued the informal
opportunities for influence with little vigor. Groups that interacted
"infrequently" or not at all were negligible factors in the agency's
relations with its constituency.

Drawing the line as generously as possible, below the level of
sporadic interaction, the following attentive constituency of oil regulation emerges. Environmental groups are virtually unrepresented.
Only Ralph Nader's PIRG maintained even sporadic contact with
the oil regulators, and its involvement ceased in early 1977 when its
oil expert resigned. By and large, public interest group participation
involved but one group, the Consumer Federation of America. Although the CFA's interactions can only be described as sporadic
because they included formal participation on one single, major
issue and occasional informal lobbying, its significance should not be
underestimated. The issue in which it was involved was resolved in
its favor, and the agency in its final years increasingly sought the
group's advice. The CFA's Energy Policy Task Force, which conducted its strategies, was organized in 1973 to advocate the consumer's interest in oil and gas price regulation. It speaks for fifty large
organizations, among them the AFL-CIO, the American Public Gas
Association, the National Rural Electric Cooperative Association
(NRECA), the National Farmers Union (NFU), and the U.S. Conference of Mayors. The scope of its membership makes it an obviously
attractive object of agency political interest.

Of the eight sectors examined, the oil and gas industry was the
most thoroughly involved. Associations and corporations alike maintained constant contact with agency staff, submitted written comments on hundreds of proposed rule makings, and testified at countless public hearings. The involvement of 69 percent of the groups
sampled from this sector is best described as constant. Moreover, the
only two groups that did not maintain sporadic or more contact with
the regulators are natural gas groups; they kept their distance out of
deference to the petroleum representatives.

The other interests that figured prominently in oil regulation are commercial users, 38 percent of whom had at least sporadic involvement with the regulators. Three transportation associations—the American Public Transit Association (APTA), the ATA, and the Transportation Association of America (TAA)—played brief but important roles: the last two were constantly involved during the oil shortage in 1974, attempting to secure priority allocations of fuel for their respective members, and the Transit Association participated vigorously in the consideration of diesel fuel decontrol in 1976. During times of ample supplies, however, these groups had virtually no contact with the regulatory program. The NFU, by contrast, submitted written comments frequently, testified sporadically, and lent its name to the CFA Task Force. The only user group that sustained frequent involvement was the Petrochemical Energy Group (PEG), composed of twenty-one major petrochemical firms, including E. I. duPont, Firestone Tire and Rubber, Goodyear Tire and Rubber, Monsanto, and Union Carbide, that use petroleum gases as feedstocks in their manufacturing processes. The PEG was organized in 1972 for the explicit purpose of participating collectively in regulatory programs (at that time administered by the Federal Power Commission) that affected the price and supply of feedstocks. Although the group has no permanent staff, it employs a Washington law firm, Baker and Botz—experienced in the petroleum and natural gas fields and headquartered in Houston—to monitor and participate constantly in regulatory programs. For the duration of the oil regulatory program, its rate of participation, formal and informal, qualifies as frequent.

A total, then, of twenty-one groups in this study made significant efforts to convey their views to the agency that administered the program. That represents a 42 percent reduction from the thirty-six groups that took a position on the issues of oil regulation. One sector that was solidly in favor of continued regulation, organized labor, made no effort to affect the implementation of the program or to develop political alliances with the agency. Indeed, every sector, except petroleum, that had some groups actively concerned with the issue had far fewer groups actually engaged in administrative politics. Those roles are played out among a limited number of actors, dominated by representatives of the oil industry and balanced by a handful of spokesmen for consumers and commercial users.

These are the general parameters of the relationships between the oil regulatory bureaucracy and its constituency, but the model still lacks important specifications. What strategies different groups pursued, how effective their strategies were in realizing policy goals, and how the bureaucracy contributed to interest intermediation are all important questions. Answers to them will elaborate the organizational politics of oil regulation and provide a basis for understanding policy in this important area of the energy problem.

Interest Group Initiatives

Interests affected by oil regulation had many means by which they might try to influence the program. As both the theory and the foregoing discussion of nuclear regulation suggest, however, the available methods of influence can be understood in terms of two general types: formal participation and informal lobbying. The varied activities subsumed by each category tend to have major causes in common and are therefore best analyzed as distinct types.

Formal Participation

The administrative procedures followed by the Federal Energy Administration and its successor, the Economic Regulatory Administration of the Department of Energy, are very different from those used by the Nuclear Regulatory Commission.* The ERA is not required by any of its enabling statutes to adhere to the formal adjudicatory or rule-making procedures spelled out in the APA; it may make decisions without judicial hearings and without relying solely on evidence adduced through hearings. Oil regulation needs to adhere only to the informal rule-making procedures specified in the APA: the agency must publish notice of a proposed rule at least 30 days before it becomes effective and may receive comments from interested parties during that period. The FEA act made two important revisions in these loose guidelines. It reduced the minimum comment period to a mere ten days, but it required oral hearings whenever a decision was "likely to have a substantial impact on the Nation's economy or large numbers of businesses and individuals" and prohibited waiver of notice and comment procedures except where strict compliance was found to cause serious harm or injury to the public health, safety, or welfare.[10] Within these guidelines oil regulation was administered by substantial, informal rule making to

---

*Although the oil regulations were eliminated in January 1981, the ERA (and its administrative procedures) remains part of the DOE.

establish general policy, and informal adjudication of exceptions and appeals to relieve specially burdened firms. This study concentrates on the rule-making process.

By all appearances the oil regulators strove to establish policy through general statements thereof rather than through the ad hoc adjudicatory method favored by nuclear regulators. What is more, the oil regulators usually seemed to incorporate extensive public input. In the FEA's first year of operation it conducted a full seventy-one rule makings and provided opportunity for prior public comment in forty-five of them. In twenty-seven instances a prior public hearing was held. Where prior public input was not allowed, hearings were held in twelve cases and written comments accepted in sixteen after the regulation took effect.[11] Through 1978 this formally open process continued apace, tallying well over two hundred rule makings in four years.

The amount of formal interest group participation, through written comments and oral testimony, varied predictably with the scope of the issue. Rule makings that promised broad and heavy impacts could generate hundreds of written comments and consume several days of hearings. Minor issues might yield rules with the benefit of only a few comments. For example, the FEA's proposal in April 1976 to decontrol the prices of diesel fuel and home heating oil prompted 125 groups to submit written comments and 22 to offer public testimony. In contrast, an August 1977 rule making to extend the crude oil buy/sell program's current allocation quarter produced only ten written comments and no oral statements.

To evaluate and explain this formal participation, the groups in the study were asked several questions that elaborate the play of influence in the comment and hearing procedures: (1) the proportion of relevant rule makings in which they participated formally; (2) the reasons why they participated in this manner; and (3) their assessment of the effectiveness of these channels relative to other modes of influence. This method omits the views of many small and independent refiners and marketers who frequently mailed comments to the regulators; however, their experiences are represented adequately by their national associations that are included in the study. All of the corporations, including the two large independents—Ashland and Clark—routinely submitted written comments on virtually all rule makings of relevance to corporate interests. Estimates of the precise frequency of written submissions vary from

85 to 100 percent of all relevant proceedings. Typically, oral presentations, offered less frequently, were made by company presidents or executive vice-presidents flown into Washington from corporate headquarters. This time-consuming form of participation was reserved for the most significant issues and was intended to demonstrate that significance to the agency hearing board.

Trade associations, particularly the largest, most heterogeneous ones, offered written and oral comments much less frequently than individual companies. The API took part in the formal processes only sporadically, and the NPRA only infrequently. The reticence of these major voices in the oil industry stems from the divisive structure of the regulations, which determined (and tried to equalize) the average cost of crude for every domestic refiner, specified what suppliers had to sell to what buyers, and controlled the competitiveness of different size refiners. Rule makings on such issues would pit one firm against another—sometimes large against small, but often large against large. The NPRA represents all domestic refiners and, as a consequence, could not achieve consensus on the many issues singling out small refiners. The API represents a wide range of oil interests, but speaks primarily for the largest integrated firms. Even so, the majors could not agree on those frequent issues involving entitlements and the equalization of crude oil costs; hence, the API often remained silent. Only on consensus issues such as average crude oil prices and product decontrol would it participate, and on these important issues the API put its full analytical forces behind its input.

Formal participation was more frequent by the smaller, homogeneous associations that were not divided by the regulations. The APRA, which represents small refiners, SIGMA, and the NOJC, which represents independent wholesale distributors of gasoline and retailers of home heating oil, had little difficulty achieving consensus. Written comments were submitted as a matter of course, and oral testimony was added where an emphatic statement seemed warranted. Although resource limitations kept participation down to about half of the relevant issues, that rate of involvement by small firms was comparatively regular.

A number of commercial user groups responded to agency requests for written or oral comments. The TAA submitted comments on a half-dozen allocation priority issues during the 1974 oil shortage, and testified once. The ATA and the APTA had similar concerns at that time, and utilized all available means of communication. After those issues dissipated, the TAA and the ATA absented themselves from regulatory decision-making. The APTA, on the other hand, continued to submit written comments and to testify on diesel fuel issues. The NFU testified infrequently, but routinely submitted comments on major issues such as gasoline or heating oil decontrol. The most frequent regulatory participant in this sector was the PEG, which was involved on every rule making dealing with allocation and averaged one rule making per month through 1978.

Consumer representatives were conspicuously absent from rule-making hearings and seldom filed comments with the agency. At times state or local governments would represent the consumer interests of their locales or regions; fuel-poor New England states, for example, were the most prominent in this category. National consumer and public interest groups, however, made only infrequent appearances before the agency. The Energy Policy Task Force of the CFA was extensively involved in the formal process in 1977 to establish a price monitoring system for home heating oil, and Consumers Union filed written comments several times. Relative to oil industry and even commercial user participation, the formal involvement of consumers can only be characterized as negligible.

The overall pattern of formal participation in oil regulation is peculiar. It includes much less involvement by public interest groups than occurs in environmental regulation. It is particularly out of line with the commitment of consumer organizations to the issues. The Energy Policy Task Force of the CFA and Energy Action were expressly established to address problems of escalating oil and gas prices, and broader groups such as Congress Watch and Consumers Union devoted substantial resources to oil price matters. Participation is also inconsistent with the cost of formal involvement. Because oil regulations were promulgated without quasi-judicial hearings, the minimum cost of formal participation was low. Legal counsel was unnecessary, and expertise was not challenged by cross-examination. Participants needed to be armed with no more than their opinions to contribute formally to oil regulation.

Why then were so many major interest groups unrepresented in the formal forums? The main reason is that formal channels were not the means by which the oil regulators *really* received input; informal channels were all-important. Partly because the notice and comment procedures seemed a poor way to adduce facts, and partly because methods of interest intermediation better suited to agency interests emerged, the formal decision-making procedures of the oil bureaucracy became perfunctory. Written comments on proposed rules were dominated by assertions of probable impacts without cogent analysis.[12] Oral testimony typically offered more of the same; time did not allow fully substantiated presentations.

The defects and ineffectiveness of the formal channels of participation were mentioned by every group interested in the regulatory program. For example, the director of governmental relations for a major oil company complained that "petroleum regulation hearings are a joke." He elaborated, "the hearings have no adversarial, evidenciary procedures, so there is no way to sort out the facts." A spokesperson for the Energy Policy Task Force of the CFA equated FEA hearings with "dog and cat shows," that is, "whoever cries the loudest wins." The strong consensus among corporate lobbyists, trade association representatives, and public interest advocates was that the probability of altering a proposed oil regulation through hearing participation was negligible. The impact of written comments was judged to be only marginally greater. Few of the concerned groups could cite instances in which they believed their written comments or public testimony had affected a proposed rule.

It was far more common for groups to view these formal channels as opportunities to "go on the record." They enabled interests to establish their views on regulatory issues officially, and prevented the agency or the courts from subsequently dismissing appeals on the grounds that groups failed to express objections at the appropriate time. Only one group, the PEG, regarded formal channels as effective means of influencing policy. Its spokesman argued that reliable analytical comments, documented with substantial technical data, had proven most effective among its various efforts to influence regulatory decision making. Although many groups agreed that high-quality technical analysis was basic to the exercise of influence, only the PEG regarded the formal channels as the most propitious means of conveying this information.

Informal Participation

Informal participation, which includes all modes of involvement other than written comments and hearing testimony, was widely and decisively regarded as the most effective means of influencing oil regulation—by thirteen of the fifteen groups familiar enough with the program to have an opinion.[13] Moreover, most groups agreed on how informal participation translated most successfully into influence. Agreement was so strong that a veritable law of influence emerges: the earlier in the decision-making process informal participation took place, the higher the probability that it would be influential.

The law-like properties of this assessment are a straightforward consequence of the three-stage process that typically was followed in promulgating oil regulations. The first and longest stage, which on major issues might last a year or more, was the transformation of a regulatory problem into a proposed rule. It occurred through successive revisions of draft proposals circulated through relevant agency channels. By all accounts, and by simple logic as well, regulations underwent the greatest change at this stage. Moreover, the rules governing ex parte communication did not prohibit informal interest group involvement. Groups consequently attempted vigorously to influence the problem agenda and proposed rules.

The second stage in the process began with the publication of the proposed rule in the *Federal Register* and concluded with the public hearings or, if no hearing was held, with the close of the public comment period. By statute this stage had to last at least ten days and, in practice, ran up to one month. Again, ex parte rules did not prohibit off-the-record input by interest groups. The final stage was a different story. After the close of public comments, the agency spent a short period ostensibly reviewing oral and written input, and reaching a final decision. Off-the-record communication during these deliberations was improper; only at the agency's request might groups introduce further information.

With two exceptions, every group with sufficient experience to comment explained that petroleum regulation was influenced mostly in the early, formative stages,[14] and that once proposed regulations reached the *Federal Register* they could not be changed. At that point, as several oil company representatives put it, "regulations are cast in cement." After two hundred or so rule makings it was clear to the overwhelming majority of nongovernmental participants that the agency seldom promulgated a final rule that differed significantly from the published proposal.

Although informal participation was organized whenever possible to complement this decision-making timetable, interest groups did not always direct their efforts toward the same public authorities. With respect to oil regulation, it is instructive to consider three arenas of informal participation: the agency staff, the agency administrator, and the Congress.

Lobbying the Agency Staff

Because oil regulations were promulgated informally and were open to extensive group input at the formative stages, the agency staff became the favored target of all groups that could afford to cultivate their favor. During the formative stage of rule making, groups had three basic objectives, each of which the staff could substantially further: (1) they wanted advanced intelligence about probable administrative actions so that they could increase their time for developing a response; (2) they hoped to acquire drafts of proposed regulations on which they might comment informally; (3) they strove to establish trusting, two-way flows of information between themselves and the agency—what groups referred to as "working relationships." The types of initiatives taken to reach these ends varied little from one interest group to the next; differences were largely in quantity.

The large trade associations, particularly the API and the American Gas Association (AGA), made the most extensive efforts to cultivate the agency staff. Each group has a team of five or six professionals whose sole responsibility is monitoring executive agencies.[15] Technical, legal, and analytical support is provided by other association staff. There is little doubt that these executive agency relations teams were successful in accomplishing the above objectives. According to sworn testimony before a congressional oversight committee,[16] and corroborated by several API members in interviews, their group was regularly able to obtain internal drafts of proposed rules. In fact, just four weeks after an API representative was berated by Senator Howard Metzenbaum for obtaining advance drafts of regulations, he was again providing drafts to member companies.[17] Once a week a committee composed primarily of the agency liaison specialists of major oil companies, and chaired by the director of agency relations for the API, met to review pending FEA/ERA decisions and to circulate and discuss drafts of proposed actions and regulations. The drafts were analyzed by API or corporate staff, depending on the impact of the proposal, and revisions were suggested to the agency. At least on limited technical issues the API and the majors acknowledged good success in having suggestions incorporated.

This type of informal influence is made possible largely through the cultivation of working relationships with agency staff. All but two of the industry groups claimed that the overwhelming majority of their FEA/ERA liaison work occurred at the staff level.[18] The preponderance of these staff contacts involved career managers and analysts at the GS-15 and GS-16 levels. The AGA, for example, made 85 percent of its contacts in the FEA/ERA at this level, while only 3 percent of its contacts involved secretaries or assistant secretaries, and the remainder involved lower-level clerks. The primary medium of exchange in relationships between group representatives and agency staff was technical information. Every industry group commented that the agency staff was hungry for any information or advice that prevented them from later appearing misguided or incompetent. The job of the group representative is to provide information and to demonstrate over time that the information serves the staff's needs. The manager of government relations for the AGA explained that his team approaches the agency staffer with the philosophy, "our job is to make you look good to your boss."

Gaining the trust of the agency staff is a lengthy process. All things being equal, the more constant the contact, the more rapid the build-up of trust. Every group with the time and resources to do so tried to keep in daily contact with at least a few staff members. The wealthiest groups might cultivate friendships with 25 or more key bureaucrats in a single agency. For example, the AGA's executive branch relations team maintained a file of 1,200 persons in relevant agencies who were called frequently to share informally in association intelligence, and presumably to pass on valuable information on agency decision making. The manager of the team also constructed a short list of 104 "key people" with whom he met personally and who could be counted on to provide information on agency decision making. In exchange, these staff members were routinely recipients of all forms of association analyses, forecasts, and recommendations.

The agency relations programs of the AGA and the API are significantly more ambitious than those of other groups concerned with petroleum regulation, but they are very similar in kind to the programs of smaller Washington operations. Virtually every group representative responsible for executive relations tries to develop working relationships and friendships with career regulators. Representatives are concerned primarily with the stable, nonpolitical administration, and not with the transient bureau chiefs, assistant secretaries, or administrators who serve at the president's grace. Technical information and credibility are the major tools of his trade, and his ability to tailor the information he provides to the needs of his group is the source of his influence. At the same time, the representative's influence is constrained by his need to maintain credibility. Information and advice that are solely self-serving threaten the bond of trust that facilitates the informal play of influence. In view of the fact that groups invest so heavily in this approach to governmental relations, it is reasonable to infer that, despite the constraints, this strategy of influencing regulatory policy has proved profitable.[19]

The picture of early and often staff-level involvement is an accurate description of the strategy pursued by most groups in this study to affect oil regulation. There exists considerable variation, however, in the extent to which the strategy was exploited. Successful cultivation of the regulatory staff required substantial investments of time and money. The technical expertise that provided the basis for working relationships is an extremely expensive medium of exchange for a group without a natural source. Public interest groups, which cannot use the cost of servicing regulatory agency staff as a tax deduction or pass the cost on to consumers, have difficulty competing in a market where corporations, which participate in regulation directly and finance the work of trade associations, develop expertise as part of normal business operations. Cultivation of regulatory staff is also time-consuming. Credibility develops slowly and must be nurtured with frequent meetings, phone calls, and successful technical assistance.

An indication of the relative ability of different sectors to utilize this strategy is provided by the resource figures for the organizations most concerned with oil regulation. Data on these indicators are provided in Table 5.3. Although the same caveats apply in the interpretation of these data as in the last chapter,[20] there is little question that the data provide valid indicators of relative organizational capability for cultivating the cooperation of the regulatory staff.

Only those organizations classified in Table 5.2 as having had at least "infrequent" involvement with the petroleum regulatory programs are included in these two tables. The variation in sectoral

TABLE 5.3
Washington Offices of Petroleum Regulation Constituents

Amount	Consumers	Majors and independent producers	Small refiners, independent marketers and retailers	Commercial users
Staff size				
200 and over		10% (1)		20% (2)
150–199				
100–149				10% (1)
50–99				
25–49		10% (1)		10% (1)
10–24		50% (5)	25% (1)	30% (3)
0–9	100% (3)	30% (3)	75% (3)	30% (3)
Median staff	5	16	4	14
Total staff of five largest groups	15	364	33	902
Annual budget				
Over $30 million		14% (1)		
$20–$30 million				
$10–$20 million				11% (1)
$5–$10 million				22% (2)
$1–$5 million		14% (1)		11% (1)
$500,000–$1,000,000		43% (3)	25% (1)	22% (2)
$250,000–$500,000		28% (2)	25% (1)	22% (2)
$100,000–$250,000	67% (2)		50% (2)	11% (1)
$50,000–$100,000	33% (1)			
$0–$50,000				
Not ascertained		—% (3)		—% (1)
Median budget	$200,000	$1,000,000	$310,000	$745,000
Total resources of five wealthiest groups	$485,000	$34,900,000	$1,750,000	$37,145,000

resources is dramatically large. Public interest groups even marginally involved in the implementation of oil regulations numbered only three, and had a total staff of fifteen and total expenditures of $485,000—only a small fraction of which was devoted to oil regulation. In light of the heavy demands of regulatory agency relations, this compares exceedingly unfavorably with the potential of the major integrated oil companies and independent producers. The five largest groups in that sector employed a total staff of 364 and had nearly $35 million to work with annually. I am not suggesting that policy influence is directly proportional to professional and financial resources, but these assets do determine which groups will have the greatest success in gaining the favor of the agency staff.

The small refiners, and the independent marketers and retailers, were also rather poorly represented by interest groups in Washington. These firms comprise that portion of the petroleum industry that was intended to benefit from oil allocation and price controls. The individual businesses are too small to have their own Washington offices. Some of the larger ones retained legal counsel to assist with application for exceptions and interpretations, but they did not engage in the full range of informal liaison activities that characterize the interest group approach. Even if the subsector is augmented with a major association that was unfortunately omitted from the sample, the total staff of the five largest groups was less than 40, and their total finances no more than $2 million.[21] While these beneficiaries were better equipped than consumers to utilize the important staff strategy of influence, they did not have the potential to match the effort expended by the dominant producing sector of the industry.

Commercial users were an entirely different story. Their organizations are among the best financed and staffed in the nation's capital. Ten of them that played some role, however small, in petroleum regulation had a median staff of 14 and a median budget of $745,000. The five largest were better financed and staffed than the largest organized representatives of major oil interests, yet only one group utilized its potential to participate informally and extensively at the staff level. Petroleum regulatory issues rarely impacted significantly and uniformly on the membership of the organizations. When issues did call for a response, these groups worked through formal channels and also, as we shall see, with other informal methods. Regular staff liaison was not, except for one group, a strategy used by commercial users of petroleum. As a consequence, organizational resources are indicative only of unused potential.

While the early and frequent cultivation of agency staff emerged as the preferred method of influence in oil regulation, other avenues of informal persuasion also proved important—all the more so because they were less dependent on financial and professional group resources than the staff relations that major oil companies dominated.

Lobbying the Political Leadership

Although the permanent regulatory staff took responsibility for the promulgation of rules, the political leadership of the oil regulatory agencies was not without influence. The leadership was, after all, accountable for all regulatory decisions and vulnerable to congressional veto on major decisions such as product decontrol or large crude oil price hikes. The political appointees heading the FEA or ERA may not have had the expertise to match arguments with the staff, but they were sufficiently threatened by political repercussions to constrain or veto staff policy with which they generally disagreed.

Two forms of interest group pressure were aimed at the political leadership of oil regulation: direct pleading and indirect political persuasion. The latter occurred largely through congressional intermediaries for the groups, and will be treated in the next section. The direct approach involved combinations of two basic tactics. The first was to treat the political leadership to the same technical input offered to the staff. The administrator is deluged with data, analyses, and forecasts with which to support a decision favored by a particular interest. This information aids him in his internal and external relationships, and eventually fosters for the group a position as trusted adviser. Administrators are sensitive also to a second, and overtly political, tactic. Unlike agency staff, political administrators are wary of the consequences that their decisions may have for the president or their congressional allies and opponents. Groups that cannot compete in the expensive technical game of staff relations may participate effectively in higher competition by simply providing political intelligence or threatening political repercussions.

Fortuitously, interest group use of the direct approach to political level regulators is easily described. Beginning in September 1974 the FEA required each of its employees holding the rank of GS-15 and above to maintain detailed records of "oral communications received from 'non-involved' persons expressing an opinion or viewpoint on a specific application, interpretation, request, appeal, petition for special redress, investigation, or enforcement proceeding before the FEA."[22] The stipulation was designed to increase the integrity of FEA decision making by establishing a public record of any informal conversations that might influence rule making or other agency decisions.[23]

While the FEA was in existence, the assistant administrator for regulatory programs—Gorman Smith, from July 1, 1975 (the first date for which information is available) through January 1977—was the highest authority responsible for oil regulation. After the Department of Energy was created, comparable authority was vested in the administrator of the Economic Regulatory Administration, David Bardin, who assumed responsibilities similar to those previously held by Gorman Smith. Although the Department of Energy does not require that substantive communications from outside interests be recorded, Bardin continued to do so through June 30, 1978.

Tables 5.4 and 5.5 present the distribution, by sector, of outside communications received respectively by Smith and Bardin. Table 5.5 also includes contacts with Bardin's assistant, Barton House, who also was a political appointee. Contacts with House comprise only 10 percent of the total contacts in Table 5.5 and do not impair the comparison with data on Gorman Smith. Interest group contacts with each administrator are aggregated over six-month periods to indicate any political change that might be occurring.

While Gorman Smith, a Gerald Ford appointee, was in charge, informal input from outside interests was thoroughly dominated by the petroleum industry. During the nineteen months for which records are available Smith met with outside interests 106 times; over three-fourths of the meetings were with oil industry representatives. The remaining communications were with commercial users (15%) and utilities (8%). Incredible as it may seem for an administrator ostensibly responsible for protecting individual consumers, not once in this period did Smith interact with a public interest group representative.[24] Moreover, the variety of informal input he received diminished over time. During Smith's last seven months in the position 81 percent of his interest group meetings involved petroleum industry representatives.

When David Bardin became administrator a dramatic change

TABLE 5.4

Frequency of Meetings Between Interest Groups and FEA Assistant Administrator of Regulatory Programs

Sectors	7/1/75– 12/31/75	1/1/76– 6/30/76	7/1/76– 1/15/77	Totals
Environmental groups	0% (0)	0% (0)	0% (0)	0% (0)
Consumer and PIGs	0% (0)	0% (0)	0% (0)	0% (0)
Petroleum and gas industry	77% (24)	72% (31)	81% (26)	76% (81)
Electric power	6% (2)	14% (6)	0% (0)	8% (8)
Conservation and renewable energy	0% (0)	0% (0)	0% (0)	0% (0)
Labor unions	0% (0)	0% (0)	0% (0)	0% (0)
Commercial users	16% (5)	14% (6)	16% (5)	15% (16)
Financial institutions	0% (0)	0% (0)	3% (1)	1% (1)
TOTALS	99% (31)	100% (43)	100% (32)	100% (106)

Table 5.5

Frequency of Meetings Between Interest Groups and ERA-DOE Officials

Sectors	9/19/77–12/31/77	1/1/78–6/30/78	Totals
Environmental groups	3% (1)	0% (0)	2% (1)
Consumer and PIGs	13% (4)	14% (5)	14% (9)
Petroleum and gas industry	60% (18)	43% (15)	51% (33)
Natural gas	3% (1)	14% (5)	9% (6)
Major oil	33% (10)	9% (3)	20% (13)
Independent producers	0% (0)	0% (0)	0% (0)
Small refiners	13% (4)	0% (0)	6% (4)
Independent marketers and retailers	10% (3)	11% (4)	11% (7)
Miscellaneous	0% (0)	9% (3)	5% (3)
Electric power	20% (6)	23% (8)	22% (14)
Conservation and renewable energy	0% (0)	0% (0)	0% (0)
Labor unions	0% (0)	0% (0)	0% (0)
Commercial users	3% (1)	20% (7)	12% (8)
Financial institutions	0% (0)	0% (0)	0% (0)
TOTALS	99% (30)	100% (35)	101% (65)[a]

[a] This total underestimates the total number of meetings held over this period, because records for several weeks were missing from agency files.

took place. The frequency of informal input from the petroleum and natural gas industry decreased by one-third to 51 percent. Even more striking, meetings with consumer representatives increased from zero to 14 percent, which does not compare unfavorably with the frequency of meetings with major oil representatives—a relatively low average of 20 percent. Bardin also divided his time about evenly between the two general classes of petroleum interests. Major integrated firms and independent producers received an average of 20 percent of his time while small refiners and independent marketers and retailers received 17 percent. Under Bardin the utility industry also became more involved, tripling its access to the chief regulator.

The changing pattern of informal group access to petroleum regulation parallels not only the changing pattern observed in nuclear regulation but also the change in presidential administrations and political appointees. After David Bardin, a Carter appointee, took the regulatory reins from the Ford appointee, interest group communication grew decidedly more pluralistic.

Lobbying the Congress

Because regulatory agencies are formally accountable to democratic authorities, they can be influenced without direct entreaties from interest groups. Congress became a particularly important intermediary for the interests of several groups affected by oil regulation. Indeed, its intervention on behalf of various interests was a common complaint by major oil companies.[25] Overt intervention was possible because the informal administrative procedures of oil regulation precluded almost no efforts at influence. The NOJC and SIGMA, for example, utilized congressmen as informal intervenors on critical rule makings and exceptions to rules for independent marketers. The APRA, which represents small refiners, counted on their congressional connection to influence "energy actions," i.e., regulatory decisions subject to legislative veto. In essence, groups with large memberships distributed throughout the country found Congress to be relatively sympathetic. Because major oil companies could not generate genuine grass roots pressure, they were unable to exploit the congressional avenue as effectively, and their plight failed to generate the sympathy heaped upon small oil businesses.

These conclusions, gleaned from the interviews, are reinforced by the behavior of interest groups at congressional hearings between

TABLE 5.6
Interest Group Participation in Congressional Hearings on FEA/ERA, 1974-78

Sectors	Authorization		Oversight		"Energy Action"[a]	
	Support	Oppose	Support	Oppose	Support	Oppose
Environmental groups						
Consumer and PIGs	100% (5)			100% (1)		100% (1)
Petroleum and gas industry						
Natural gas						
Major oil		100% (2)		100% (2)	100% (3)	
Independent producers		100% (1)		100% (2)	100% (1)	
Small refiners	100% (10)				25% (2)	75% (6)
Independent marketers and retailers	90% (18)	10% (2)	29% (2)	71% (5)	60% (6)	40% (4)
Miscellaneous	100% (1)					
Electric power						
Conservation and renewable energy						
Labor unions	100% (1)					100% (2)
Commercial users	100% (7)		100% (1)			100% (2)
Financial institutions				100% (4)		
TOTALS	89% (42)	11% (5)	18% (3)	82% (14)	42% (11)	58% (15)

[a] This portion of the table includes only those energy actions on which there was some interest group opposition. Therefore, of the eleven energy actions recommended through 1978 (see text and n. 27), only numbers (2), (3), and (4) are included in this table. Of the remainder, (1), (5), (6), and (7) were noncontroversial, and (11) was pro forma. Numbers (8) and (9), which would have provoked opposition, were withdrawn through action (10) before Congress reviewed them.

1975 and 1978. Although groups communicate their views to Congress through means other than testimony at appropriations, authorizations, and oversight hearings, the transcripts of the hearings provide a valid and ready indicator of the indirect strategy of regulatory influence.[26]

During House and Senate appropriations hearings (1975–78 and 1975–77 respectively) not a single interest group testified either in support of or in opposition to the FEA or the ERA. In the same periods the House Appropriations Subcommittee on Interior and Related Agencies, which evaluated the FEA budget requests, heard an average of 185 nongovernmental witnesses per year for the other agencies under its jurisdiction, and its Senate counterpart, an average of 164. The absence of witnesses is not explained by any dearth of important issues under debate in the appropriations process. The FEA was questioned at considerable length each year by the subcommittees, and its requests for large increases in regulatory program funding prompted tough questions about enforcement and compliance practices, yet no constituents spoke for or against the agency. If it was accommodating or courting interest groups, it was not receiving appropriations support in exchange.

From 1974 through 1978 Congress held numerous other types of hearings concerned with the FEA and the ERA—at least twenty of them explicitly concerned with authorizations or oversight. The distribution of authorization support and opposition by sector for the FEA/ERA, as shown in Table 5.6, corresponds closely to what one might expect, given the impact of the EPAA and the EPCA, which the agencies administered. The two acts defined petroleum allocation and price regulation, and were decidedly beneficial to consumers, commercial energy users, small refiners, and independent marketers and retailers—the groups that provided nearly all of the support for the regulatory programs. Except for a few expressions of opposition by some independent marketers, the intended beneficiaries of regulation provided solid support for continued authorization of the regulatory programs. Likewise, the interests most burdened by regulation, i.e., major oil companies and independent producers, unanimously opposed reauthorization, but not in great numbers. Over four years only two major oil representatives and one independent producer group testified in authorization hearings. This tremendous understatement of their position is a stark contrast to their unrivaled effort to influence the regulatory agency directly. Congressional influence simply was not an important part of major oil's strategy to influence regulation.

Oversight hearings, also analyzed in Table 5.6, differ from authorization hearings in a fundamentally important way. While the latter are concerned primarily with the substance of policy, the former are concerned more with the agency's performance in implementing the matters delegated to it in authorizing legislation. This difference is reflected in the dissimilarity of their respective patterns of interest group support and opposition. At FEA/ERA oversight hearings the groups that strongly supported the regulatory *programs* were either silent or critical of the agency's *implementation* of the programs. Small refiners chose to avoid comment; consumers also remained silent, except for a single, unequivocal indictment of the agency by Ralph Nader. Commercial users, among the most ardent supporters of the programs, largely avoided the implementation issue. Independent marketers and retailers, less reserved, accounted for nearly half of the total interest group participation. Their position was nearly as clear in the oversight hearings as in the authorization hearings. While they were 90 percent in favor of the regulatory programs, they were 71 percent opposed to the agency's implementation of them! Major oil companies and independent producers again failed to participate at a level consistent with their capability. Only four representatives chose to criticize the agency.

The patterns of agency support and opposition are reinforced by group participation in one other important area of congressional involvement. Pursuant to the 1975 Energy Policy and Conservation Act Congress could veto any "energy actions" by the oil regulators that would alter regulations with statutory status. Major examples of energy actions included proposals to decontrol prices of individual products and change the small refiner entitlement bias. Of the eleven energy actions proposed by the FEA and ERA in 1976 and 1977, three provoked sufficient concern and opposition to prompt Congress to consider a veto seriously.[27] Energy action (2), which reduced the competitive advantage enjoyed by all small refiners with better than average access to lower priced oil and provided benefits to branded independent marketers, major oil companies, and small refiners without access to lower priced crude, provoked an intra-industry dispute. Energy actions (3) and (4), which removed all allocation and price controls from home heating oil, diesel fuel, and other middle distillate refined products, stimulated a clash along different lines. The proposal had the perceived impact of benefiting petroleum producers and refiners at the expense of consumers, commercial users, and independent marketers. The Subcommittee on Energy and Power of the House Commerce Committee and the Senate Interior Committee held hearings on these three controversial actions as well as on five noncontroversial ones. The interest group testimony on actions (2), (3), and (4) is summarized in Table 5.6.

The distribution of testimony is almost precisely the opposite of the congressionally intended pattern of support for oil regulation. Three classes of intended beneficiaries—consumers, labor, and commercial users—unanimously opposed the deregulation of middle distillates while two classes of intended cost-bearers—major and independent producers—unanimously supported the proposal and the change in small refiner entitlements. The other two classes of beneficiaries—small refiners and independent marketers—were divided by the proposals. Energy action (2) offered benefits to a subset of small refiners without easy access to cheap lower-tier crude oil; however, it also reduced the benefits to virtually all other small refiners and was perceived as weakening their position as a class. The majority of small refiners therefore opposed the action while a minority of them, in the name of self-interest, lent support. The middle distillate decontrol issues did not divide small refiners; they all stood to benefit, yet they chose not to support the agency publicly on the issues. Independent marketers were affected oppositely: they were largely unaffected by energy action (2) and sent only a single representative to testify in support; on energy actions (3) and (4) they were divided, however, because the security and prices of supplies available to marketers differed in a decontrolled middle distillate market. A majority of the testimony from this sector supported the proposal, but a significant minority saw the move as a serious threat to their businesses.

Because none of these energy actions was successfully vetoed by Congress it is tempting to conclude that the agency was satisfying congressional intent. Too many other factors, however, could also impede a veto within the prescribed time limit of only fifteen days. The only prudent conclusion is that, regardless of the genuine congressional support for these actions, the regulatory agency was not drawing its support from its originally intended constituency. The controversial actions were opposed by a majority of the intended supporters of regulation and supported by a majority of the intended opponents.

The consistent patterns of group participation in congressional hearings provide insight into the nature of agency-group relationships. First, they suggest that the agency lacked strong political support. While many individual and commercial consumers, and small refiners and marketers, continuously extolled the virtues of regulation, they provided no support for the implementation of the program. Major oil companies and independent producers, being the agency's intended cost-bearers, could not comfortably provide support either. Their reticence before Congress was the only "support" the agency really enjoyed from its constituency. The second insight is that whatever support the agency was cultivating among its constituents, it was among its intended cost-bearers. The disapproving testimony of intended beneficiaries, which indicated that the agency was not providing adequate benefits during implementation, pointed to generally uncooperative group-agency relationships. By contrast, major oil companies and independent producers approved the agency's major decisions and maintained a low profile during critical oversight hearings. These cost-bearers would have much preferred no regulation at all, but, given no choice on that issue, their behavior before Congress indicates a satisfactory relationship with the regulatory agency. In sum, Congress became the major arena for participation by the beneficiaries of oil regulation, but not to voice support for the benefits actually being provided. Beneficiary initiatives were largely critical of the behavior of the agency where, as we have seen, group initiatives were monopolized by cost-bearers.

Bureaucratic Strategies

How did the oil regulators respond to the pattern of group pressures brought to bear on them? Did they accept and reinforce it? Did they attempt to alter it substantially? These questions raise the issue of the bureaucracy's independent contribution to the political relationships that underpin public policy. Group behavior is only a partial determinant; it is the bureaucracy that completes the relationships by choosing its political allies and allocating its costs and benefits in a manner that promotes its chosen objectives.

A quantitative summary of the oil bureaucracy's group strategies

TABLE 5.7
Informal Lobbying of Petroleum Regulatory Agencies

Dimension	Consumer and PIGs	Majors and independent producers	Small refiners, independent marketers and retailers	Commercial users
Mean frequency of informal interaction[a]	2.33 (3)	3.78 (9)	3.75 (4)	2.2 (10)
Mean percentage of contacts initiated by agency[b]	50% (2)	35% (9)	32.5% (4)	21.5% (10)
Mean effectiveness rating: informal vs. formal participation[c]	3.0 (1)	2.88 (8)	3.0 (4)	1.0 (2)

[a] On the basis of numerous open- and closed-ended questions (see Appendix A) the informal initiatives made by each group toward the petroleum regulatory agencies were coded as constant, frequent, sporadic, infrequent, or nonexistent. To summarize the data in this table the categories were assigned scale scores of 5, 4, 3, 2, or 1, respectively.

[b] Responses to question C.2.d.3 are reported in the mean here.

[c] In answer to question C.2.d.6: if the respondent believed informal contacts were most influential, the response was coded 3; responses attributing greater influence to formal contacts were coded 1; responses attributing equal influence were coded 2.

is provided in Table 5.7, which reiterates two important points already established as a basis for assessing bureaucratic efforts. Each group's assessment of the relative importance of formal and informal channels of influence is measured on a three-point scale (line 3) and averaged across participating sectors. With two exceptions the knowledgeable groups strongly affirm the greater importance of informal participation for regulatory influence. The table also summarizes the mean frequencies of informal interaction (line 1)—a large part of the total interactions reported in Table 5.2. On a five-point scale the table reports mean interactions of a "frequent" nature for the two subsectors of the oil industry and of an "infrequent" nature for consumers and commercial users. These two sets of statistics provide context and justification for a measure of bureaucratic strategies. Each group estimated the proportion of its informal interactions that resulted from the initiative of the agency, and the proportions are averaged in line 2. Interpreted relative to the frequencies of interaction, they offer a gauge of bureaucratic efforts at cooperation or co-optation.

The plainest fact about bureaucratic strategies is that the regulators did little to alter the pattern of participation initiated by the groups. Among the thirteen oil industry groups that averaged frequent participation, the agency initiated one-third of the contacts—most of them with major oil interests and independent producers, who had many more Washington representatives. The agency, in other words, did not attempt to interact with the beneficiary interests in the oil industry any more than it attempted to relate to the cost-bearers, and thereby did not counteract the cost-bearer's representational advantage. In fact, several cost-bearer groups including the API and Standard Oil of California attributed half of their regulatory interaction to agency initiative. The agency's effort to communicate with its consuming constituents was by contrast meager. Although half of the contacts between consumers and the agency, and one-fifth of those between commercial users and the agency, were initiated by the regulators, these portions are based on a very small number of meetings and do not amount to a significant bureaucratic effort.

How did the agency come to pursue this communication strategy? The answer differs between the political and professional levels of the regulatory agency.

The behavior of political regulatory authorities was already documented in Tables 5.4 and 5.5. On average, during 1975 and 1976 the regulatory chief spent 76 percent of his meeting time with the oil industry, 15 percent with commercial users, and absolutely none with consumers. In 1977 and 1978 the new regulatory leader distributed his time very differently: 51 percent to the industry, 12 percent to commercial users, and a full 14 percent to consumers. These data make it clear that while the industry dominated political level interaction, the agency made a significant difference in whose interests were heard. The decline in the industry's share and the increase in the consumers' share of the leadership's time after 1976 cannot be attributed to changes in group resources or effort, but rather to the wishes of the new regulatory administration.

In 1977 political support of increased consumer participation also emerged at the very top of the energy bureaucracy. The new administrator of the FEA, and later deputy secretary of energy, John O'Leary, took several steps to pluralize interest representation. In early 1977 he broke with traditional FEA opposition by awarding public funds to Consumers Union to assist their participation in a formal proceeding. His consumer sympathies were aired before the House Subcommittee on Energy and Power in the spring of 1977: "I think that it is a very, very useful precedent for our agency. . . . I think that the history of government agencies, with the best will in the world, is that they haven't represented that set of interests very well. So I am really pleased to see a very cautious and very well modulated entry of this consumer interest into the regulatory process."[28] O'Leary continued the participation experiment by awarding a larger sum to the CFA in mid-1977 to help develop a rule for monitoring the price and supply of decontrolled home heating oil. The CFA reported that their satisfaction and success resulted from their ability to hire expertise and participate in staff-level deliberations throughout the informal rule-making process.[29]

Because agency staff were so important to oil regulation, the sympathy and support of political administrators were not adequate protection for any interest. Somewhere in the vicinity of 90 percent of all FEA-initiated contacts with the regulatory constituency were made by the professional staff.[30] In contrast to more recent political-level overtures, virtually all of these contacts were made with the representatives of the petroleum industry. They involved intended cost-bearers (e.g., major oil firms) as well as beneficiaries (e.g., small refiners) but effectively excluded the largest classes of interests ostensibly served by regulation, i.e., consumers and commercial users. The only staff-initiated contacts consumer representatives had through 1978 occurred during the two instances of funded participation. The staff also appears to have had little use for commercial user participation. Except for the PEG the Washington representatives of commercial user interests seldom heard from the regulatory staff.[31] In sharp contrast, many oil representatives received phone calls from the agency staff every week, if not more often, requesting various forms of assistance.

An important reason for such staff behavior emerges from the nature of the assistance being sought. The oil regulatory staff, perhaps more than any other federal regulatory staff, felt desperately in need of technical assistance. Quite apart from the means they used to mediate interest conflicts, the agency staff wanted help with such basic matters as data on prices, supply and demand, as well as estimates of policy consequences and suggestions of practical alternatives. The inadequacy of the decision-making apparatus at the FEA was deeply rooted. The staff was inherited from the FEO, which had assembled it hastily from lawyers and administrators in the Cost of Living Council and the Department of Interior to deal with the oil emergency of 1973. This group had limited experience with the oil industry and made numerous errors guiding the country through the problems of the oil embargo.[32] The crisis forced the staff to rely on fast and frequent rule making, in the hope of learning from its errors, and to eschew lengthy public hearings in favor of consultation with the most knowledgeable source, i.e., the oil industry.

After the embargo ended, the agency had the time and resources to terminate such consultative policy making. The FEA became an established entity with policy responsibilities extending beyond crisis management, and its staff accumulated experience. In its first months the FEA issued rules prohibiting agency employees from accepting free lunches from the oil industry, and requiring all staff rated GS-15 and above to log meetings with outsiders. The agency was also free from the conventional taint of too many ex-industry employees; in March 1974 only 2.5 percent of its workforce rated above GS-12 had oil industry experience.[33] Finally, the Department of Energy Act of 1977—by establishing the Energy Information Administration to collect and independently verify information necessary for energy policy making—aimed to minimize the need for technical consultation.

The early habits of the regulatory staff, however, showed no signs of breaking. The routine pursuit of industry assistance was reported over and over in the interviews and is confirmed in the public record. A particularly enlightening account of agency consultation emerged in 1978 Senate oversight hearings. The inquiry was prompted by an internal API memo, leaked to the *Washington Post*, in which agency lobbyist John Iannone reported to his superiors that he received from the agency drafts of twenty proposed rules and privileged studies before they became public domain. None of the drafts had been released to consumer groups or nonindustry representatives. Asked why the API was given an advance draft of an amendment to the price regulations, Peter Holihan, a member of the regulatory staff, replied innocently: "I was having a little problem with one technical matter in the rule making, and Mr. Iannone stopped by and asked me if he could help me with this matter." Senator Metzenbaum criticized Holihan's acceptance of API assistance with the natural question: "There are 20,000 employees at the Department of Energy. . . . Not one of these employees could help you with the technical problems you were having, and you needed instead to go to the representative of the API in order to get the technical matters resolved. Is that what you are testifying?"[34] Holihan did not dispute the possibility that he could have relied instead on internal agency assistance.

Why did the regulatory staff fail to circulate the drafts of its proposals to nonindustry interests? Its public justification was that they had "ample opportunity to speak and comment in the formal rule-making process," and that in general "public interest groups [had] not shown an active interest."[35] Since the formal procedures were widely known to be ineffective, the first justification is hardly sincere; the second is the more informative. The agency staff plainly had little appreciation of the substantive sphere of interests it was mandated to protect nor of the organizational problems that impaired the participation of many of its intended beneficiaries; also, it had little expressed or revealed concern for playing a really independent role in the mediation of interests. The oil industry made itself a rich and ready source of advice that the staff gratefully employed to reduce the many costs of decision making. While the political levels of the oil bureaucracy adjusted their behavior to changing political stimuli, the regulatory staff locked its consultative behavior into a pattern that fit most comfortably the incessant routine of informal rule making monitored closely by the industry.

The Consequences of Captured Consultation

Despite the modest shift toward pluralist bureaucratic strategies after 1976, the organizational relationships of oil regulation generally were characterized more by capture than by pluralism. Cost-bearing interests dominated group initiatives and bureaucratic strategies, while beneficiary interests were weakly represented by small refiners and independent marketers. Consuming beneficiaries had but a negligible relationship with the regulators. Much of the policy making by the agency was consistent with, and arguably caused by, these organizational connections.

The major purposes of petroleum allocation and price regulation were to distribute petroleum products equitably during shortages, to prevent inflationary price increases, and to maintain competition in the industry. Many of the goals were substantially accomplished, but not through the efforts of the regulatory agency. Consider the rewards of the major beneficiaries in turn. Consumers and commercial users indeed paid lower prices for oil products throughout the 1970s than they would have paid in an unregulated market.[36] While the consumer benefits of lower prices can be disputed within the context of long-term energy problems, lower prices were clearly an intended benefit from the perspective of lawmakers in the 1970s. Consumers do not, however, owe this benefit to the regulators. Congress eliminated most bureaucratic discretion over consumer prices in 1975, when it passed the EPCA. That act overruled the FEA by rolling back administered prices, and prohibiting average annual increases in excess of 10 percent. By regulating oil prices by statute Congress became the major producer of consumer benefits; the agency, for its part, used its remaining discretion to whittle away at these benefits. In particular, the FEA decontrolled oil product prices for all products except motor gasoline. During periods of ample supply, product prices are minimized through competition, and consumers do not suffer. The problem for consumers is that during subsequent shortages, such as occurred in 1979, the burden is upon them to demonstrate that product controls should be reimposed. This is why they opposed these agency decisions.

Small refiners also owe far greater thanks to Congress than to the agency for their benefits, the greatest of which was the "entitlement bias." The FEA established the original bias in 1974, but not out of evident sympathy with the small refiners' plight. The bias was designed to duplicate the subsidy these refiners had always enjoyed under the oil import quota program terminated earlier that year. In the 1975 EPCA Congress eliminated administrative discretion over the bias by legislating its size and duration.[37] Whether the bias would have been just as secure under agency discretion is unknown. The FEA's successful effort to pare it down in Energy Action (2) and its enforcement behavior suggest, however, that bureaucratic support for small refiners was weak relative to that expressed in Congress.[38]

The only beneficiary interests to benefit unambiguously from agency policy were independent wholesalers and marketers. During the shortages of 1973 and 1974 the allocation regulations indeed protected them from being squeezed out of business by integrated companies. After 1974, however, these firms really shifted position, from beneficiaries to cost-bearers, as they came to view allocation regulation as unnecessary, but price regulation as anathema.

The message of this substantive evidence is that Congress rather than the bureaucracy provided most of whatever benefits the designated beneficiaries of oil regulation enjoyed. Partly this is explained by Congress' desire to claim credit and reap political support for lowering prices and aiding small businesses. Partly, though, it is explained by congressional judgment that the agency would not otherwise provide the benefits—an explanation consistent with the agency's organizational relationships. The latter explanation is reinforced by the agency's efforts to enforce the regulations.

Oil regulations were enforced through a multi-stage process that began with an audit and the determination of a violation, and followed with a notice of probable violation, to which firms had ten days to respond or begin corrective action. If a firm did not respond satisfactorily, the agency had a number of means available to it, including civil penalties, to gain compliance. While the FEA was in existence, enforcement actions took place through six programs in which different sectors of the industry were audited for compliance. Data through April 1975 on FEA investigations, refunds, penalties, and other administrative actions are reported by program in Table 5.8.

The most striking pattern in these data is the gross imbalance of

TABLE 5.8
Summary of FEA Compliance and Enforcement Efforts,
by Program, 1974–75

Program	Investigations		Refunds	"Bank" adjustments
	Total	Violations		
Refinery	Unknown	Unknown	$74,800	$418,200
Propane	45	22	4,038	NA
Utility	18	2	494	NA
Producer	48	11	794	NA
Retail-wholesale	Over 90,000		80,484	NA
TOTALS	Over 90,000		$160,610	$418,200

Program	Unresolved cases		Penalties	
	Number	Amount	Number	Amount
Refinery	18	$148,600	0	$0
Propane	13	29,983	2	23
Utility	1	710	0	0
Producer	2	Unknown	8	47
Retail-wholesale	Unknown	Unknown	144	864
TOTALS	34	$179,293	154	$934

SOURCE: Rycroft, "Bureaucratic Performance," p. 623, adapted from "Recap of FEA Compliance and Enforcement Efforts By Program," in United States House, Committee on Interstate and Foreign Commerce, Subcommittee on Oversight and Investigations, *FEA Enforcement Policies*, 1975, p. 201.
NOTE: All dollar amounts in thousands.

enforcement effort across the different programs and sectors of the industry. In its first year and a half of operation the FEA conducted over 90,000 investigations of wholesalers and retailers (e.g., gas stations), but completed only 48 investigations of producers. Similarly, the marketers were assessed $864,000 in penalties while producers were assessed only $47,000. A December 1974 investigation by the General Accounting Office found that the FEA had assigned 762 of its 850 auditors to wholesale and retail outlets, but not a single one to the country's 19,000 producers.[39] Such an allocation of resources was completely at odds with the potential for dollar violations. Price cheating at the producer level occurred through mislabeling of old oil as new, with payoffs of several dollars per barrel. Among marketers, cheating occurred at the rate of several cents per gallon on comparatively small volumes of product. FEA investigations indeed confirm this; the average refund per audit was only $894 for retail-wholesale investigations, but $16,541 for producer investigations.

The refining industry also benefited from a weak enforcement effort. During its first year of operation the FEA assigned only 88 auditors to the nation's 250 refineries and only two auditors to each of the 31 largest.[40] The potential for cost passthrough violations at a 300,000-barrel-per-day refinery was infinitely greater than at a 5,000-gallon-per-day gas station. The Refinery Audit and Review program detected nearly a half billion dollars in violations—six times the amount of retail and wholesale violations—but required only $75 million in refunds—less than was required of marketers. Refiners were permitted to write the remainder off against "banked costs" (i.e., potential legal price increases that had been postponed, or "banked," because the market would not yet absorb them). What is more, refiners were not assessed one dollar in penalties.

The thrust, then, of the FEA's early enforcement effort was to pursue violations among the small and independent firms the agency was mandated to protect, and to tolerate or trust the behavior of the producers and refiners it was intended to police. Over 50 percent of the refunds, and nearly all of the penalties, were assessed against marketers, while only 14 percent of the dollar violations were found at that level. The entire crude oil producer investigation focused on independent firms that produced only 30 percent of domestic crude, and left uninvestigated the major firms that produced the remaining 70 percent. Finally, FEA investigators were consistently underallocated to the refineries of major firms.[41] Reliable evidence indicates that the FEA continued this enforcement pattern through 1975 and 1976. In July 1977 an executive task force investigating FEA performance concluded: "Unfortunately, to date the FEA's efforts to secure compliance from our nation's major refiners have been a failure. There are entirely inadequate audit resources and no lawyers assigned on a full-time basis to any of the major refiners. Given the size of the problem, the limited work that has been done to date, and the enforcement problems that necessarily accompany any effort to remedy aged violations, a major new undertaking is required."[42]

Subsequent audits and settlements revealed that FEA performance in enforcing compliance by major oil companies was poor indeed. In December 1977 the new Department of Energy established an Office of Special Counsel (OSC), headed by Stanley Sporkin, who had also led the executive task force, to investigate regulatory compliance since 1974. The OSC was specifically directed to concentrate on thirty-four major domestic refiners. It chose to focus on the fifteen largest, and was well prepared with a staff of six hundred and a timetable of two years to audit the largest companies carefully. Exxon, for example, had sixty-five staff assigned to it alone; the FEA had assigned only two. By the summer of 1978 more than thirty administrative or judicial proceedings were initiated, charging more than one billion dollars in violations. Although legal battles over the charges continue to drag on, major violations have been admitted and settlements effected. Gulf Oil Corporation, for example, agreed to pay $42.2 million to its customers and the United States Treasury for overcharges.[43]

The reasons for the lax enforcement effort by the FEA and the more vigorous effort by the DOE are multiple. The FEA offered Congress several plausible explanations. Administrator John Sawhill's rationale for the emphasis on marketers in 1974 was that "the retail sector was the source of the overwhelming majority of complaints received by the agency. We felt a clear responsibility to be responsive" to them.[44] Because agencies are interested in minimizing complaints, both to make their own existence easier and to head off congressional pressure, this is a reasonable justification for attention to retail and wholesale violations. It falls short, however, in view of the fact that marketers are the only members of the oil industry with contact with consumers, and therefore the only portion of the industry likely to generate price complaints. The FEA had to recognize the potential for unnoticeable yet substantial violations among pro-

ducers and refiners. In its view, there was good reason not to investigate them carefully: "It's a question of more capable. They [the
majors] have more qualified lawyers who spend their time analyzing
every line and phrase in our regulations. They have the high-
powered auditors who have access to the numbers and the com-
puterized capabilities, so that they have a greater capability to understand, interpret and comply with our regulations than does the
small independent crude producer, who's running his records out of
a log book kept in the back of a pick-up truck."[45] The argument is
not without merit, but it does not justify complete trust. Legal staffs,
after all, are also adept at identifying minimal compliance options.
The FEA also defended its enforcement imbalance on cost grounds:
it was cheaper and faster to train a staff to audit retail outlets than to
investigate large refineries. Again, this is reasonable behavior to a
point, but surely time and money limitations cannot explain the
failure of the FEA to prepare a staff for investigating large firms by
1977.

The shortcomings of the official explanations, and the clear consistency of enforcement behavior with the nature of interest group ties
to the agency, suggest that this consistency is not coincidental. It is
arguably causal. That is, the shifting pattern of emphasis from small
to major firms is substantially a product of the political relationships
between the agency and its constituency. Prior to 1977 the organizational relationships of oil regulation were essentially of the captured
type. The FEA's decision making was dominated by large cost-
bearing interests, with agency reinforcement. By the fall of 1974, in
fact, the FEA was already recommending its own termination.[46]
Forced to press on with its statutory enforcement responsibility, the
agency opted for investigations that could be carried out quickly
and that would not cost it important political support. Small firms
were easy targets and were already the agency's political opponents
(although they wanted the regulations). Investigations of major producers and refiners would have promised prolonged proceedings and
threatened the political and technical support the agency enjoyed.

After 1977 the organizational relationships evinced greater pluralism at the highest level of decision making. President Carter's FEA
Administrator, John O'Leary, in fact, made the restoration of confidence in the regulatory program his number one priority.[47] The
commitment at that level, coupled with the Carter White House's
antipathy for major oil, was sufficient to produce the targeted en-

forcement effort by the new Office of Special Counsel. The organizational relationships at lower levels in the agency remained unchanged; however, the staff was relieved of control over compliance in the late 1970s. The shift reinforces, moreover, the conclusion that the politics of capture was the major cause of lax and imbalanced enforcement of oil regulations through 1976.

Theories and Explanations

Interest Group Initiatives

Oil regulation presents a different test of the organizational theory of political influence than does nuclear regulation. Because it was not a classic, social regulatory program and did not rely on formal decision-making procedures to produce policy, it created quite different incentives for interest group participation. The differences are potentially problematic for the theory because interest group initiatives in the two programs are similarly patterned: they tend toward monopoly. In oil regulation group initiatives were thoroughly dominated by the efforts of corporate and associational representatives of the regulatory cost-bearers, major oil. The efforts of the two major beneficiaries, consumers and commercial users, were meager, while those of the partial beneficiaries, independent refiners and marketers, were more frequent but nonetheless swamped by major oil. How, then, does the theory account for the repetition of the pattern despite the important differences between oil and nuclear regulation?

The answer begins with the resources available for political action. In the case of social regulatory problems such as undesirable nuclear byproducts, the incentives for collective action are inevitably skewed in favor of the producers of the byproducts. Producers are economic firms with large or concentrated stakes in the resolution of the issue while the sufferers of the byproducts are usually individuals with small or diffuse stakes. Given rational decision making about collective action, the producers are far more likely to become well organized for political participation. The result is a bipolar constituency characterized by a gross resource disparity. This is the outcome predicted in Table 3.4 and observed in nuclear regulation.

Oil regulation, however, only partially fits the classic regulatory model. The price regulations were intended to protect consumers from an imperfection in the market, i.e., the OPEC cartel, that would otherwise have drastically inflated oil prices and awarded domestic producers a windfall profit. In this respect oil regulation is mostly consistent with the classic model. Producers obviously had much larger individual stakes than consumers. Oil regulation deviates from the model, however, with the interests of commercial users, whose stakes in oil prices were also large at the individual level. Airline companies, for example, were seriously concerned that higher fuel costs, and therefore higher plane fares, would discourage travel and depress gross profits. Petrochemical firms, for another illustration, feared the loss of market shares to substitutable products that did not require expensive petroleum feedstocks. These interests, like producers, were provided ample individual-level incentives to amass resources for collective political action.

Oil regulation differs further from the classic regulatory model in the functioning of its allocation and intra-industry programs, where the cost-bearers were primarily the major oil companies but the beneficiaries were no longer the individual consumers. The beneficiaries of allocation regulations were the independent marketers, who stood to lose their suppliers during shortages, and the commercial users, who were able to achieve priority allocation status. The intra-industry programs also made beneficiaries out of the small refiners through the entitlement bias. While the nonconsumer beneficiaries included about 200,000 small businesses, their individual level stakes in the preservation of the regulations were larger than those associated with classic regulatory policy.

The collective resources available to this more complex set of constituents nonetheless fits the predictions rather well. Large firms—in this case not only cost-bearing major oil companies but also benefiting commercial users—experienced the greatest regulatory impacts and enjoyed the greatest organizational resources. Individual consumers reaped the smallest regulatory benefits and generated the least organizational resources. The small firms in the refining and marketing sectors felt moderate impacts, both positive and negative, and developed an intermediate level of resources. The results are summarized in Table 5.9 for groups having at least infrequent contact with the regulators. On the average an organized representative of the major cost-bearing firms had over 150 times the financial resources and over 30 times the staff of a group representing consumers. In sectoral terms the total disparity becomes

TABLE 5.9

Material Resources of Petroleum Regulation Constituents

Resource statistic	Consumers[a]	Majors and independent producers[b]	Small refiners, independent marketers, and retailers[c]	Commercial users[d]
Annual budget of Washington office				
Mean	$162,000	$25,217,000	$540,000	$4,301,000
Median	$200,000	$30,000,000	$400,000	$745,000
Paid, full-time Washington staff				
Mean	5	164	10	94
Median	5	190	4	14
Number of organizations	3	3	3	10

NOTE: Excludes corporate governmental relations offices, which are not organizations.

[a] Includes Energy Action Committee, Energy Policy Task Force of CFA, and Consumers Union.

[b] Includes AGA, API, and NPRA.

[c] Includes APRA, NOJC, and SIGMA.

[d] Includes APTA, ATA, Americans for Energy Independence, Business Roundtable, United States Chamber of Commerce, Electricity Consumers Resource Council, National Association of Manufacturers, NFU, PEG, and TAA.

staggering because the producing sector is also represented by more than twenty corporate governmental relations offices, each with resources that dwarf those of the typical consumer group. The disparity is, in fact, much greater than that separating the producing and nonproducing interests in nuclear regulation. The major integrated oil companies constitute the largest industrial interest in the United States and are probably the richest lobbying force in Washington; in any case their governmental relations resources easily exceed those of nuclear power.[48] Consumers, by contrast, constitute the most diffuse interest in society and are poorly organized in comparison to environmentalists and other more specialized "public" interests.

Consumers were not, however, the lone beneficiaries of oil regulations. Large firms such as public transit systems, trucking companies, heavy industry, airlines, and petrochemical businesses, which consume large quantities of petroleum products, profit from lower oil prices. These interests were predictably well organized. Although the resources of individual groups varied greatly—the average group had a budget of $4.3 million while the median had only $745,000—the sector totaled over $43 million per year in expenditures and was staffed by over nine hundred Washington personnel. Less well organized were the independent refiners and marketers, whose small firms supported interest groups with average budgets of $540,000 and average staffs of ten.

The magnitude of the group resources cannot, of course, be attributed only to the stimuli of oil regulations. Most of the groups were in existence long before 1973 (see Table 3.3) and in pursuit of many other collective and selective goals. The oil regulations did prompt the organization of three consumer groups and one commercial user group,[49] and they led established groups and corporate offices to augment or initiate their energy lobbying. The major theoretical point, however, is not the distribution of new organizing stimulated by a program; the key point is that among different interests organizational resources are distributed predictably according to the policy stakes they encounter at the individual level. The group resources of the constituents of oil regulation were consistent with the policy impacts they experienced individually.

Resource disparities among the interest groups do not, however, fully explain the imbalanced pattern of regulatory constituents, or why consumer groups had negligible contact with the agency, or why commercial users stayed away in droves. Consumers could not have been deterred, like environmentalists at the NRC, by the high costs of formal participation, nor could commercial users have been discouraged from participating by inadequate resources. Even the huge resource advantage of major oil does not account for its near-monopolization of group initiatives.

Solutions to these puzzles lie in the strategic decisions of interest group leaders who hypothetically assemble a set of political tactics through a series of benefit-cost analyses: decreasingly profitable tactics are cumulated until strategic resources are exhausted. As groups confront limited and unequal budgets, tactics that promise relatively low net benefits will be characterized by the least and most imbalanced group participation. This effect occurred in nuclear regulation because the agency employed expensive formal procedures to establish a minimum of policy in licensing proceedings. In oil regulation the same effect occurred, but for different reasons.

The informal process through which oil regulations were developed made effective participation quite expensive because it required the cultivation of "working relationships" with the regulatory staff. Such relationships demanded daily monitoring of the agency, quick and technically competent responses to agency inquiries, a record of credible and sympathetic assistance to the agency, and—in resources—one to two persons engaged full-time in agency liaison; a supportive staff of lawyers, economists, and petroleum specialists; and a large and reliable data base. At least $1 million per year was necessary to exploit the strategy on major issues, and considerably more to employ it fully.

As in nuclear regulation, other strategies such as congressional lobbying or media ploys could be pursued at lower costs; they also usually promised greater benefits. Because oil regulations were developed through an incremental learning process of fast and frequent rule making, the payoffs from successful participation in any single rule making were relatively small. Much as the NRC discouraged the participation of national interest groups by making policy through numerous licensing proceedings, so the oil regulators discouraged participation by multiplying the number of decisions comprising its policy. Because this practice effectively reduced the expected value of bureaucratic participation below that of alternative strategies, only groups with sizable budgets could cultivate the agency as well as pursue the more profitable options. For groups such as consumers and independent refiners and marketers, with annual budgets of several hundred thousand dollars, resources were simply insufficient to cover more than just the congressional arena, where their participation was most frequently observed.

This is reinforced, and other aspects of regulatory initiatives are explained, by the second, strategic leadership consideration. Interest organizations depend for their maintenance on—and leaders must accommodate themselves to—factors besides policy influence that affect organizational survival. One such factor affecting the behavior of the constituents of oil regulation was selective incentives. Organizations that produced for their members technical information pertinent to the oil regulations enjoyed a natural advantage in regulatory participation. Their research activities enabled them to assist the regulators at comparatively little extra expense. Most of the oil industry associations in fact conducted research as a membership service. Groups such as consumer or commercial user organizations that did not produce such information as a selective incentive had to pay much more to produce the information so valued by the regulators and collected no membership dividends from it. This factor further explains major oil's dominance of the agency and the greater involvement of the independent oil sector than of consuming interests despite their nearly equal financial resources. The sources of consumer group support—several large philanthropists enjoying purposive benefits and numerous large interests concerned with lower prices—strongly encouraged political strategies that reaffirmed the efficacy of contributors and that promised large net payoffs in public goods.[50] For satisfying these member needs, Congress was a more favorable arena than the bureaucracy.

The second organizational maintenance factor affecting group participation was the long-term consequence of the oil regulations themselves. Most affected by this factor were commercial users, whose unit sales and total profits fall as energy prices rise. Oil price regulation supported their profits, yet they either favored deregulation of prices or took no position (see Table 5.1). The major reason is clear. Commercial users were torn between their short-term interest in profits and their long-term interest in stability and survival. The regulations served the former, but they interfered with the latter by discouraging domestic oil production. At the industry level the user associations resolved this conflict by favoring their maintenance interest or remaining neutral. Either way, caution dictated nonparticipation in bureaucratic policy making.

Bureaucratic Strategies

The oil regulators faced a pattern of group initiatives that tended toward monopoly and threatened to capture regulatory policy making. Rather than try to counteract it, however, they mostly reinforced it. The regulators chose to employ decision-making procedures that discouraged participation by all but the wealthiest organizations. What is more, they exacerbated the pattern with their consultative behavior. The regulators made a great deal of effort to involve interest groups in policy making: over one-third of the interactions between the agency and its constituents (see Table 5.7) were initiated by the regulators; however, at least 85 percent of those overtures were directed at the regulated industry, and the overwhelming majority of those toward cost-bearers.[51] Why the agency chose this essentially co-optive strategy is an important question because it had the discretion to choose otherwise.

The organizational theory proposed an explanation for the bureaucracy's choice of interest group strategies that emphasized external political influences. Let us consider, in turn, how congressional, presidential, and judicial constraints affected the oil regulators and whether the effects worked as hypothesized.

Congressional Constraints. As proposed in the organizational theory, congressional influence over bureaucratic strategies is a function of the structure and practice of congressional oversight, broadly defined. That is, the more heterogeneous the interests in the oversight structure, and the more vigorous the practice of oversight, the more pluralistic will be the bureaucracy's interactions with interest groups. This proposition was operationalized through four hypotheses that identified the number of committees, subcommittees, and special oversight subcommittees with jurisdiction over an agency as the key structural variables, and the quantity and quality of oversight as the key practice variables. Evidence on nuclear regulation indicated that congressional influences may indeed operate in the hypothesized manner; presidential influences, however, provided a stronger explanation of NRC behavior. The behavior of the oil regulators provides a valuable check on this tentative conclusion.

Data bearing on the structural hypotheses are summarized in Table 5.10, which describes the congressional oversight structure in the periods 1974–76 and 1977–78. What do these structures lead us to expect of bureaucratic strategies? First, the oversight structure of oil regulation was neither highly centralized nor highly fragmented; in a formal sense it did not represent an unusual pluralism of interests or an unusual paucity of interests. Only a single standing committee held jurisdiction in each house; however, at least two subcommittees shared responsibility within each committee. Based on hypotheses (1) and (2) (see Chapter 2), the agency should not have felt compelled to accommodate a diversity of interests, but neither should it have felt safe in catering to only one. The second salient feature of the structure is that it included special oversight subcommittees in the House over the full period of this study, and in the Senate through 1976. The hypothetical effect of the special panels is to encourage agencies to address the demands of more interests in order to minimize complaints and investigations.

A third important aspect of the oversight structure is that it underwent little substantive change from 1974 through 1978:[52] of sole significance was the elimination of the Senate Special Subcommittee on Legislative Oversight. Any changes that occurred in bureaucratic behavior from 1974 to 1978, therefore, cannot be attributed to structural change unless they entailed a modest decline in concern about

TABLE 5.10

Congressional Oversight Structure for Petroleum Regulation, 1974–78

Committees	Subcommittees	Chairpersons
FEA, May 1974–Dec. 1976		
Senate Interior and Insular Affairs		Jackson (D-Wash.)
	Minerals, Materials, and Fuels	Metcalf (D-Mont.)
	Special Subcommittee on Legislative Oversight	Jackson (D-Wash.)
House Interstate and Foreign Commerce		Staggers (D-W.Va.)
	Communications and Power[a]	MacDonald (D-Mass.)
	Special Subcommittee on Investigations[a]	Staggers (D-W.Va.)
	Energy and Power[b]	Dingell (D-Mich.)
	Oversight and Investigations[b]	Moss (D-Calif.)
FEA, Jan.–Sept. 1977, and ERA, Oct. 1977–Oct. 1978		
Senate Energy and Natural Resources		Jackson (D-Wash.)
	Energy Conservation and Regulation	Johnston (D-La.)
	Energy Production and Supply	Haskell (D-Colo.)
House Interstate and Foreign Commerce		Staggers (D-W.Va.)
	Energy and Power	Dingell (D-Mich.)
	Oversight and Investigations	Moss (D-Calif.)

[a] Through 12/74.
[b] After 1/75.

investigations. A final structural feature of potential significance is the leadership of the relevant committees. Two House subcommittee chairmen, John Moss and John Dingell, and a Senate subcommittee chairman, Lee Metcalf, were among the staunchest defenders of consumer interests and the strongest critics of the oil industry in Congress. While the oversight committees also included many oil district representatives, consumer interests were not only represented—they enjoyed key leadership support.

Although the structural congressional cues and constraints were less clear for the oil regulators than for the nuclear regulators, they were not ambiguous; and they remained nearly constant. In essence, the oversight structure should have stimulated bureaucratic concern for its beneficiaries as well as its cost-bearers. The presence of oversight subcommittees, pro-consumer committee leaders, and multiple subcommittee overseers should have deterred the agency from accommodating a limited clientele. The effects of these structural signals on bureaucratic strategies did not, however, occur as predicted. The regulatory staff devoted virtually all of its contact with interest groups to cost-bearing interests. The political leadership also pursued a co-optive strategy during the Ford years, but became decidedly more pluralistic during Carter's presidency. Neither the general pattern of co-optation nor the late shift toward more pluralistic contacts was consistent with the structural constraints issuing from Congress.

When structural cues and constraints are not having their expected effect, the first place to look for an explanation is the practice of oversight. If active congressional oversight fails in its support, the interests represented in its oversight structure can no longer be assured of bureaucratic accommodation. In the case of oil regulation, infrequent and/or uncritical oversight would at least partially explain the co-optive bureaucratic behavior.

The available evidence indicates, to the contrary, that the oil regulators were the subjects of both frequent and critical congressional supervision. From 1973 through mid-1976, when the average number of congressional hearings for a federal regulatory agency was 61.6 (see Table 4.5), the FEA was the topic at nearly twice that number—more often than any other regulatory agency except the EPA.[53] During the 95th Congress of 1977–78 the number of hearings dropped to only 48, while for prior years the average had been 69. Despite the decline, the amount of attention paid the oil regulators by Congress was substantial. The agency's behavior was a top congressional priority among regulatory programs.

Qualitative indicators also describe vigorous oversight of oil regulation. Congress often criticized the FEA for its co-optive relationship with major oil, its failure to protect consumers and small business, and its biased enforcement program; it even accused the FEA of obstructing federal criminal prosecution of pricing violators.[54] The hearings regularly provided consumers an opportunity to vent their frustrations in dealing with an agency that was presumably providing benefits to consumers. On April 28, 1975, for example, before the Senate Interior and Insular Affairs Committee, Peter Schuck of Consumers Union lambasted the FEA for its cooperation with the cost-bearing clientele:

> In short, FEA, while still in its very infancy, has managed to behave almost precisely like the most seasoned regulatory agency—excluding consumers from its decision-making processes, delaying difficult decisions as long as possible, acting only when compelled to do so by threat of litigation, public exposure, or congressional pressures, suffering potential conflicts of interest to exist, making decisions of the most enormous magnitude without adequate economic data and with excessive reliance on ex parte industry representations, and all too often acting in violation of the law.

There is no evidence that Congress used oversight hearings to show support for the FEA or to meet its oversight responsibilities in a pro forma manner.

After Carter took office and the FEA was absorbed by the Department of Energy, congressional attention and antagonism toward biases in oil regulation showed no signs of waning. The Senate Energy and Natural Resources Committee became a particularly vociferous critic. Senator Howard Metzenbaum (D-Ohio), in particular, used his post on the committee to lead consumer opposition to major oil at every turn in the continuing energy debate. In June 1977 he chaired one of the most embarrassing oversight hearings for both major oil and the Department of Energy, where the infamous "Iannone Letter" was revealed.

The practice of congressional oversight was, then, as inconsistent with observed bureaucratic behavior as was its structure. Despite substantial congressional efforts in support of interests other than those of regulatory cost-bearers, the oil regulators continued to pursue their co-optive strategy. Moreover, the late movement of the regulatory leadership toward broader consultation is inconsistent with congressional changes at the same time; after 1976 the incidence of congressional oversight declined and the agency was under somewhat less, rather than more, pressure to pluralize its political support. In short, congressional oversight had little to none of its intended impact on bureaucratic behavior toward interest groups.

Presidential Constraints. The cues for the oil regulators that emanated from the White House during the Ford and Carter administrations could not have been any sharper. The Ford administration began recommending to Congress the termination of oil price and allocation controls in the fall of 1974.[55] Higher oil prices through deregulation were also the keystone of Ford's energy policy proposals of 1975 and 1976. In his last month in office he proposed, subject to congressional veto, the decontrol of motor gasoline prices.[56] By contrast, President Carter, in his first month in office, proposed the revocation of Ford's proposal and thereby prevented gasoline decontrol.[57] Carter's energy policy proposals also opposed price decontrol. Although his recommendations accepted the conservation value of higher prices, they sought to raise prices through taxation and regulation. Throughout his presidency Carter demonstrated only antipathy for major oil interests. In the spring of 1977 he formed the presidential commission on FEA enforcement that identified probable noncompliance of large oil companies. In 1979, when gradual oil decontrol became the only way to achieve price conservation, he successfully led Congress to adopt the Windfall Profits Tax that major oil had so strongly opposed.

The presidential policy preferences were reflected clearly in the consultative behavior of the political administrators of oil regulation. During the Ford administration the FEA had virtually no contact with consumers but extensive interaction with its large regulated clients. During the Carter administration its leadership initiated far more contacts with regulatory beneficiaries, and consultation at that level approached pluralism. At the staff level, however, consultation remained co-optive. Since the FEA developed its standard operating procedures under Ford, the staff's behavior was initially consistent with presidential interests. The lack of change with the succession of Carter further supports the conclusion that presidential cues, as opposed to other environmental stimuli, influenced bureaucratic strategies. Presidential directives and preferences permeate the bureaucracy from the top down. When bureaucratic strategies change among political appointees but not among professional staff, the most probable cause is presidential influence. There is no question that the regulators understood presidential wishes. President Ford used the FEA leadership as his main advocates of oil decontrol while Carter appointed an FEA administrator whose first objective was to revitalize regulatory enforcement.[58] Congressional cues for the oil regulators were also loud and clear, but the political behavior of the regulators indicates that primarily presidential preferences were heeded.

The pattern of accountability is similar to that observed in nuclear regulation and reinforces the conclusion that presidential cues and constraints influenced bureaucratic behavior more than congressional efforts. It is important to note, however, that responsiveness of the independent regulatory agency, the NRC, was not appreciably different from that of the executive regulatory agency administering oil controls. The organizational theory hypothesized that presidential constraints would affect the behavior of independent agencies less than the behavior of agencies directly accountable to the White House. This difference was not observed. The staffs of the NRC and the FEA/ERA were equally loath to change their consultative behavior to suit presidential policy while the regulatory leaders were about equally willing to adapt their group contacts to presidential preferences. Whether institutional independence generally matters so little for the control of regulatory consultation cannot be said with the limited data of this study. What can be stated with greater confidence is the degree to which alternative lines of accountability control the bureaucracy, and the conditions under which they do so. The four cases provide independent tests of those controls. Our tentative conclusion at this juncture is that presidential cues have the greatest effects, however small, over bureaucratic relationships with interest groups.

Judicial Constraints. The behavior of the courts in this regulatory arena lend weight to the conclusion. In fact, the term "constraint" is a misnomer for the posture assumed by the courts on issues of oil regulation. Unlike Congress and the White House, which articulated strong preferences concerning how the FEA conducted its business and how its decisions affected major interests, the courts provided the oil regulators with no constraining signals. The general issues of judicial relevance in oil regulation were substantive and procedural due process.[59] That is, the major issues for the courts were whether regulatory decisions reflected due concern for all the interests at stake and whether those interests were afforded proper opportunity to be heard.

On both issues the courts endorsed FEA behavior. The EPAA and subsequent legislation gave the regulators a great deal of discretion in implementing the goals of fair prices, equitable burdens during shortages, and protection for small oil businesses. As a consequence the courts continually deferred to agency judgments on substantive issues. In eighty-five lawsuits during the FEA's first year of operation the courts reaffirmed time and again the regulators' broad substantive discretion.[60] Likewise, the courts chose to accept the

agency's adherence to the truncated notice and comment procedures specified in the FEA act as sufficient provision of procedural
due process; they did not attempt to impose more elaborate leasing
procedures as they had for the NRC; and they did not insist, as they
do for many agencies, that the FEA/ERA demonstrate a "hard
look" at all affected interests by developing a substantial record.[61] In
one important decision, the FEA was judged to lack good cause for
waiving notice requirements,[62] but as long as the notice and comment requirements were met, the courts accepted FEA policy making in substance and in procedure. Without significant judicial constraints the regulators were free to choose those administrative and
political strategies that best suited their individual and organizational goals.

Conclusion

When President Reagan abolished oil price and allocation controls
in January 1981 he ended a program that lacked the support of the
organizations controlling it. For most of its existence oil regulation
was a captured process, with the initiatives from its constituency
nearly monopolized by large cost-bearers. The implementing agencies pursued essentially co-optive strategies to accommodate their
constituency and moved only sparingly toward more pluralist tactics
in the last years. Finally, the decisions and practices of the regulators
often reflected the captured nature of the process. Why the process
came to operate this way is in many respects explained by the
organizational theory.

In one important respect, however, the theory appears inadequate. Contrary to expectations the regulatory staff were largely
immune to all legitimate pressures for accountability. Congressional
inquiries and entreaties held no sway with the staff despite years of
such efforts. The change in presidential administrations and preferences also produced no strategic change comparable to that observed at the top of the organization. As in nuclear regulation, the
staff were largely uninterested in playing independent political roles
and manipulating their constituencies. They were passive professionals rather than active politicians. They accepted the configura-
tion of pressures and assistance that confronted them—as long, that
is, as those groups would facilitate their technical responsibilities.
Since it is almost always the regulated industry with the greatest

incentive and capacity to be so effectively involved, it follows that the staff will typically try to co-opt them. If the political environment affects staff behavior, it does so through well-established patterns of policy preferences, such as the Joint Committee on Atomic Energy long provided for the Atomic Energy Commission, and not through anything as transient as single presidential administrations, several years of congressional oversight, or occasional court decisions. Political control of the permanent regulatory bureaucracy requires far more persistence.

What were the policy consequences of the capture of oil regulation? First, the agency was a permanent supporter of decontrol. Second, the agency implemented decontrol at its earliest opportunities. Third, enforcement of oil regulation favored the large cost-bearers until a presidential directive forced a shift in emphasis. Finally, the benefits enjoyed by consumers, small businesses, and other intended beneficiaries had to be secured from Congress; a captured regulatory agency could not be trusted to produce them.

6

ENERGY RESEARCH AND DEVELOPMENT

Although we have become accustomed to hearing that the United States lacks a national energy policy, that assessment is not entirely true. The United States has not yet resolved all of the environmental and economic tradeoffs associated with future energy supplies. It is not, however, without, nor was it ever without, ambitious programs for ensuring future energy supplies. The de facto national energy policy that these programs have long constituted is straightforward and fairly coherent: to provide assistance and incentives for the private discovery and production of energy. Much of the stimulus has been provided through tax laws, such as the oil depletion allowance, and regulatory programs, such as oil import quotas; however, the increasingly important form of such aid is government research, development, and demonstration (hereafter, R&D) programs. Especially since the energy scare of the early 1970s the government has accepted responsibility for many of the start-up costs and high-risk investments that the private sector hesitates to accept. By supporting new technologies before they are commercially profitable, the government hopes to smooth market adjustments to new energy supplies and avert nationally damaging shortages.

Federal policy making during the 1970s consistently reaffirmed the central place of R&D policy in the nation's fledgling energy plans. In 1973 President Nixon likened the energy problem to the challenges of the first atomic bomb and the first man on the moon. Just as crash programs in technology development successfully met those challenges, a massive R&D effort called Project Independence would vanquish the energy challenge. In 1974 President Ford approved the creation of a new agency, the Energy Research and

Development Administration (ERDA), solely responsible for the R&D mission. In 1977 the energy policy apparatus was made more comprehensive with the creation of the Department of Energy (DOE), but the department was, and still is, mostly an R&D bureaucracy. Forty-five percent of the DOE's original staff and 67 percent of its initial budget authority came from the ERDA.[1] Throughout the decade Congress demonstrated little of its characteristic sluggishness when it came to making energy R&D policy. Over the seven fiscal years prior to 1981, federal spending for energy R&D increased 600 percent.[2] Given the relative size and the technological scope of this commitment, it is not unreasonable to regard research, development, and demonstration as the essence of national energy policy in the United States today.

What sort of energy future will this de facto policy produce? The answer to that important question depends on many imponderable factors: for example, the comparative rates of discovery in different fields of research, the price of competing sources of energy, and the evolution of local, state, and federal regulations. The answer also depends on one factor about which this study can have much to say, namely, that the size of government subsidies going to alternative energy technologies over time will directly affect the relative rates of their development. Understanding how the government establishes its R&D spending priorities is therefore important for understanding how the production and distribution of energy will be constituted in the long run. Among the many reasons for these priorities the political support for alternative technologies provided by interest groups and the R&D bureaucracy is of obvious importance. The major purpose of this chapter is to explain the exercise of that support and its effects on R&D policy making.

Allocation Politics

Preliminary to an analysis of actual patterns of support, a great deal can be inferred from the simple observation that energy R&D is an "allocation" policy,[3] capable of providing many concentrated benefits and imposing only small, diffuse costs. The nuclear industry can be given breeder reactors and fusion energy research; the solar industry, subsidies for photovoltaic electricity; the fossil fuel industries, support for synthetic fuels; and environmentalists, aid for biomass, wind, or gasohol energy. The subsidy costs can normally be assessed against taxpayers without substantial resistance because the individual burdens are so small. The total 1980 energy R&D budget of under $4 billion could have been supported with only $16 from each man, woman, and child in the United States. As long as unusual conditions of fiscal austerity, such as those of the early 1980s, do not preclude new spending, Congress can build political support for such policies by providing funds to a large number of beneficiaries. During the 1970s the normal support for allocation policy was indeed forthcoming. While other energy proposals, usually involving regulations, became bound up in heated controversy, Congress aggressively expanded energy R&D programs, which by 1980 had become the keystone of national energy policy.

In essence, energy R&D is politically attractive for many of the same reasons that porkbarrel programs have traditionally been so well received. Like public works projects and defense contracts, energy R&D can satisfy the particular political needs of numerous congressmen. They can claim personal credit for the highly visible benefits; they can expect few of their supporters to recognize the economic costs; and most interested congressmen can participate in the distribution of benefits if they are willing not to interfere with the benefits allocated to other congressmen. This much about political support for porkbarrel and similar "distributive" programs is clear and familiar; however, important questions about these policies remain.[4] In particular, the pattern of distribution associated with the policies is far from obvious and, indeed, prevailing hypotheses and empirical research suggest very different possible patterns. The benefits appear in some research as flowing disproportionately to the members of committees and subcommittees with substantive and budgetary jurisdiction over the policy, but in other research as more widely and equitably dispersed throughout the Congress.[5] With respect to energy R&D the unresolved issue is how and why resources are allocated among the many possible projects and technologies.

Although the issue is similar to questions about the allocation of military contracts, river and harbor projects, and water and sewer grants addressed in the leading literature on distributive politics, energy R&D policy cannot be most effectively studied with the methods employed for the traditional porkbarrel programs. Distributive politics research has been most concerned with the geographic allocation of many particularized and separable benefits, under a committee structure catering to special constituency needs. Unlike traditional porkbarrel programs, however, the benefits of energy R&D cannot be allocated to nearly as many congressional districts or separated as easily into independent decisions. Only one district in Tennessee, for example, has a breeder reactor project, only a half dozen have synthetic fuel projects, and only a few western districts have geothermal projects. Subsidies for solar power are only somewhat more widely distributed. What is more, choices between alternative R&D programs have vastly greater policy consequences than choices between traditional public works projects. The choice between a gasohol demonstration plant and a coal gasification plant, for example, is not simply a political decision between a farm district and a coal district; it is a clear choice about energy futures. It is consequently inappropriate to focus on the committee representation of congressional districts to explain energy R&D policy.

This analysis focuses on the organizational alliances that support the major energy alternatives. Energy R&D is a field where interest groups are multiple, resourceful, and competitive. Its programs are monitored, not by a single group or a small number of cooperating groups, but by a heterogeneous collection of beneficiaries. It is also a field where the bureaucracy has been preeminent, making many of the allocation decisions, proposing most of the new projects, and wielding the greatest expertise. Understanding the relationships of multiple interest groups with each other and with the policy makers in the energy bureaucracy is thus an important task in explaining energy R&D policy. While the interest and influence of congressional committees on R&D policy has also to be considered, the relationships between the bureaucracy and interest groups must be accorded *special* attention. In this R&D program, in contradistinction to those for, say, national defense or space exploration, the government will not be the user of the technological breakthroughs. Energy technologies must be commercialized before government R&D can be considered a success. Ensuring private acceptance of them therefore demands closer than usual collaboration between the R&D agency and the groups that will employ the technologies.

The R&D Constituency

The prominence of research and development programs in United States energy policy is reflected in the large number of interest groups that expressed formal positions on R&D issues. As Table 6.1 reports, 64 percent of the sample groups had organizational opinions. The interest was widespread; in no sector were less than 31 percent of the groups concerned, and in several sectors more than three-fourths. Given that groups do not trouble themselves with position formulation and consensus building on issues that little affect them, it is fair to conclude that more than a majority of the relevant groups held serious R&D interests.

The probability that a group would take a position on energy R&D was highest, not surprisingly, for sectors composed of energy supply industries or firms developing alternative energy or conservation technology. Put simply, interest groups with members that benefit directly from government R&D projects were most likely to take a position in the political debates surrounding these projects. The conservation and renewable energy sector, which had the highest probability of participation, includes groups such as United Technologies, the Solar Energy Industries Association, and the

TABLE 6.1
R&D Issue Positions, by Sector

Sector	Percent groups with formal position	Dominant issue position in sector	Total groups in sector
Environmental groups	67% (6)	Increase spending for solar, "soft," and small technology	9
Consumer and PIGs	78% (7)	Increase solar, renewable spending	9
Petroleum and gas industry	56% (9)	Increase spending for synthetic fuels	16
Electric power	78% (7)	Increase spending for nuclear fission, fusion, and coal utilization	9
Conservation and renewable energy	100% (7)	Increase spending for solar, conservation, and decentralized energy	7
Labor unions	75% (6)	Increase government spending everywhere	8
Commercial users	31% (4)	Increase spending for synthetic fuels	13
Financial institutions	50% (1)	Increase conservation and solar spending	2
TOTAL	64% (47)	Increase government spending for R&D	73

American Institute of Architects—groups that directly represent alternative energy technology interests. For similar reasons 78 percent of the electric power sector advocated positions on energy R&D issues. Interest groups such as the Atomic Industrial Forum, the National Coal Association, and the Edison Electric Institute represent companies that benefit directly from R&D in such areas as breeder reactor technology and coal gasification.

The only parts of the energy industry not uniformly concerned with the politics of energy research and development were some members of the petroleum and natural gas sector, where only 56 percent of the groups took positions. Several factors account for this comparatively low level of interest. First, the oil and natural gas industries are technologically mature and are nearing the limit of recoverable reserves. Although there is room for increasing conventional oil and gas supplies through technology development, the long-term payoffs are small compared to the potential yield of R&D in other areas.[6] What is more, private industry has been more willing to invest capital in oil and natural gas R&D than in the more risky alternative sources, making government R&D less imperative.

A second reason the petroleum and gas industries were less than uniformly interested in R&D policy is the diversity of firms among them. Those most concerned about government R&D were primarily large, horizontally integrated corporations with significant interests in coal, uranium, solar, or other energy technologies. In this sample, Ashland Oil, Exxon, Gulf Oil, Shell Oil, Standard Oil of California, and Sun have significant coal reserves as well as interests in oil shale, tar sands, solar and/or other energy-producing or -conserving technologies; Gulf and Exxon also have significant uranium reserves and uranium milling capacity.[7] They are, in short, energy conglomerates with interests extending well beyond the issues of conventional oil and gas production. The gamut of interests of such a conglomerate is not represented by any single interest group. Groups such as the National Petroleum Refiners Association, the Natural Gas Supply Committee, and even the American Petroleum Institute represent the major oil and gas corporations on many political issues—but not on R&D issues. Major oil company interests today cut across the association boundaries established in response to earlier needs of the oil business. The groups that speak for the industry on traditional issues are therefore silent on R&D issues, leaving the majors to speak either for themselves or through associations representing other sectors such as coal or nuclear. Similarly, the smaller oil businesses that are so concerned about other energy issues—firms such as Clark Oil, and groups such as the American Petroleum Refiners Association and the Council of Active Independent Oil and Gas Producers—abstained from these issues. In sum, the R&D interests of the petroleum and natural gas sector were those advocated by the horizontally integrated major corporations.

Both the environmental and consumer sectors were actively concerned, with 67 percent of the former and 78 percent of the latter groups formally advocating positions. A comparable level of concern with energy R&D was expressed by labor unions. Given the basic role of energy in economic productivity, and the potential jobs created in new energy industries, it is not surprising to find 75 percent of the unions taking a position. In the final analysis, interest group concern with government R&D was pervasive.

It is also important to note that the positions advocated by interest groups help to account for the political popularity of R&D programs. In this regard it is particularly significant that the groups uniformly favored an expanded government role in energy R&D. In seventy-three interviews only one group, the National Taxpayers Union (NTU), voiced opposition to increased government spending for it. The other groups that took positions were in consensus on the need for increased federal support. Such consensus obviously reduces the usual obstacles to energy policy making. Also politically significant, and characteristic of group positions, is the fact that only a small minority of the groups advocated selective cuts in spending in one area and increases in another. The norm was simply to advocate spending in a particular area and take no position in other areas. None of the major oil corporations, for example, advocated more spending for synthetic fuels and less for fusion or solar. Likewise, none of the nuclear power advocates claimed that the government was overinvesting in solar energy or other "soft" alternatives. In fact, the only groups that took positions with negative as well as positive recommendations were a few environmental organizations that opposed further nuclear development. Even in those cases the negative position was understated in terms such as "a need to redress historic imbalances favoring nuclear research and development."

The formal group positions suggest the possibility of mutual noninterference among sectoral interests in R&D policy making. The paucity of negative positions indicates a willingness among interest groups to suppress objections to competing energy technologies, and to logroll political support—in short, an acceptance among interest groups of one of the norms of porkbarrel politics. Solar energy and other soft alternatives are supported not only by firms and industries that produce and finance them but also by environmental, consumer, and other public interest groups; synthetic fuel R&D by the petroleum and natural gas industries, the coal industry, and several commercial user groups; government investment in nuclear fission and fusion research by the nuclear industry and electric utilities; and all technologies by organized labor. Each major R&D area, then, had a solid core of interest group support, and none faced strongly expressed opposition.

This overview suggests that energy R&D policy making attracts a large and diverse constituency, dominated by beneficiaries, virtually devoid of organized cost-bearers, and willing to overlook policy differences in order to maximize respective allocations of R&D resources. It says nothing, however, about the actions groups take to carry out their positions, nor anything about the relative success of the technologies in the policy process. The overview merely suggests the potential for the politics of mutual noninterference and the equitable allocation of benefits. It remains to be seen whether this collective tunnel-vision of energy R&D is actually supported by the political alliances necessary to sustain quasi-autonomous research and development subgovernments.

Interest Group Initiatives

If energy R&D policy is formulated to minimize conflict among contending beneficiaries, the relationship between the constituency and the bureaucracy should approach pluralism. That is, multiple beneficiaries should find participation in bureaucratic politics attractive, and the agency should strive to accommodate many of its various constituents. The relationship may exclude direct cost-bearer interests; it should not, however, be monopolized by only a few beneficiaries. Interest diversity should be reflected in both bureaucratic strategies and group initiatives—the latter qualified only by the organizational advantages and disadvantages normally associated with interests composed of different-sized units.

The interview questions used to elucidate R&D politics (Appendix A, Part D) attempted to distinguish the major forms of consultation in different areas of administrative policy making, especially (1) differences between consultation on the implementation of established programs and on the formulation of new or revised programs, and (2) differences in consultation across the successive stages of basic research, technology development, and demonstration or commercialization. The first distinction was drawn because the policy consequences and the incentives for political relationships clearly differ between implementation and formulation activities. Implementation decisions determine who will receive grants on contracts, how internal projects will be designed, and how external projects will be evaluated. Formulation decisions, usually made in the context of budget submissions, have greater effect on the relative level of commitment to different technologies and to different stages of assistance. Both types of decisions have important consequences, but budget activities should prompt greater agency interest in political support, and greater group incentives for participation.

The distinctions among stages of R&D were drawn for similar reasons. The political support that is provided to different stages of R&D can affect the very logic of government support for private energy development. Government emphasis on basic research reflects a concern with truly long-term energy problems and a belief that private investment ought to assume risks for near-term alternatives if they are commercially feasible. Government emphasis on demonstration projects, by contrast, indicates a reluctance to accept private investment decisions about the comparative advantage of near-term alternatives, and entails direct subsidies to established industries. Because the immediate payoffs increase as R&D priorities shift from the long to the near term, the likelihood of group involvement should also increase. In any case, understanding the structure of political support for different stages is important for comprehending the basic logic of government R&D. After the creation of the Department of Energy, variation across the several stages should have been observable because R&D was then organized into separate offices according to commercial readiness.

These descriptive goals turned out to be impracticable. Interest groups tended to mix the purposes of the initiatives; implementation and budgetary goals could be pursued through a single strategy. Groups also made little effort to differentiate stages of commercial readiness in their efforts to arrange desirable government support. At any and all appropriate stages support was pursued with equal vigor. To ensure reliable measures, interest group initiatives had to be measured with fewer indicators and fewer categories than was theoretically desirable. The indicators are: (1) frequency of participation—a four-point scale based on all areas of bureaucratic R&D decision making in which a group was involved, and ranging from none, to sporadic, to frequent, to regular; (2) area of emphasis—a three-point scale estimating the predominant focus of group initiatives, and ranging from implementation, to both implementation and budgeting, to budgeting; and (3) level of emphasis—a three-point scale gauging the relative use of staff and political contacts, and ranging from staff, to both staff and political, to political. The scores of each group were averaged within the sectors, and their means reported in Table 6.2.

Perhaps the most striking feature of group participation is its depressed level. Repeating a pattern established in the two regulatory arenas, group involvement in the bureaucratic R&D arena occurred with less than sporadic frequency (0.68) for the average group. In terms of the raw frequency distribution this means that 59 percent of the groups had no contact with the R&D bureaucracy. Of the 41 percent that had contact, almost two-thirds were only sporadic participants who limited their initiatives to a *maximum* of one bureaucratic communication per month. Only ten groups were frequent or regular participants—a substantial drop from the forty-seven that advocated positions on R&D issues.

Another finding of general importance is that implementation issues were emphasized more often than budgetary issues, and likewise that staff contacts, more often than political contacts, were emphasized in group strategies. Scores of less than two—1.89 for area of emphasis and 1.75 for level of emphasis—indicate that the typical group fell just short of covering both activities and both bureaucratic levels, and concentrated more on implementation and staff relations. In raw terms, 32 percent of the groups favored implementation involvement while 21 percent favored budgeting; 46 percent interacted primarily with the staff while only 21 percent concentrated on political appointees. Substantial portions of the sample, however, strove for balance; 46 percent divided their time evenly between implementation and budgetary questions, and 32 percent cultivated with equal efforts the agency staff and leadership.

These results, coupled with the finding of generally meager participation, suggest that most groups did not regard the R&D bureau-

Table 6.2
Interest Group Initiatives Toward Energy R&D Bureaucracy:
Summary Measures

Sector	Mean frequency of participation	Area of emphasis	Level of participation emphasized
Environmental groups	0.75	2.60	2.80
Consumer and PIGs	0	—	—
Petroleum and gas industry	1.07	1.29	1.29
Electric power	2.12	1.86	1.71
Conservation and renewable energy	1.43	2.00	1.50
Labor unions	0	—	—
Commercial users	0.15	2.50	1.50
Financial institutions	0.50	1.00	1.00
TOTALS	0.68	1.89	1.75

NOTE: Answers with respect to group initiatives were coded summarily as follows: (1) Frequency of participation: none 0, sporadic 1, frequent 2, regular 3. (2) Area of emphasis: implementation 1, both 2, budgeting 3. (3) Level of participation: staff 1, both 2, political 3.

cracy as the appropriate place to voice their typically unsophisticated positions on energy R&D. The positions of most groups were not developed beyond crude advocacy of some form of government support for particular energy alternatives. Although the bureaucracy is certainly a sensible place to begin providing budgetary support, groups did not employ it for that exclusive purpose. Implementation issues were the more frequent concern, and professional staff the far more frequent target, of group initiatives. Indeed, 78 percent of the groups devoted equal or greater effort to implementation, and the same percentage were more or as much concerned with the staff as the leadership. The norms of bureaucratic participation are thus clear: you do not interact with the bureaucracy unless you can be a service on implementation issues and can deal capably with the professional staff.

The general level and nature of group participation only begins to reveal the politically significant aspects of constituency influence. How the participation is distributed among the energy sectors and between beneficiaries and cost-bearers must still be considered. The sectors most involved with the R&D bureaucracy—petroleum and gas, electric power, and conservation and renewable energy—represent firms and industries that benefit directly and financially from federal programs. None of the other sectors averaged even sporadic involvement. Consumers and labor, which regarded themselves as both beneficiaries and cost-bearers, were completely uninvolved. Commercial users, obviously concerned with future supply security, and financial institutions, attentive to investment effects, were effectively nonparticipants too. The environmentalists were the only interest besides direct beneficiaries that came close to sporadic participation. Group initiatives, then, were dominated by three sectors of beneficiaries.

Energy R&D has traditionally been devoted primarily to nuclear power and electrical generation. Electric power is the only sector that averaged more than frequent (2.12) interaction with the agency. Indeed five of the groups in that sector—the American Nuclear Energy Council (ANEC), the American Public Power Association (APPA), the Edison Electric Institute (EEI), the National Coal Association (NCA), and the National Rural Electric Cooperative Association (NRECA)—maintained regular, or virtually daily, contact; only three other groups in the entire sample claimed that amount of involvement.

The other two benefiting sectors represent newer areas of government research and development activities, and were less closely involved with agency decision making. The conservation and renewable energy sector represents interests in a wide variety of technologies ranging from the "hard," such as fuel cells and photovoltaics, to the "soft," such as solar heating and cooling, biomass, wind, and passive solar construction.[8] The sector's average rate of involvement (1.43) falls midway between frequent and sporadic. Two of its groups, however, were regular participants in agency business. United Technologies, a growing conglomerate involved with fuel cells, gas turbines, photovoltaics, wind power, laser fusion, and other energy technologies, maintained daily contact with the R&D portion of DOE, as did the Solar Energy Industries Association, a trade association of small and large companies (such as General Electric). The other groups had only sporadic contact.

Petroleum and natural gas groups averaged just better than sporadic (1.07) involvement. This figure is depressed by the inclusion in the average of seven groups that did not take positions on the issue and had no involvement with the agency. Even those groups that did take an interest in R&D matters, however, were for the most part only sporadic participants on the administrative side. The exceptions were the American Gas Association, a regular participant, and Gulf Oil, a frequent participant, in bureaucratic decision making. The relatively low level of oil company involvement is a stark contrast to the constant involvement of major oil in the regulatory bureaucracy.

Environmentalists, the only other groups of any consequence in the R&D bureaucracy, occupy an ambiguous position vis-à-vis R&D policy. In the strict sense they do not represent beneficiaries, because their members do not profit economically from the policy, and they do not represent cost-bearers, because their primary concern is not costs, but environmental benefits. In the political process they act as advocates for soft energy development, but not as direct beneficiaries. In any case, their participation at the agency averaged less than sporadic (0.75). Only one environmental public interest group, the Sierra Club, was frequently involved with administrative policy making.

What were the goals and strategies of these active sectors in their participation? Scales scoring area of emphasis and level of emphasis (in columns 2 and 3 of Table 6.2) help in distinguishing three forms of group involvement. Groups that score low, i.e., near 1.0, on both scales are primarily technical advisors who concentrate their efforts on affecting implementation through contacts with the professional staff. Groups that score high, i.e., near 3.0, on both scales are essentially political counselors who hope to influence the general direction of energy R&D by providing input to budget formulation through political officials of the agency. These groups do not attempt to court the support of program officials or other staff; they lack the technical expertise to interact below the level of policy generalists and politicians. Between these polar cases are groups that operate at all levels of the agency with about equal frequency. They have the expertise and interest to interact on implementation matters, and the potential political power to play an effective role in budgeting. Their relationships likewise extend to the top and bottom levels of the agency. Inspection of the mean scores for the two scales reveals immediately the distinctly different strategies pursued by the four major sectors. Environmental public interest groups tended to be politicians while petroleum and gas groups had a strong propensity toward the technocratic role. The other two sectors—electric power, and conservation and renewable energy—pursued more balanced strategies.

None of the environmental groups emphasized implementation matters or focused primarily on the administrative staff in their agency relations. Of the five that interacted with the agency, four placed decided emphasis on political level liaison; the other worked both levels. Likewise, three were concerned primarily with budgetary recommendations, while two were about equally interested in budgets and implementation. All these groups regarded R&D staff at the Department of Energy as unsympathetic to environmental interests and biased in favor of central electrification, nuclear power, and technology development on a large corporate scale. They complained that the staff was largely a holdover from the Atomic Energy Commission (which is true) and had no appreciation for soft path technologies that could provide energy on a decentralized basis and be supported by small businesses. Although a DOE staff was responsible for solar energy and other soft concepts (as was an ERDA staff before it), it was criticized for its small size and its preference for working with large companies. Environmental groups cited its hostility or indifference to explain their failure to interact at that level; however, the relative poverty of technical expertise in the groups cannot be ignored as an alternative explanation. Because the staff is less interested in political support than in technical advice, it would be relatively unreceptive to the unsophisticated advice of environmental groups, regardless of policy preferences. In any case, only the Sierra Club, which monitored the environmental impact statement process at the commercialization and demonstration stages, and advised the solar and geothermal programs on environmental externalities, had staff contacts of apparent significance.

What little additional participation environmental groups enjoyed was at the political level. Three groups met sporadically with assistant secretaries or their deputies to discuss general budgetary recommendations. These leadership meetings were, however, of recent origin. While the ERDA managed energy R&D, environmental groups reportedly had no access at either the staff or the political level. In contrast, all the groups in this sector that took positions on R&D, including those with agency contacts, stressed that their effective point of access on the issues was the Congress. In that regard the strategy of environmental groups was similar to that of consumers and other public interest groups that dealt only with Congress on these matters. Despite the inroads environmental groups made at the political level, they did not have a mutually supportive or "working" relationship with the R&D bureaucracy. The significance of the budding relationship between environmentalists and the R&D administration mostly remains to be seen.

The petroleum and natural gas sector pursued much the opposite strategy from that of environmental groups. Their industrial representatives had a strong tendency (1.29 on both scales) to emphasize implementation and staff-level liaison. None of the groups focused their efforts preponderantly on budgetary decisions or political administrators. In fact, five of the seven administratively active groups emphasized implementation and staff-level liaison. The industry's liaison was not, however, very frequent: of the seven groups with agency relations, five had only sporadic contact. The greater involvement of the other two groups stemmed from their management of federally subsidized R&D projects.[9] For the most part the oil industry maintained a cautious and unenthusiastic relationship with the R&D bureaucracy. Through diversification the industry developed interests and expertise in oil shale, tar sands, and coal gasification and liquefaction technologies. The DOE technical staff valued its expert advice, and consultation occurred sporadically on synthetic fuel technologies. There was no effort on the industry's part, however, to cultivate relationships with the R&D staff comparable in influence to those developed with the regulatory bureaucracy.

The limited nature of oil and gas industry involvement has at least two causes not suggested directly by the organizational theory. First, the heterogeneity of their non-oil energy interests prevents major oil companies from speaking as an industry through their national association, the API. Second, many members of the oil industry, and a majority of those in this study, are unsupportive of joint R&D programs with the government because patent rights are foregone. They prefer policies that stimulate R&D through tax incentives.

The electric power sector maintained yet another type of relationship. The mean area of emphasis score (1.86) reflects a balanced concern with implementation and budgetary decisions, albeit tilted in favor of the former. The sector also tried to balance its preponderant staff-level interactions with frequent contacts with political decision makers. In fact, six of the seven active groups strove for equal attention to implementation and budgeting, while four of them worked both levels of the agency hierarchy with equal vigor. In important contrast to the other sectors, five of the seven groups pursued these strategies through *regular* interaction.

Although the strategies and specific objectives of the groups in this sector differed, they share a common interest in electrical generation and together covered all bases in the R&D bureaucracy. All the groups that worked regularly with the agency provided technical advice in the implementation of demonstration or commercialization projects. Virtually none of this advice was a consequence of contractual relationships.[10] Except for the American Nuclear Energy Council (ANEC), all are trade associations with a wealth of expertise on their respective industries.[11] Four of the associations—the APPA, EEI, NCA and NRECA—plus the ANEC, based their relationships on the exchange of technical advice on implementation with the program staff, and at this level regarded them as trusting and mutually supportive.

The groups that cultivated close working relationships at the staff level used the ties to affect administrative activities other than just implementation. In fact, the ultimate objective was to build bureaucratic support for new and expanded programs in the budgetary process. The staff and the trade associations representing this traditionally dominant sector have a mutual interest in increasing government programs. By providing the R&D staff credible technical assistance over the years, the electric power sector had established close relationships that permitted significant private input in program development. The staff accepted group advice on budget recommendations, and groups reciprocated by supporting the staff request through the remainder of the budgetary process. The groups that had working relationships with the agency staff regarded them as crucial to successful appropriation politics.

Given the importance of budgetary recommendations, it is not surprising to find that these groups also interacted frequently with political decision makers. All the active groups reported sporadic to frequent consultation with the R&D leadership. It is nonetheless clear that they placed greater value on their relationships with the permanent R&D bureaucracy. They uniformly complained that the political administrators with whom they dealt during the Carter administration were less receptive toward them than their predecessors. This change notwithstanding, most of the sector continued to have regular, mutually supportive interactions with the career bureaucracy.

The final major class of beneficiaries, the conservation and renewable energy sector, evidenced yet another type of administrative relationship. On the average their emphasis was equally divided between budgeting and implementation (mean score 2.00), and their level of interaction (mean score 1.50) tended more toward the permanent staff. On the surface their relationship was much like that maintained by the electric power sector, with staff-level inter-actions and technical assistance providing the foundation for broad-er influence. Below the surface a key difference stands out. Only United Technologies and the Solar Energy Industries Association had regular contact with the agency. Like the electric power groups they regarded their staff relationships in favorable terms, but their efforts were simply less extensive. The other groups in this new sector were only sporadically involved and did not have close rela-tions with the staff. In several instances their communications are completely explained by contract interest. Those that were adminis-tratively active reported at least pro forma access to political deci-sion makers, but none regarded the access as particularly effective. The relationships maintained by this sector were best developed at the staff level and effective largely on implementation matters. The groups recognized the importance of agency liaison for budgetary goals, but they did not yet have the network of working relationships within the bureaucracy to support those larger objectives.

Overall, group participation in the R&D bureaucracy was more competitive than in the two regulatory arenas already examined, but still limited to a small minority of the interested groups. While the pattern is not monopsonistic, the potentially monopsonistic sec-tor of electric power interests did not receive a lot of competition from other beneficiaries or cost-bearers.

Bureaucratic Strategies

Group participation can be mostly a result of the political calcula-tions of group members and leaders, or it can be strongly influenced, as we have seen, by government incentives or disincentives and direct government efforts to incorporate groups into the policy pro-cess. To consider the role of the R&D bureaucracy in structuring group participation, all its efforts to interact with interest groups—whether for political or technical reasons—are measured by the frequency of its initiatives toward each group. Group reports of agency initiatives are used to code each group as a frequent, sporad-ic, or non-recipient of agency contacts. The categories correspond respectively to daily or weekly, monthly or less, and never in the tabulation of mean frequencies of agency initiatives (Table 6.3).

The R&D bureaucracy's apparent strategy was to concentrate its

TABLE 6.3

Outside Initiatives by Energy R&D Bureaucracy

Sector	Mean frequency of agency initiatives[a]	Groups asked for congressional support
Environmental groups	0.25	43% (3)
Consumer and PIGs	0	11% (1)
Petroleum and gas industry	0.50	0% (0)
Electric power	1.62	25% (2)
Conservation and renewable energy	0.86	0% (0)
Labor unions	0	0% (0)
Commercial users	0.23	15% (2)
Financial institutions	0.50	0% (0)
TOTALS	0.49	12% (8)

[a] Means are based on a three-point frequency scale: none 0, sporadic 1, frequent 2.

constituency contacts upon those groups that represented the traditionally dominant areas of energy R&D. Only the electric power sector averaged close to frequent (1.62) contact from the bureaucracy. In fact, no other sector received even a sporadic (1.00) average rate of agency initiatives. The next most likely recipients—conservation and renewable energy groups—were contacted by the agency at an average rate of 0.86. The mean frequency for the petroleum and gas sector fell midway between sporadic and none, and for environmental groups at the negligible average of 0.12.

Six of the eight groups in the electric power sector reported that the R&D bureaucracy contacted them frequently, and one that it did so sporadically. Most of the outreach was to tap the technical expertise for which the trade associations had developed reputations of high credibility. The staff came to rely so heavily on this advice that, in fact, a regular two-way flow of communication characterized their relationship with the electric power sector.

Political administrators also frequently contacted these groups for expert input on broader policy proposals. Demands on the time of the agency leadership precluded, however, the development of working relationships comparable to those at the staff level. Consultations between political administrators and groups were not overtly political. Except in technical specificity they did not differ from the substantive interactions occurring at the staff level. For example, there was not a great deal of discussion between groups and political administrators of strategies to be used in the annual congressional appropriations process. The agency politicians did not usually suggest or request that the groups testify at appropriation hearings or provide other forms of support in Congress. As Table 6.3 reports, only two of the groups in this sector ever received explicit requests from the R&D bureaucracy for congressional support. This does not mean that the bureaucracy did not desire political support. Rather, it indicates the clear mutuality of interests between the bureaucracy and the groups, which acquired a stake in budget requests through their participation in the administrative formulation of the proposals. Group support for the requests in Congress followed automatically from self-interest.

No other sector could claim a comparable relationship with the R&D bureaucracy. The next closest relationship was maintained by the conservation and renewable energy sector, where two groups reported frequent contacts and two, sporadic contacts; three claimed, however, never to have been contacted by the agency. The relationship between these groups and the bureaucracy was not fundamentally different from that maintained by the nuclear, coal, and utility groups; it was simply far less developed, in part because their value as credible and readily accessible sources of technical assistance had not yet been demonstrated. The new technologies lacked the organizational structure to play the regular role of technical assistant to the agency. The SEIA, for example, had a small budget of $350,000 and a meager staff—almost completely administrative—of five. Because the organizational staff was not technically competent to engage in extensive staff-level administrative liaison, the sector had to rely on corporations such as United Technologies to provide technical assistance to the bureaucracy. Since many of the large corporations have interests in a variety of energy technologies, including nuclear power, the sector did not have the undivided support that would maximize its growth.

The bureaucratic initiatives that the conservation and renewable energy sector did receive were exclusively from the technical staff. The collaborative relationship was not such that the agency asked the groups to provide support for budget requests in Congress. In fact, if it had asked, the groups would undoubtedly have rejected the request, for they always had to make a case in Congress for significantly greater funding than the agency had recommended. As the analysis of policy consequences will demonstrate, the bureaucracy and these groups never agreed on the rate at which R&D in this sector should be expanded, and contact at this point was initiated almost solely for technical assistance, not for broader policy development.

The R&D bureaucracy showed similar interest in the petroleum and gas industry. The low mean rate of agency initiatives (0.50) is somewhat deceiving, since it is depressed by the large number of sectoral representatives that made no effort to deal with the bureaucracy. Of the seven groups that had some interaction with the agency, five had been contacted only sporadically or less. The two recipients of frequent contacts had been involved with the agency through contracts or cost-sharing projects. Naturally, project involvement engendered close, technically based relationships; however, the groups hoped also to cultivate their technical linkages into staff level support for, and cooperation in the development of, expanded liquid and gaseous fuel R&D. Agency initiatives toward this sector were at least as frequent as those directed toward the representatives of conservation and renewable energy technology. Although the petroleum and gas sector as a whole was not a political force in R&D policy, a number of individual corporations and a couple of major associations were building working relationships with the permanent staff. At the political levels there was not yet overt cooperation on congressional budgetary strategies. The frequency of two-way technical interaction between the bureaucracy and part of this sector suggests, however, that there was at least as much agency support and interest in technologies such as synthetic fuels as there was in conservation and renewable energy.

The groups in the aforementioned sectors were direct beneficiaries of the R&D bureaucracy. They were also virtually the only targets of agency initiatives toward interest groups. The only cost-bearing sector that interacted with the bureaucracy was the environmentalists, who represent the diffuse population that experiences the negative environmental externalities, or indirect costs, of energy R&D. To protect their interests as cost-bearers and at the same time establish grounds for working with the R&D bureaucracy, the environmental groups became vocal advocates of soft energy development. By emphasizing this positive route, rather than a negative strategy of R&D opposition, they were potential allies of the agency. Nonetheless, of the five environmental groups having contact with the bureaucracy, only the Sierra Club had ever been the recipient of administrative initiatives of any kind: namely, sporadic requests for technical advice by the solar and geothermal programs.

There were signs, however, that the neglect of indirect cost-bearing constituents might be abating. Three of the environmental groups, and one consumer group, reported that the administration asked for support in the congressional budgetary process (Table 6.3). In each case the request came from Carter appointees seeking support for the administration's recommendation that the Clinch River Breeder Reactor Project be terminated. These requests did not signify the beginning of substantive policy-making contributions by public interest groups or the start of much improved relations with the R&D bureaucracy. They were part of a coalition-building process, conducted by new political appointees in 1977, that was not supported by the permanent bureaucracy. Indeed, the ERDA establishment is reported to have lobbied covertly against the termination recommendation.[12]

Nevertheless, political level changes in group-agency relations were apparently occurring in other sectors as well. A number of the groups commented on differences in their bureaucratic access in the Ford-ERDA period vis-à-vis the Carter-DOE period. None noted any changes in staff-level relationships, either coterminal with the Carter presidency or with the reorganization of ERDA into DOE. The reported changes occurred at political levels, i.e., with Executive Schedule officials such as assistant secretaries, deputy assistant secretaries, and directors. The advocates of soft energy and conservation reported significantly improved access (see Table 6.4). The public interest group community and parts of the conservation and renewable energy sector found that it was newly possible to meet with political decision makers and to make suggestions for budget

TABLE 6.4
Post-1977 Changes in Access to R&D Bureaucracy

Sector	Improved	Declined	Unchanged
Environmental groups	75% (3)		25% (1)
Consumer and PIGs	100% (2)		
Petroleum and gas industry		67% (2)	33% (1)
Electric power		100% (3)	
Conservation and renewable energy	80% (4)		20% (1)
Labor unions			
Commercial users		100% (1)	
Financial institutions			
TOTALS	50% (9)	33% (6)	17% (3)

policy. They reported no such opportunities in ERDA. It is important to note, however, that direct economic beneficiaries in the conservation and renewable energy sector were not experiencing these improvements. Access by United Technologies and the SEIA was at least as effective while ERDA was in operation.

Complementing the improved access of the soft energy advocates and the public interest group community was a decline in effective access reported by the electric power, petroleum, and gas groups. None reported any improvement, but that does not imply any serious deterioration. Only one group complained of anti-nuclear or "soft-headed" biases of Carter appointees; the rest attributed minor deterioration to the reorganization of the bureaucracy. Because DOE was less than a year old at the time of the interviews, the complaints had much to do with reorganizational confusion. Whether the structural changes in R&D management at DOE permanently alter the effective access of these sectors to political decisionmakers remains to be seen. It is prudent to speculate that, as the reorganized bureaucracy settles into its routines, they will reestablish that access upset by the transition.

The bureaucratic strategy of the R&D administration falls between the categories of pluralist and corporatist consultation, but much closer to the latter. Only the electric power sector was approached frequently by the agency and could claim a working relationship with it. The agency did not ignore its other beneficiaries, but made less than sporadic efforts to interact with them. Agency efforts to involve cost-bearers in R&D policy making were meager to none. Only one environmental group, which qualifies only indirectly as a cost-bearer, was approached sporadically. The outreach came predominantly from the agency staff, and served primarily to inject projects and proposals with technical industry knowledge and at least tacit assent. The targets of consultation did not differ greatly, however, between the staff and the politicians. Both levels concentrated on the traditional beneficiaries. The only perceptible difference between levels was the sincere effort by politicians after 1977 to consult with environmentalists.

The Policy Consequences of Quasi-Corporatism

Contrary to the initial perception of R&D policy making as a classic pluralist process in which conflicts are resolved through cooperative logrolling rather than competitive compromise, pluralism does not characterize the bureaucratic politics of energy R&D. Interest group initiatives and bureaucratic strategies evidenced the dominance of a single sector more than the involvement of a variety of interests. The relationship was not as limited as those observed in the regulatory arenas, and it was certainly not captured by cost-bearers. It was restricted, however, to a sufficiently small number of beneficiaries to be labeled "quasi-corporatism." Further support for this designation is provided by the policy decisions of the R&D bureaucracy over the period of study.

An obvious place to begin an analysis of R&D policy outputs is with the awards of R&D contracts. Research on congressional allocation decisions has often focused on the geographic distribution of defense contracts and other easily disaggregatable government benefits. Since the Department of Energy's R&D budget is second only to that of the Department of Defense, and between 60 and 80 percent of the DOE's budget flows through procurement, contract allocation might seem to be a reasonable starting point for evaluating energy R&D policies.[13]

Contracting is not, however, what the relationships between the R&D bureaucracy and major interest groups are all about. Most of the contracts do not go to the major energy corporations, or even the smaller firms, represented by the interest groups in this study. Most DOE contracts are awarded to research organizations that survive on government contracts[14]—consulting firms such as Arthur D. Little, SRI International, and the Mitre Corporation. While R&D procurement decisions may favor organizations and firms located in key congressional districts, and these decisions may even grease the congressional machinery, they are not the major stake for national interest groups.

In support of this conclusion, Table 6.5 reports evidence that only 22 percent of the groups studied ever held or even applied for energy R&D contracts. In two of the administratively active sectors—environmental interests and electric power—virtually no contract interest existed. Individual firms in the latter sector were attracted to R&D grants, but their associational representatives left the issuance of these awards untouched. Only the NCA in this sector held an R&D contract, one that was far indeed from the focus of its Washington administrative relations. Research and development contracts are simply not benefits that associations of competing

TABLE 6.5
Interest Group Role in Energy R&D Contracting

Sector	Groups holding or applying for energy R&D contracts	Total groups in sector
Environmental groups	0% (0)	9
Consumer and PIGs	0% (0)	9
Petroleum and gas industry	38% (6)	16
Electric power	11% (1)	9
Conservation and renewable energy	100% (7)	7
Labor unions	12% (1)	8
Commercial users	0% (0)	13
Financial institutions	50% (1)	2
TOTALS	22% (16)	73

N O T E : Of the sixteen groups holding or applying for contracts, six are individual energy corporations; ten are associations.

firms can pursue consensually. The primary goal of national groups is to influence larger policy decisions in which all their members can potentially share.

In the two other active sectors the contract motivation for bureaucratic liaison appears larger than it really was. Six oil and gas interests held or applied for R&D contracts, but only the Gulf Oil Corporation attributed most of its administrative involvement to "grantsmanship." All the groups representing conservation and renewable energy interests had contract connections with the bureaucracy, but the majority of them were also pushed into administrative liaison by larger goals. Only three of the groups—the Institute for Local Self-Reliance, the National Association of Home Builders, and the National Congress for Community Economic Development—interacted with the R&D bureaucracy almost entirely because of extant or desired contracts. Although contractual relations were important also to the American Institute of Architects and to United Technologies, they expressed equal concern with broader implementation and appropriation goals. The final two groups, the SEIA and Consumer Action Now, were motivated to a negligible degree by procurement interests. Their objectives lay almost entirely in the general expansion of government support for conservation and renewable energy technology.

In sum, the dominant purpose of administrative relations was not contract procurement. At most, contracts were the major motivation for the initiatives of a portion of the conservation and renewable energy sector. The major objective of almost all national groups was to cultivate technically and politically supportive relations with the R&D bureaucracy in order to affect policy implementation and budgeting. To understand the significance or effects of group-agency relations it is therefore important to examine decisions in those areas. Our analysis of policy consequences, which focuses on the allocation of R&D funds in the budgetary process, will not only reveal the significance of quasi-corporatist organizational relations; it will also explain how the government's important choices among alternative energy futures are made.

Budgeting for Energy R&D

Although energy R&D has been administered through a bewildering array of projects and programs over the years, most of it can be classified within six general program areas: fossil energy, nuclear fission, nuclear fusion, solar energy, geothermal energy, and conservation. Using the disaggregated program expenditures reported annually in the appendix of the federal budget, I reconstructed executive budget requests and actual budget authority granted for these areas for fiscal years 1976–79. Table 6.6 traces the change in actual appropriations for the programs over the four-year period, during which actual budget authority nearly tripled. All areas of R&D benefited from this dramatic growth. Because the United States government had not committed itself to any single course of future energy development,[15] it may well have been a rational strategy simply to distribute the increased funds across all areas of R&D until there was sufficient information to warrant commitment to a particular path of development.

As long as there is no long-term plan for R&D appropriation decisions, the allocation of funds is an annual political contest. Failing any central allocation criteria, funds may be increased in equal proportions to all programs—in the traditional incremental fashion of budgeting.[16] Or, funds may be dispersed in unequal proportions to reward certain political constituencies—a pattern representing real program competition.[17] The latter appears to have been the case with R&D funding. Incremental decisions that provide all claimants with their "fair share"[18] would tend to increase each program area

TABLE 6.6

Energy R&D Funding: Program Shares of Actual Annual Funding

Program	FY1976 Dollars (millions)	FY1976 Percent of total	FY1977 Dollars (millions)	FY1977 Percent of total
Fossil energy	$253.9	20.3%	$505.5	22.8%
Nuclear fission	629.0	50.2%	945.2	42.6%
Nuclear fusion	226.0	18.0%	391.8	17.7%
Solar energy	66.1	5.3%	200.1	9.0%
Geothermal energy	30.2	2.4%	49.3	2.2%
Conservation	47.0	3.8%	124.9	5.6%
TOTALS	$1,252.2	100.0%	$2,216.8	99.9%

Program	FY1978 Dollars (millions)	FY1978 Percent of total	FY1979 Dollars (millions)	FY1979 Percent of total
Fossil energy	$719.1	25.9%	$823.7	23.9%
Nuclear fission	1,051.0	37.9%	1,095.4	31.8%
Nuclear fusion	396.5	14.3%	471.0	13.7%
Solar energy	305.6	11.0%	443.0	12.9%
Geothermal energy	80.8	2.9%	135.2	3.9%
Conservation	221.8	8.0%	473.4	13.8%
TOTALS	$2,774.8	100.0%	$3,441.7	100.0%

by the same percentage each year and thereby maintain the priorities of each program in the overall policy. That was not the case in R&D appropriations.

The four-year growth rates of the six programs varied widely. Nuclear fission R&D experienced the lowest rate of growth, and appropriations did not quite double; fusion energy more than doubled its funding; fossil energy research and development received a still greater injection of funds, increasing by well over 300 percent. These growth rates were small, however, compared to the fortunes of the new technologies. Geothermal energy spending increased more than 400 percent, solar energy funding more than 700 percent; and budget authority for conservation R&D skyrocketed over 1,000 percent.

Naturally, these disparate growth rates changed the shares of total R&D devoted to these general areas. Nuclear fission was the major loser in relative terms. In fiscal 1976 it accounted for more than half of the energy R&D subsumed by the six programs; by 1979 it accounted for only 31.8 percent. Fusion also declined in relative emphasis; its share of the total dropped from 18.1 percent to 13.7 percent. The other areas—fossil, solar, and geothermal energy (the smallest program)—gained at the expense of the two nuclear programs, as did conservation, which jumped to third position in priority. In four years the energy R&D budget was completely reoriented. The split between nuclear and non-nuclear programs changed from 68 percent versus 32 percent in 1976 to 46 percent versus 54 percent in 1979. The general R&D priorities (at least, as reflected in dollars) reversed, to the benefit of the newer technologies.

On the surface, at least, the nonincremental changes run counter to the apparent quasi-corporatist relationships between the R&D bureaucracy and its clientele. The bureaucracy's only thoroughly developed, mutually supportive relationships were those with the electric power sector. Except for the NCA, which represents fossil fuel interests besides those in electrical power, all the groups in this bureaucratically dominant sector are nuclear energy advocates. How could it be that those interests with the most bureaucratic support prospered least, while those with the least support prospered most? Could it be that the relationships were not quasi-corporatist at all, or that the relationships were not having their hypothesized effects?

The data on final budget authority reported in Table 6.6 are not suitable for analyzing agency budget policy because they are contaminated by the decisions of other budgetary actors in the Office of Management and Budget and in the Congress. The ideal data are the agency's initial and final budget estimates submitted to the OMB many months before the president's budget is finalized. Since those data could not be located in consistent form, it was necessary to devise less direct measures of the agency estimates.

The closest readily available indicators of agency budgetary requests are the recommendations for spending authority in the president's annual budget—as a result of negotiations between the OMB and the agency. Because agencies condition their requests on the expected reaction of OMB, and the OMB is inadequately equipped and often indisposed to scrutinize their requests, agency preferences are frequently reflected clearly in the president's recommendations.[19] To understand their meaning, it is necessary to evaluate the absolute presidential requests against clear standards, in this instance (Table 6.7) as percentage changes in the status quo. Two versions of the status quo—previous executive requests and previous congressional appropriations—are employed because the agency and the

TABLE 6.7
Presidential Requests as Percentages of Energy
R&D Funding, FY76–FY79

Program	Absolute request as percentage of previous		Budget share[a] request as percentage of previous	
	Request	Appropriation	Request	Appropriation
Fossil energy	+43.0%	+57.1%	+4.9%	+12.7%
Nuclear fission	+16.3%	+23.7%	−16.0%	−11.4%
Nuclear fusion	+33.6%	+35.9%	−1.8%	−1.7%
Solar energy	+91.7%	+51.5%	+40.9%	+9.2%
Geothermal energy	+75.7%	+50.3%	+30.4%	+13.5%
Conservation	+131.6%	+63.2%	+84.0%	+18.2%
Total R&D	+35.9%	+38.5%		

[a] A budget share is the percentage of the six-program total contributed by a single program. The percentage-change scores reported are calculated with the formula: $[(BS_t - BS_{t-1}) / BS_{t-1}] \times 100\%$, where BS_t represents the requested budget share, and BS_{t-1} the previous year's budget share as requested or appropriated.

president do not know exactly what level of appropriations will exist in a given year when they make requests for the next. Appropriation bills are usually not enacted before executive budget preparation takes place; hence, final appropriations provide only a late estimate of the status quo as perceived by the agency. Previous executive requests, on the other hand, have usually been modified by congressional committees by the time the agency makes its decisions, so those data provide preliminary estimates of the status quo. Because a single, superior estimate does not exist, both imperfect bases are used to estimate the average program funding changes requested in the presidential budgets.

Regardless which measure of the budgetary status quo is employed, the important patterns in executive requests for the R&D programs are the same. First, the executive branch recommended rapid expansion of all energy R&D, with proposed annual increases in total R&D expenditures averaging at least 35.9 percent. Second, the recommended increases were typically least for nuclear programs, most for solar, geothermal, and conservation programs, and somewhere in between for the fossil fuel programs. Relative executive support for the six programs is even clearer in Table 6.7, where the average recommended changes in program budget shares highlight sizable shifts in executive R&D priorities. If budget share changes are measured by comparing successive executive requests, the reordering of priorities is particularly dramatic. At the extremes, the budget share of nuclear fission programs was slated for annual reductions of 16 percent, while the budget share of conservation programs was recommended for annual increases of 84 percent. In between, solar and geothermal energy programs received strong yearly endorsements, but fossil energy's share was proposed to increase only slightly and nuclear fusion's to drop 1.8 percent per year.

These executive recommendations of large increases in total R&D and greater relative growth in non-nuclear programs appear to support the very same interests that Congress ultimately funded. If this is true, of course, it calls into question the quasi-corporatist political relationships associated with the R&D bureaucracy. Why would an agency strongly supported by one set of beneficiaries recommend policies that favor another, competing set of beneficiaries? Appearances are somewhat deceiving. In at least two respects the bureaucracy's support for non-nuclear over nuclear programs is exaggerated by these data.

The first source of bias is the filtering of agency requests that occurs before they become presidential recommendations. Usually the filter makes only equitable reductions in ambitious agency programs; on matters of great presidential concern, however, program priorities may be reordered.[20] During the 1970s energy policy was such an important political issue that presidential influence could have played this exceptional role in the budgetary process. In fact, the Ford and Carter administrations recommended very different changes in funding for the six R&D programs. President Ford's requests gave greater priority than Carter's to nuclear fission and fossil energy, and less to geothermal energy and conservation. The differences, summarized by budget share changes in Table 6.8, were substantial. For example, the Carter administration recommended a 21.4 percent annual reduction in the budget share for nuclear fission and a 55.0 percent increase in the share for conservation; the Ford Administration asked for only a 6.4 percent reduction in the nuclear fission share, and a small *reduction* in conservation. Undoubtedly some of the impetus for the dramatic shift in priorities between administrations came from the R&D bureaucracy. A small shift toward non-nuclear programs would, indeed, be consistent with the modest efforts by its leadership to expand interest group alliances. So large a change in priorities, however, is simply too much to attribute to any established bureaucracy—let alone one that demonstrated so

TABLE 6.8

Energy R&D Funding: Comparison of Ford and Carter Requests for Changes in Program Budget Shares, FY76–FY79

Program	Requested change relative to previous appropriations	
	Ford administration	Carter administration
Fossil energy	+16.9%	+4.2%
Nuclear fission	−6.4%	−21.4%
Nuclear fusion	−4.0%	+2.8%
Solar energy	+9.3%	+9.1%
Geothermal energy	−2.1%	+44.8%
Conservation	−0.2%	+55.0%

NOTE: Ford administration change scores are based on averages of FY76 to FY77 and FY77 to FY78 changes; Carter administration change scores are based on FY78 to FY79 changes.

little interest in political change. It is more plausible to credit the disparate interests of two unusually concerned presidents.[21]

Even if the agency did provide greater support for non-nuclear programs than one can reasonably infer, a second factor eliminates any doubt about the agency's support for its entrenched clientele of electric power interests. In Table 6.9 the presidential requests for R&D program funding are compared with final congressional appropriations. The first two columns again illustrate differences in priorities between administrations that are too large to explain with agency initiative alone. Congress had to subtract 1.4 percent from the Ford Administration's enthusiastic annual requests for nuclear fission, but had to add 18.3 percent to the Carter administration's anemic requests for that program. Similarly, the Carter administration fell 23.0 percent short of the congressional appropriation for conservation, but the Ford administration fell 33.6 percent short in its requests.

The apparent influence of presidential preferences on executive requests is not, however, the major point of the table. In the last column, where the average congressional responses to all executive requests over the period 1976–79 are reported, the interests of the R&D bureaucracy become obvious. Notwithstanding the strong presidential preferences in the requests, the data indicate that the executive branch was a strong supporter of traditional R&D programs. On the average, the presidential budget *overrequested* for nuclear and fossil fuel programs and grossly *underrequested* for solar, geothermal, and conservation programs. The congressional appropriations process had to pare back the executive proposals for the one group and to augment them for the newer programs up to an average of 36.5 percent per year. As the political system shifted its support toward a more diversified R&D policy, the executive requests continued to support a more traditional pattern of allocation. Even allowing that bureaucratic priorities are obscured by the politically sensitive preferences of presidents, they still shine through. The bureaucracy emerges as the strongest governmental supporter of the traditional R&D programs in nuclear, coal, and electric power. The key support for alternative technologies, at least in the 1970s, was to be found in Congress.[22] The shift in R&D priorities that is so evident in final appropriations was not, then, a product of bureaucratic initiative. To the contrary, agency budgetary recommendations were generally consistent with the quasi-corporatist political alliances between the R&D bureaucracy and several large, established beneficiaries.

The groups that years ago cultivated working relationships with the permanent R&D bureaucracy, and maintained those relationships through the energy crises and political tumult of the 1970s, were rewarded for their efforts in the budgetary process. While the rest of the political system pushed enthusiastically ahead with nonnuclear and nontraditional R&D programs, the R&D bureaucracy remained a strong advocate of the interests of its dominant clientele. That is no small payoff for administrative liaison. Indeed, nuclear fission and fusion funding increased by $711.4 million, and fossil

TABLE 6.9
Energy R&D Funding: Congressional Appropriation as Percentage Change in Executive Request, FY76–FY79

Program	Ford administration FY76, FY77	Carter administration FY79[a]	Four-year average[b]
Fossil energy	−6.4%	−1.8%	−7.3%
Nuclear fission	−1.4%	+18.3%	−1.2%
Nuclear fusion	+5.0%	+3.3%	−1.5%
Solar energy	+35.6%	+18.6%	+25.2%
Geothermal energy	+5.9%	+4.2%	+8.6%
Conservation	+33.6%	+23.0%	+36.5%
Total R&D	+2.0%	+10.7%	+0.7%

[a] The budget for FY78 was prepared by the Ford administration during 1976 and submitted to Congress in January 1977 prior to Ford's leaving office, but budget requests were subsequently revised during 1977 by the Carter administration. Because actual FY78 appropriations reflect responses to both administrations, that fiscal year is excluded from this column.
[b] Because this column is intended to indicate the general, relative preferences of Congress and the Executive, FY78 is included here.

energy funding (of which coal is the largest part) by $569.8 million in four years. No other program area even approached growth of that magnitude. Whether other programs come to enjoy similar success in the future will depend, in large measure, on the ability of their beneficiaries to develop strong bureaucratic alliances. The chances of that occurring are a function of the same factors that produced the quasi-corporatism of the late 1970s.

Theories and Explanations

Interest Group Initiatives

The basic structure of interest group participation in R&D policy making is explained by the characteristics that define an allocation policy. The costs of allocation policies, normally, are widely dispersed and therefore provide little individual level incentive for supporting collective action in defense of cost-bearing interests. Energy R&D fits this model, with its direct economic costs borne by every taxpayer and its indirect environmental costs absorbed by large populations subject to spillovers from R&D projects. The cost-bearing interests were, as we have seen, poorly organized. Numerous organizations represented environmental interests, but the diffuse impacts of policies such as energy R&D did not add up to strong individual membership incentives. Environmental groups suffered from small budgets and staffs as a result of these weak incentives. Taxpayer interests *per se* were represented by only one group that paid attention also to energy policy, the National Taxpayers Union. It is one of the more affluent diffuse interest groups but could afford a full-time staff of only eight persons. The organizational weaknesses of the other consumer and public interest groups, though similar, were irrelevant in this policy arena because they chose not to oppose the swiftly rising costs of energy R&D. The poor organization of cost-bearing interests in R&D, then, was an outcome to be expected of allocation policies. Insofar as their absence affected policy making, concern for the costs and efficiency of allocation programs was diminished.

A less certain but equally important consequence of constituency representation is the distribution of policy benefits among contending beneficiaries. Allocation policies usually create strong incentives for their beneficiaries to organize in pursuit of the benefits. At the very least, the incentives are stronger for beneficiaries than for cost-bearers. The individuals or firms subsidized by allocation policies experience relatively large governmental impacts and are therefore likely to be motivated to support collective action. Energy R&D policy was predictably monitored by a sizable collection of often wealthy organizations advocating beneficiary interests. The R&D programs did not provide the only incentives, of course, that sustained these collectives, but they did enhance their political stakes. The simple dichotomy between beneficiary and cost-bearer incentives promotes a general pattern of beneficiary dominance in allocation policies that was realized in energy R&D. That pattern says nothing, however, about the representation of different beneficiaries—an issue of particular importance in energy R&D.

The organizational theory suggests that variation in participation is caused, at root, by variations in the number and political stakes of the different beneficiaries. If individual beneficiaries in a sector are numerous and stand to prosper in only a small way from favorable government action, they will find contributions to interest groups to be not economically rational and will be prone to take a "free ride." In contrast, sectors with smaller numbers of large beneficiaries will have more willing contributors to collective action. The financial and staff resources of beneficiary groups should, *ceteris paribus*, increase with the size of beneficiaries and as the number in any sector decreases. The differences in organizational resources should then be reflected in different rates of group participation. These effects were strong, though imperfect, in the R&D constituency.

The electric power sector is composed of industries with larger and fewer firms than the industries that could have benefited from other forms of R&D. In the coal industry twenty firms accounted for 55.1 percent of domestic production in 1972; eleven of them are subsidiaries of, or are themselves, *Fortune 500* companies.[23] In the nuclear power industry seven firms hold three-fourths of the domestic uranium mining and milling capacity, and the vendors of nuclear reactors number even fewer.[24] Of the significant electric power producers, who are more numerous than coal, uranium, or reactor producers, a comparatively small number predominates. Over 77 percent of U.S. electric power is produced by the 250 investor-owned utilities, the rest by the more than 1,900 municipally owned utilities and 1,000 co-ops.[25] Industries so structured face relatively low organizational obstacles; a few large firms have sufficient economic incentive to sustain interest groups regardless of the industry's contribution, and free-ridership is minimized by its conspicuousness. The electric power sector benefited from these theoretical advantages. Its six national associations enrolled most of their eligible firms and enjoyed budgets that averaged nearly $4 million per year in 1978;[26] five of them were regular participants in the R&D bureaucracy.

By contrast, only one interest association in the conservation and renewable energy sector was a regular participant.[27] Much of the difference in participation rates can be attributed to the problems of collective action. The industries that stand to profit from R&D on renewable energy are generally less concentrated than the industries in the electric power sector. The solar energy industry, for example, includes some large diversified energy corporations but is dominated by thousands of small businesses. In the most developed sector of the industry, solar heating, no manufacturer has more than 3 percent of the market.[28] Another potentially strong segment—farming, foresting, and processing of biomass energy—is very decentralized and just beginning to expand production. Photovoltaic electricity, a more developed sector of the industry, is also highly dispersed, being linked to the dynamic semi-conductor industry. The only relatively concentrated portion of the industry is that with interests in centralized electric power produced with high technology systems such as solar thermal "power towers," ocean thermal conversion, and microwave space power satellites.

The many and varied firms in the fledgling solar industry are impeded in collective action by their sheer number, as well as by their diverse goals. Solar heating interests, for example, are most in need of policies that will modify obstructive building codes, establish tax incentives for solar conversion, and help finance solar heating systems. Photovoltaics and central solar electricity, by contrast, need government research and development. The result of decentralization and diversity is a poor political association. The SEIA had only 950 members, an annual budget of $350,000, and a staff of five in 1978. To maintain a regular presence at the R&D bureaucracy it had to rely heavily on the assistance of corporate lobbyists on loan from large members with Washington offices. This constraint necessarily pushed solar advocacy in the direction of centralized, high-technology projects favored by major corporations. It is probably no coincidence that one-fourth of the federal solar budget in 1978 went to centralized thermal projects with payoffs no sooner than the twenty-first century.[29]

The other major renewable energy source, conservation, is probably shortest on political organizational incentives. It may also have the greatest potential for reducing American dependence on foreign oil. By many estimates a 30 to 40 percent reduction in energy consumption could be achieved without any significant diminution of the American quality of life.[30] The barriers to such efficiency, moreover, are not primarily technological. The major obstacle is the extremely decentralized energy consumption market, which is frequently uninformed about conservation options and nearsighted about the payoffs of conservation investments. Higher energy prices are important and appropriate signals to encourage conservation, but they are not nearly enough to maximize energy efficiency. Millions of individual and commercial consumers need further information and incentives such as tax credits, favorable financing, and energy-efficiency labeling. They could benefit also from government research, development, and especially demonstration projects. Some of the more promising areas for government expenditure include passive solar and other energy-conscious forms of building design, industrial cogeneration of electricity and heat, conservation retrofitting, and mass transit.[31] Whatever the policy option, however, conservation is hampered by a highly diffuse constituency of potential beneficiaries.

An assistant administrator of the FEA recognized the political problem of conservation early in the energy crisis: "Outside of perhaps the insulation manufacturers, there is no organized conservation industry in this country. So we have nothing to compare to the energy producers in terms of marketing, distribution, and lobbying. The oil companies and utilities are busy talking about how much they need to produce. But no one's out there wholesaling conservation by the ton and barrel."[32] The environmental and public interest groups that advocated conservation programs were predictably weak. Consumer Action Now, for example, devoted itself exclusively to the promotion of conservation and solar power. In 1978 it played the key role of coordinator for the congressional solar lobby; its annual budget, however, was a meager $18,000, and its paid staff one-and-a-half. Another prominent conservation and decentralized energy group, the Institute for Local Self-Reliance, enjoyed a budget of $250,000 per year, but that too was quite small by Washington standards. Each group could manage only sporadic contact with the R&D bureaucracy. Variation in industry concentration and, by association, in the potential impacts of R&D policy are, then, clearly reflected in the organizational resources of R&D beneficiaries. Differences in resources in turn help explain differences in beneficiary participation in the R&D bureaucracy.

Inasmuch as some beneficiaries were well organized despite their diffuse nature and some well-organized beneficiaries did not participate up to their potential, this causal chain is imperfect. In the conservation and renewable energy sector, the American Institute of Architects enlisted the support of 28,000 licensed architects, and the National Association of Home Builders attracted 104,000 small builders into its fold. Their annual budgets in 1978 were $7 million and $12 million respectively, and their Washington staffs 110 and 200. Like many professional and trade associations they overcame the problems of collective action by providing substantial selective material benefits to their members.[33] They were, however, no more than sporadic bureaucratic participants, by reason of their inadequate resources—not in the absolute sense, but in terms of opportunity costs. Architects and homebuilders are concerned with the implementation of energy conservation goals because they stand to profit from any reductions in the energy consumption of their buildings; however, other government policies have a far greater effect on their profits than conservation R&D. Policies affecting interest rates, for example, have greater impacts on profits, and therefore receive more political attention. In fact, after membership programs and top political priorities are financed, they have few resources left for energy policy. The AIA assigned only two professionals to energy policy, and the NAHB six. In the energy arena, moreover, other issues promised larger impacts than energy R&D. Both groups allocated most of their energy policy effort in the late 1970s to the formulation of building efficiency standards by the DOE and the Department of Housing and Urban Development.

Opportunity costs likewise discouraged the participation of other concerned groups in the R&D bureaucracy. Groups representing environmentalists, consumers, commercial users, and organized labor were interested in the direction of energy R&D policy (see Table 6.1), but they had little or no contact with the R&D bureaucracy. The reason is not simply that they lacked resources. If the expected value of participation had been high enough, they would have participated. The potential benefits of bureaucratic relationships were severely taxed, however, by the costs of effective involvement. The R&D bureaucracy, like the oil and nuclear regulatory agencies, placed a premium on technical exchanges with interest groups. Although the formal costs of participation were not great, as they were in nuclear regulation, political alliances with the R&D bureaucracy commanded a high price. Only groups that were already in the business of generating technical information as a service to members, or that could tap member sources of information, could afford effective bureaucratic communication. Groups not so constituted simply could not afford the technical investment; expenditures for more profitable political strategies, such as lobbying a nontechnical Congress, exhausted group resources before marginal tactics such as administrative liaison could be attempted.

In sum, group participation in R&D policy making in the energy bureaucracy tended toward monopsony for two reasons. First, the industries in the electric power sector are relatively concentrated and were able to generate substantial organizational resources, while the remaining beneficiary and cost-bearing interests are relatively decentralized and were unable to become well organized. These differences in resources were then translated into vast differences in participation by a second factor: the high level of technical expertise required to establish a close relationship with the R&D bureaucracy. Unless groups could draw on the expertise of members or produce expertise in the course of maintaining memberships, administrative participation became a costly strategy and an early victim of limited organizational budgets. For most of the many cost-bearers and beneficiaries interested in energy R&D policy, bureaucratic participation was ruled out by one or both of these factors. Large coal producers, electric utilities, and nuclear interests consequently dominated all potential bureaucratic participants.

Bureaucratic Strategies

The energy R&D bureaucracy generally behaved so as to reinforce the pattern of interest group initiatives it was receiving. Its strategy was not fully corporatist, but it nonetheless encouraged a quasi-corporatist relationship with its constituency. In comparison with the agency's overtures toward the electric power sector its efforts to interact with other sectors can only be described as meager. Table 6.4 summarized the bureaucracy's strategy clearly: the average frequency of agency-initiated consultation with nuclear, coal, and utility groups was two or more times as great as with any other sector.

The cues hypothesized to cause or condition the strategies of bureaucracies responsible for allocation policies (Table 3.4) are those given by Congress. Allocation policies such as energy R&D have great legislative appeal because they reward large numbers of congressmen without severely penalizing anyone. Bureaucratic behavior should reflect this ready opportunity for political approval by attending to the interests of key congressional supporters. Presidential and judicial cues or constraints may also force allocation agencies to modify their political strategies, but the demands of Congress should take precedence.

In Table 6.10 a fundamental component of congressional cues for the R&D bureaucracy is summarized. The basis of a politically successful allocation program is the accommodation of the key interests represented on the committees that authorize and appropriate funds for it. The table describes those key committees for the two halves of the period under study: 1974–76 and 1977–79.

From the onset of the energy crisis through 1976 the R&D bureaucracy was the ward of a heterogeneous set of congressional overseers. Three Senate committees, four House committees, and the Joint Committee on Atomic Energy held some substantive jurisdiction over energy R&D. The number of standing subcommittees claiming jurisdiction was greater still. Primary responsibility for the bureaucracy was claimed by fewer committees—Senate Interior, House Science and Technology, and the JCAE—but several significant programs were authorized elsewhere. In both House and Senate appropriation responsibility was also divided as subcommittees on Public Works and Interior split the funding responsibility for R&D. Finally, four special subcommittees on oversight gave the R&D bureaucracy reason to believe that its allocation decisions and other politically sensitive actions were being closely watched.

After 1976 the congressional oversight structure for energy R&D became more consolidated. Although three Senate and four House committees retained some substantive authority, the JCAE relinquished its important nuclear R&D responsibility. The new Senate Energy committee and the House Science and Technology committee were awarded nuclear jurisdiction, and thereby assumed dominant roles as R&D authorizers. Significant fragmentation remained, however, with appropriations still divided between two subcommittees. Environmental and conservation R&D had other committee homes, and jurisdictions over single subjects were claimed by multiple committees. President Carter's 1979 synthetic fuels bill, for ex-

TABLE 6.10

Congressional Committees and Subcommittees with Jurisdiction over Energy R&D, 1974–76 and 1977–79

1974–76	1977–79
SENATE	
Appropriations	No change
Subcommittee on Public Works	
Subcommittee on Interior	
* Banking, Housing, and Urban Affairs	No change
* Interior and Insular Affairs†	Energy and Natural Resources†
Subcommittee on Energy Research and Water Resources	Subcommittee on Energy R&D
Public Works	Environment and Public Works
JOINT	
Atomic Energy†	Eliminated
HOUSE	
Appropriations	No change
Subcommittee on Public Works	
Subcommittee on Interior	
* Banking, Currency, and Housing	No change
Interior and Insular Affairs	No change
Subcommittee on Energy and Environment	
Subcommittee on Water and Power Resources	
* Public Works and Transportation	No change
Science and Technology†	Science and Technology†
2 Subcommittees on Energy R&D	Subcommittee on Advanced Energy Technologies and Energy Conservation R&D

NOTE: Asterisks designate committees that have special oversight subcommittees; daggers, those that have primary substantive responsibility.

ample, was marked up by several House committees, including the Committee on Education and Labor. The potential concerns of these different sovereigns continued to be underlined by three oversight subcommittees, poised to investigate complaints by various aggrieved interests. While the 1977–79 period provided a more centralized congressional oversight structure for bureaucratic contemplation, it still evidenced considerable pluralism.

Plainly, these are not the congressional oversight structures that the behavior of the R&D bureaucracy would lead us to expect. More fragmented and pluralistic congressional responsibility would be hard to imagine, yet the bureaucracy acted more as if it was under centralized controls. This is not to say that the bureaucracy was impervious to congressional wishes other than those of coal and nuclear power advocates. It sponsored a wide variety of R&D programs and indeed supported recommendations for sharp increases in conservation, solar, and other renewable energy funding. It was not unwilling to cater to a host of congressional preferences, but stopped short of satisfying congressional interests maximally. Throughout the late 1970s the R&D bureaucracy's budgetary requests for nuclear and fossil fuels (see Table 6.9) were overenthusiastic, and were subsequently reduced by Congress. Its recommendations for conservation, solar energy, and geothermal energy were grossly inadequate, and were ultimately augmented by large amounts by Congress. It also made little effort to begin establishing political alliances with groups that congressional overseers obviously endorsed. Whatever the efforts of the bureaucratic leadership in 1977 and thereafter to expand its political base, it cannot be attributed primarily to congressional demands. The movement in congressional demands after 1977 was toward jurisdictional consolidation and a reduction in the number of R&D interests with separate committee advocates. Likewise, the loss of nuclear support from the Joint Committee was probably not the key motivation behind the pluralistic shift by the bureaucratic leadership. The demise of the Joint Committee (see Chapter 3) had been underway, and similar cues available, for several years, yet neither the staff nor the leadership adjusted. The responsiveness of the R&D bureaucracy to Congress was, in short, sluggish and imperfect.

Greater responsiveness was elicited by the presidents. The influence of Congress was in the main a residuum from many years of strong support for nuclear dominance of energy R&D prior to the 1974 energy crisis. Through one of the classic subgovernments of all time, Congress and its JCAE had reinforced a promotional nuclear bureaucracy. The problem for Congress was that it could not prod the expanded energy R&D bureaucracy to follow its new political wishes immediately. The courts also had little impact on the bureaucracy's political strategies. Since the administration of R&D programs was not subject to the procedural constraints nor implemented through the extensive rules that characterized regulatory administration, court appeals were not a potent weapon for dissatisfied groups. The major judicial influence on R&D programs was the mandatory compliance with the environmental impact statement requirements of the National Environmental Policy Act. The threat of suits enabled the Sierra Club to participate occasionally in the R&D bureau-cracy's environmental assessments, but without realizing any large policy dividends. Only the demands of presidents produced substan-tial, immediate political responses from the bureaucracy.

President Ford was a strong supporter of nuclear power, while President Carter was a fierce opponent; at the same time they both regarded the fossil fuels as crucial interim energy supplies. At least during his early years Carter was a vigorous advocate of conserva-tion and solar energy. His 1977 National Energy Plan counted heavily on conservation, and his legislative coalition for its enact-ment depended on environmental group support.[34] Partially as a *quid pro quo* he cleared many of his R&D nominations with envi-ronmental groups before referring them to the Senate.[35] President Ford also regarded conservation as an important element of energy policy but believed it could be produced through appropriate price signals rather than through research, development, or demonstra-tion.

These disparate preferences were reflected in executive budget recommendations to Congress and, just as clearly, in the political strategies of the R&D bureaucracy. During the Ford administration the R&D bureaucracy continued the corporatist interest group rela-tionships it had established during its years as the Atomic Energy Commission and the Office of Coal Research. With the Carter inau-guration, and new interests to satisfy in the White House, more pluralistic outreach began. Environmental and public interest groups began to receive greater attention, and the traditionally fa-vored groups experienced minor deterioration in their bureaucratic relations. The fact that the initiatives did not occur throughout the bureaucracy but were confined to the political leadership is the best indication that the changes in strategies during the 1970s were influ-enced most by presidential turnover.

Conclusion

The most remarkable aspect of the quasi-corporative relationships that underpinned energy R&D in the late 1970s was their persis-tence in spite of substantial pressure for change. The R&D bureau-cracy was reorganized in 1974 and 1977 to expand and diversify its responsibilities. Funding for nontraditional programs increased steadily and more rapidly than any other program area; bureaucratic participation opportunities were not prohibitively expensive; congressional support and responsibility was heterogeneous; and presidential policy, even under Ford, favored a diversified R&D plan. The bureaucracy nonetheless demonstrated little interest in expanding its political base beyond the constituencies it had cultivated during its previous existences. Among nontraditional R&D interest groups only the Solar Energy Industries Association developed a working relationship with the bureaucracy. That development, however, owed more to the efforts of large corporations with interests in central electrification than to the mobilization of the huge constituency of solar energy interests. The inroads that other nontraditional groups established during the Carter years are likely to be as ephemeral as presidential administrations.

In time the R&D bureaucracy will undoubtedly make peace with its congressional sovereigns, but probably not on terms established unilaterally by Congress. The bureaucracy showed itself capable of maintaining relationships with its preferred interest groups under turbulent political conditions. When Congress and the R&D bureaucracy settle into relationships of mutual support, the new technologies are likely to play a significant role. It is also likely, however, that their representatives may be the corporations capable of large R&D projects that the bureaucracy favored, rather than the diffuse groups that enjoyed congressional support. The consequences of such a political arrangement will be a continued emphasis on centralized energy production, and slow development of conservation and decentralized solar energy.

7

NATIONAL ENERGY PLANNING

Although the 1970s were years of sharp conflict and continuous debate over the United States' energy future, consensus on one issue persisted: the country needed a national energy plan. Conservatives and liberals, producers and consumers, developers and environmentalists generally agreed; to leave the nation's energy future to a congeries of policies that lacked consistent or long-term goals, and to a market controlled by an unpredictable foreign cartel, was irrational and dangerous. Agreeing on the need for a plan and formulating such a plan are, however, two very different things. National energy planning is a difficult political task even if everyone agrees on the merits of the process.

The crux of the planning problem is that all the remedies offered by science, technology, or private enterprise are costly, uncertain, or both. Once the domestic production of inexpensive and environmentally benign oil and natural gas peaked in the early 1970s, equally attractive substitutes did not take their place. The major alternatives such as foreign oil, nuclear energy, coal power, and conservation came with real and imagined costs that provoked resistance to their introduction. Under these circumstances national energy planning faced, and still faces, a serious problem. Planning must achieve a political consensus on how important and conflicting values should be compromised in working for a better energy future.

Congress was indeed stymied by this policy dilemma time and again during the 1970s, but it had little trouble fashioning an organization to which it could delegate the planning responsibility. The Department of Energy was created, with legislative ease, to implement national energy planning. It embodied the new political consensus that energy policy making required coordination, consistency, and foresight. Although the DOE was also assigned many implementation functions previously performed by ERDA, the FEA, and the FPC, its *raison d'être* was national energy planning. The DOE's major responsibility was to address the new tradeoffs in the energy arena and formulate comprehensive proposals for achieving majority goals. In other words, the new department was directed to mediate the conflicting demands of the many interest groups concerned with national energy policy.

Planning and Politics

Although planning seems to connote expert, analytical, farsighted, and rational policy making, it is actually a thoroughly political process. It is nothing more, nor less, than the specification of clear policy priorities and the implementation of a series of related actions over time to accomplish them. The often intertwined processes require political choices among competing values.[1] So basic is politics to planning that planning, it is said, is "either political or it is decorative."[2]

Because planning is political, the planning process varies in form with the political context in which it operates. Coercive planning may be used where political authority is absolute or goal consensus is high.[3] Indicative or educational planning is more common where the targets of government control are numerous or uncooperative.[4] Corporatist planning tends to arise where political consensus is strong and the private sector hierarchically organized.[5] In the United States the national political context has generally discouraged planning of any real consequence.[6] Fragmentation among industrial and labor interests complicates government bargaining with the private sector. The separation of powers minimizes legislative willingness to authorize and support binding executive planning power. The multiple points of access to government authority on most important issues facilitate obstructionism by groups dissatisfied with planning decisions. Ideology, finally, prompts resistance to any form of policy making that even suggests direct public control of private enterprise.[7]

The national energy planning that Congress intended the Department of Energy to perform is in general consistent with American tradition. The Department of Energy Act of 1977 requires the DOE to submit biennially to Congress five- and ten-year national energy plans.[8] While the act is vague about the intended consequences of the plans, Congress will clearly not be bound by them. In essence, the act instructs the department to project the long-term energy needs and supplies of the nation, establish policy goals within the expanded time-frame, and formulate programs consistent with the goals. It does not insist that the goals be maintained for any period of time, nor does it provide the department with discretionary authority to implement them. The objectives may be changed as often as the department sees fit, and the means available to it for accomplishing the objectives are limited to those regulatory and allocation programs already authorized. The main difference, then, between the DOE's mandate and those of other cabinet departments is that it must demonstrate explicitly every two years the long-term integrity and internal consistency of its programs and proposals. By American standards, that is a significant form of planning.

Interest groups are bound to play important parts in the planning process. The DOE cannot expect its long-term goals and policy proposals to be accepted by Congress or implemented successfully unless it builds a supportive coalition during the planning process. If it does not mediate the interest conflicts that attend so many energy policy initiatives, the conflicts may subsequently be resolved in a manner inconsistent with the department's plans. In any case, the DOE act explicitly requires the department to consult with "consumers, small businesses, and a wide range of other interests" in formulating the energy plans.[9] The interesting theoretical and empirical issue is how the department will structure this group consultation.

Planning agencies such as the DOE face tricky problems in structuring their relationships with interest groups. First, because executive agencies lack the authority to ensure that their plans will be accepted and their proposals enacted, groups feel less compelled to compromise. A dissatisfied group always has the opportunity to seek a better deal in Congress. Second, because American planning agencies usually face a large number of potential group opponents and allies, the selection of interest contacts can be complex. Interest groups in the United States are not organized hierarchically, or otherwise consolidated, by sector. Oil interests, for example, are directly represented by over fifty Washington organizations, environmental interests by at least twenty national groups; labor interests are similarly fragmented. As a further complication, many interests are represented by corporate governmental relations staffs. On major policy issues such as energy, the opportunities to win or lose support by consulting or failing to consult are innumerable. It becomes a master feat to establish consensus when the interest group population provides so little help. Organizational fragmentation places most of the burden of coalition building on the back of the agency.

A third problem for national planning agencies is that institutionalized interest representation is unworkable. Multi-sector planning committees, such as those in Europe that include a country's major industry and labor association representatives, are impractical with the fragmented American group system.[10] The American executive branch recognizes this and has instead provided interest representation through single sector advisory committees. In the late 1970s, well over 1,000 of these committees were scattered through the federal government. The Department of Energy had twenty-five. The committees formalize interest articulation but do little to facilitate planning or comprehensive policy formulation. They do not permit intersectoral discussion or bargaining; they merely provide an additional source of interest group access. The agency is still left the task of sorting through committee recommendations, as well as countless informal group inputs, to develop an integrated plan. At best, advisory committees are a ready source of advice for decision makers to employ as suits their political and policy objectives. In the energy field advisory committees did not even fulfill that role. They met infrequently, were often ignored, and are widely acknowledged to have had little policy impact.*

Together these problems indicate that the relationships between planning agencies and interest groups will be based on informal consultation structured in different ways, depending on particular political contexts. Planning agencies simply have numerous group

*This conclusion is based on several sources. First, every group in the study was asked to assess the usefulness of energy advisory committees (first established by the FEA and ERDA) for accomplishing their objectives. Without exception they claimed that the committees were an ineffective means of participation and at best additional sources of information on agency decision making. Second, in January 1978 a random mail survey of 125 FEA advisory committee members (conducted by myself) indicated that committee members believed they had no impact upon policy formulation. Finally, a Congressional Research Service study of energy advisory committees (1977) criticized the ineffectiveness of FEA advisory committees. Most of the FEA's advisory committees were continued in the Department of Energy. See "Energy Advisers," pp. 38–47.

strategies from which to choose. Choices will vary with the agency's resources, the structure of the group arena, and the interests and influence of the agency's political sovereigns. Permutations and combinations of these factors allow for many explicable forms of consultation.

The organizational theory offers a means for integrating these causal factors and ultimately explaining the interest group relationships of planning agencies. An explanation must wait, however, for the measurement of the independent variables. It is difficult to predict *a priori* how planning agencies and interest groups will interact, because the political incentives and institutional constraints that condition those interactions vary across planning arenas. The hypothesis that planning agencies will be characterized by *pluralistic* relationships is based on two phenomena (see Table 3.4). First, interest group initiatives will tend to be competitive because the goal uncertainty of planning gives many groups reason to expect large policy impacts, and the costs of participation in such "high level" decision making can be defrayed with political as well as technical resources. Free-rider organizational problems will still promote inequality in representation, but in less pronounced form than in regulatory or allocation arenas. Second, bureaucratic strategies should be pluralistic because planning agencies want to maintain political flexibility over time and must obtain approval of their plans by representative institutions, i.e., Congress and the president, if they are to have any force. A pluralistic strategy involving numerous concerned groups satisfies both of these bureaucratic needs. The interaction of this strategy with competitive group initiatives produces, in turn, a pluralistic relationship. Whether such a relationship characterizes national energy planning depends, however, on the participation incentives actually provided and the institutional constraints effectively applied.

Planning and Consultation in the Federal Energy Administration

Prior to the creation of the Department of Energy responsibility for formulating national energy policy was held chiefly by the Federal Energy Administration. Indeed, the major justification for creating the FEA was to centralize responsibility for energy policy making. This was not, however, a role to which the FEA was well suited. It lacked authority and expertise in important areas of energy policy such as research and development, public lands, natural gas regulation, and nuclear regulation. Most of its organizational and political resources were devoted to the single energy issue of oil regulation, as was manifest in the Ford administration's energy policies that continually revolved around oil pricing schemes.

The FEA's preoccupation with oil issues was also reflected in its planning level consultation with interest groups. Policy planning responsibility in the FEA was centered in the office of the administrator. The apex of the FEA hierarchy was not intended to devote its time to problems of oil regulation; a separate office headed by an assistant administrator was responsible for regulatory programs. The administrator's office was charged with overseeing all FEA programs—including the strategic petroleum reserve, conservation and the environment, and energy resource development among others—and with comprehensive policy formulation; yet, the issues of oil regulation seem to have determined the constituency orientation of the administrator's office.

Table 7.1 reports the number of meetings between interest groups and FEA administrators Frank Zarb and John O'Leary. Zarb served in the final two years of the Ford administration, while O'Leary served during the first nine months of the Carter administration.

TABLE 7.1

Frequency of Meetings Between Interest Groups and FEA Administrators

Sector	Frank Zarb 7/1/75–1/15/77	John O'Leary 1/20/77–9/30/77	Total
Environmental groups	4% (6)	3% (6)	4% (12)
Consumer and PIGs	3% (4)	3% (5)	3% (9)
Petroleum and gas industry	58% (79)	52% (100)	55%[b] (179)
Electric power	12% (17)	22% (42)	18% (59)
Conservation and renewable energy	1% (1)	5% (10)	3% (11)
Labor unions	1% (2)	2% (4)	2% (6)
Commercial users	16% (22)	12% (24)	14% (46)
Financial institutions	4% (5)	1% (1)	2% (6)
TOTALS[a]	99% (136)	100% (192)	101% (328)

[a] Rounding errors cause sums to deviate from 100%.

[b] Eighty-six of these meetings involved major oil corporations. That figure represents 48% of that sector's contacts, and 26% of *all* contacts.

The data are taken from logs of outside contacts FEA officials were required to maintain. The predominant role of the oil and gas industry in FEA consultation is unmistakable. The Republican administrator and the Democratic administrator allotted 59 percent and 52 percent of their respective group contacts to oil and gas representatives. Other interests that figured prominently in national energy policy debates were barely represented at the FEA. Consumer groups and labor unions were the major opponents of oil and gas price deregulation, yet no significant effort was made by the FEA to discuss with them their views. Similarly, a major thrust of research and development spending was toward conservation and renewable energy sources, but the proponents of those programs—environmental, conservation, and renewable energy groups—were represented in a total of only 7 percent of FEA policy consultations.

The only sectors besides oil and gas that were reasonably well represented were other major business interests—commercial users and the electric power sector. In the case of the latter, moreover, utilities accounted for virtually all representation; coal and nuclear representatives did not maintain a major presence. The participation of both commercial users and utility representatives can be attributed to issues of oil regulation. Both are major consumers of petroleum and gas; both are acutely concerned about fuel allocations and supply security; and both supported the proposition that oil and gas deregulation would increase supplies. Their frequent FEA participation is consistent with the agency's preoccupation with, and its commitment to, a national energy policy based on oil deregulation.

The FEA's responsibility for comprehensive planning notwithstanding, its policy and political perspective was dominated by industrial oil interests, i.e., the oil industry and the businesses that consume its products. There is little evidence that the agency attempted to broaden its perspective or support through interest group consultation. The dominant role played by the oil industry, utilities, and commercial users is obviously explained in part by their superior governmental relations resources; however, the nonparticipating groups were not sufficiently poor to explain the extreme skew in FEA consultation. As will become clear from the very different consultation that occurred in the Department of Energy, FEA consultation was biased by the incentives and strategies employed by the agency, and not by any gross imbalance of group resources.

Planning Reorganized

Although the DOE and the FEA were similarly charged with comprehensive policy formulation, the former was better suited to the task. Unlike the FEA, the DOE does have administrative authority over the major components of the energy policy system. Only nuclear regulation, among major energy programs, is beyond its jurisdiction. Although public land use remains under Interior Department control, the DOE shares responsibility for economic regulation of leases for energy development. Its comprehensive purview provides it with the managerial basis for integrated energy policy development.

Effective responsibility for this function is housed in two DOE offices: the Office of the Secretary and the Office of the Assistant Secretary for Policy and Evaluation. The former "decide[s] major energy policy issues and act[s] as the principal energy advisor to the President." The latter "formulate[s] and recommend[s] the Department's overall policy direction, and coordinate[s] analysis and evaluation of policies and programs."[11] The latter also prepares the biennial national energy plans. In theory these two offices are responsible respectively for the political and analytical components of planning. In practice, they overlap considerably. Both offices are likely to employ interest group consultation because political support and technical advice are the basic resources of interest groups.

To understand the relationships that developed between the DOE offices and the interest group population, it is necessary to understand first how energy policy was formulated *immediately* prior to the creation of the new department. It was during that period, when President Carter's National Energy Plan was formulated, that the seeds of DOE consultation were planted.

Consultation and the National Energy Plan

The DOE did not begin operating formally until October 1, 1977, nine months after President Carter took office. Informally, however, planning began in December 1976, one month before he was inaugurated. At this early date Carter had already chosen future DOE Secretary James Schlesinger as his principal energy advisor, and the outline of the impending National Energy Plan began to emerge.

The process of assembling an ad hoc team of planners also began at this time. Finally, the Carter transition team in Washington began to accept energy policy suggestions from interest groups.

President Carter had made national energy policy the number one priority of his new administration and promised publicly to recommend a major plan within ninety days of his inauguration. To formulate this plan he did not turn to the FEA or ERDA; in fact, the established agencies were almost completely shut out of the formulation process. Carter delegated the task instead to energy advisor James Schlesinger, who in turn assembled a small team of less than two dozen energy planners to develop a proposal. Besides Schlesinger, the most influential members of the team turned out to be S. David Freeman, former director of the Ford Foundation's Energy Policy Project, and Robert Nordhaus, former counsel for the House Commerce Committee and chief aide to John Dingell, the powerful chairman of the House Subcommittee on Energy and Power. With the creation of this team executive responsibility for energy policy formulation was effectively transferred from the established bureaucracy to the future core decision makers of the DOE.

This planning experience was to become an important determinant of subsequent behavior by DOE policy formulators. The team that developed the National Energy Plan was faced with an exceedingly difficult task; comprehensive energy policy proposals had continually eluded Congress and past administrations. To make matters worse, Carter's ninety-day deadline set in train a series of new problems. In the short time available it was virtually impossible to utilize or coordinate the potentially rich input of the established energy agencies. The plan consequently omitted supply stimuli other than higher prices, and ignored such salient issues as nuclear licensing reform. The exclusion of ERDA and the NRC, among others, from the formulation process left important components of existing policy out of the "comprehensive" review. Their advice might have helped the planners avoid the objections of congressmen accustomed to existing policy approaches.

The ninety-day deadline also precluded careful quantitative analysis of direct impacts. By the summer of 1977 four congressional agencies—the Congressional Budget Office, the General Accounting Office, the Library of Congress, and the Office of Technology Assessment—had concluded that the Carter team had significantly overestimated the plan's ability to meet its goals.[12] These doubts and a number of technical flaws in the hastily designed plan reduced congressional confidence in the proposed policy.[13]

Finally, the short timetable made serious consultation with interest groups and Congress rather difficult. Ninety days does not allow the luxury of multiple drafts and wide-ranging feedback. If a comprehensive plan was to be produced swiftly, the planning team required privacy and thorough control over the process. In fact, the plan was developed in virtual isolation from external political influence by a small team of economists and lawyers led by one of the original "rational" policy makers. The then future Secretary of Energy had never been known for his political astuteness. Rather, his reputation in policy circles rested upon his considerable analytical skills. During his early years at the Rand Corporation Schlesinger had been instrumental in the development of systems analysis—the once highly touted rational-comprehensive approach to policy making that initially attracted Carter to Schlesinger.[14]

During the early part of his administration Carter too expressed support for "scientific" problem solving over politicized, incremental approaches; and he later displayed a penchant for personal immersion in the details of policy making rather than in policy salesmanship. He also held great hope for "rationalizing" the bureaucracy through reforms such as zero-based budgeting.[15] Yet, when Carter arrived in Washington he was also the political outsider, committed by campaign pledges to a populist style of government. It is dubious whether Schlesinger would have engaged in serious political consultation, given any timetable. Carter, however, was surely torn. His desire to open up the Washington establishment to fresh popular influences conflicted with his belief in analytical policy making.

The ninety-day deadline may ultimately have resolved the dilemma. Carter essentially chose to consult without really consulting. In March 1977 he initiated an ambitious program ostensibly designed to involve the public in the design of the plan. The scheme was at best a misguided attempt at genuine consultation, and at worst a slick public relations effort in the tradition of the 1976 presidential campaign. Public participation was encouraged through three forums: a highly publicized request for written comments from the general public; a sequence of ten regional "town meetings" conducted by the FEA; and a series of White House "mini-conferences" attended by some 400 interest group representatives and led by members of the energy planning team.

The request for written comments stimulated nearly 28,000 responses, and the ten meetings were attended by 2,600 persons. About 800 individuals had an opportunity to speak at the regional meetings.[16] There is little evidence that the public comments contributed in any significant way to the content of the plan. As might be expected in a conflictual problem area such as energy, no consensus emerged for government action in particular directions. There was both opposition and support for the gamut of policy options. Public responses tended to mirror the constellation of contending views that had stymied energy policy making since the embargo. But the lack of consensus was not the main reason the comments had little impact. By the time the comments were compiled and summarized during the first week of April, the National Energy Plan was essentially complete. The president's national energy address and public unveiling of the plan was only two weeks away. The planners could hardly have redesigned the complex plan in a fortnight to accommodate the myriad complaints and suggestions of thousands of citizens, nor could the White House realistically have expected any major surprises in the public responses. The energy problem was not new in 1977. The political conflicts were already crystal clear to national policy makers. In the final analysis, the White House effort to involve the public could not have been seriously intended for any purpose other than public relations—i.e., to build public support for the ambitious plan. To that end, it was probably successful. Public concern about the energy problem increased more than five-fold during Carter's first months in office.[17]

The public, of course, is not intimately involved in the legislative maze that executive policy proposals must ultimately negotiate. Unless public opinion is unambiguous and intense—as, for example, on the issues of budget and tax cuts that the Reagan administration made its first initiatives—executive policy must attempt to assemble a winning coalition of policy influentials such as congressmen and interest groups.[18] Such a strategy was imperative in the energy area because public consensus was absent. President Carter did not fully appreciate this point; the National Energy Plan initiated his administration's rocky relations with Congress.[19] Under the tight schedule energy planners had no time for consultation with key members of Congress, and the president made little effort to involve them. Those representatives and senators who would determine the fate of the plan were not seriously consulted until mid-April when they were briefed on its content and asked for their support. Evidently the planners were confident, from their knowledge of past congressional committee views, that the proposals would be favorably enough received.[20]

The administration's effort to involve interest groups in the formulation process was more extensive, but hardly more sincere. Interest group representatives were given supposedly genuine opportunities to contribute to the plan through the forum of White House mini-conferences. From March 14 to March 25 three-hour conferences were conducted by members of the energy planning team, and each attended by twenty or so representatives of a particular energy interest.[21] Consumer groups were assigned to the first conference, the auto industry to the second, labor unions to the third, and so on until twenty-one fairly homogeneous sectors had participated. Like the other forums, these conferences were thinly veiled public relations schemes; they were not forums for substantive input.

All but a few of the groups interviewed for this study took part in the mini-conferences and unanimously perceived them as sheer salesmanship. No one believed the Carter administration was sincerely interested in soliciting serious substantive suggestions. The most obvious reason for skepticism was the timing of the meetings. With the April 20 unveiling of the plan only a month away, the prospect for significantly influencing it was generally viewed as slim. Another reason for the skepticism was the conduct of the meetings. Some were largely briefings on the basic contours of the plan; others simply permitted each representative an opportunity to state general energy positions and recommendations. Obviously a three-hour conference with twenty participants does not afford anyone the chance to speak in much detail. At the most an interest group representative might be allotted ten minutes. The administration was not interested in obtaining thoughtful responses to specific policy proposals. In short, the effort did not promote a meaningful dialogue between planners and interest groups.

The conferences also failed, because of their insincerity and brevity, to foster substantial group support. This shortcoming became evident in group behavior during the congressional deliberations. The mini-conferences may even have harmed the plan's chances for enactment. Several of its eventual opponents expressed deep resentment, during the interviews, at being approached through such a transparent scheme. One might suspect that the meetings were really intended to attract the support of groups less directly concerned with energy while key groups were consulted informally. But this was not the case. Only twelve of the groups in this study reported any informal contact with the energy planning team prior to the release of the plan. Six of them felt that these meetings, which usually involved Schlesinger or David Freeman, were held for much the same reason as the mini-conferences—i.e., to provide groups a nominal form of participation.* The administration realized that certain interest groups were simply too important in the energy field to be completely ignored. Groups such as the NCA, the NRECA, and the ANEC were consequently granted pro-forma audiences with the key planners. It is possible that the planners benefited in some subtle way; however, the groups saw no evidence of their advice either in the plan itself or in the administration's political strategy to get it enacted.

Only six groups regarded their contacts with the planning team as something other than courtesy meetings. In two cases the contacts were for strictly technical reasons. The Motor Vehicle Manufacturers Association was asked for technical information pertinent to the proposed "gas-guzzler" tax, and the Electricity Consumers Resource Council, a new group of large industrial electricity users, was solicited for data relevant to utility rate reform. Only four groups, then, classified their contacts as serious, substantive policy discussions. Of those, the APPA and the NARUC were disappointed to find that their recommendations went entirely unheeded. That leaves only two groups out of the seventy-three interviewed that believed they engaged in effective policy consultation with the administration's energy planning team.

Those two groups, Friends of the Earth and the Sierra Club, initiated contact with the Carter transition team before the inauguration and had several interchanges with the planners, about half of them on the planners' initiative. Both groups had submitted specific policy recommendations early and claimed that the plan proposed incorporated most of their suggestions. The National Energy Plan was, in fact, a conservation-oriented plan and enjoyed strong support from the environmental community.[22] To conclude, however,

*The six groups were the ANEC, the AFL-CIO, the Sun Company, the Oil, Chemical and Atomic Workers Union, the NCA, and the NRECA.

that these groups had a determining influence on it is unwarranted.

The claims of the environmental groups notwithstanding, the National Energy Plan was formulated almost entirely through internal analysis and deliberation. The presence of James Schlesinger as chief planner is almost reason enough to believe the energy proposals were not externally generated. Further reason is provided by the key positions of Robert Nordhaus and David Freeman on the team. The utility rate reform and natural gas pricing portions of the plan were similar to proposals Nordhaus had worked on as counsel to the House Subcommittee on Energy and Power. The gas-guzzler tax and conservation incentives reflected ideas associated with Freeman before and during his time as director of the Ford Foundation Energy Policy Project.[23] It is unlikely, moreover, that a planning team that chose to ignore serious consultation with all other major energy interests would do otherwise with two prominent environmental groups. In the final analysis, the National Energy Plan was formulated with no significant substantive consultation. Interest groups, like all other relevant political powers, were accorded only pro forma participation in this ambitious ninety-day planning process.

Interest Groups, Planning, and the DOE

The experience of the National Energy Plan made a clear mark on interest group consultation as subsequently practiced by DOE (or soon-to-be DOE) policy makers. In the interviews each group representative was asked to estimate the number of meetings the group held after April 20 with Secretary Schlesinger or his office, and with the DOE Office of Policy and Evaluation (see Appendix A, Part E); to estimate the number of times the offices initiated contacts; and to describe the substance of the contacts. The responses were coded, and are reported in Tables 7.2–7.3.

Table 7.2 summarizes the frequency of interaction between DOE policy formulators and the eight sectors of interest groups. The period of time summarized is approximately one year, May 1977 to May 1978. Although the DOE was not established until October 1, 1977, respondents did not distinguish between interactions with Secretary Schlesinger and interactions with him or his staff before they became DOE officials. Energy planning activities did not undergo an abrupt shift the day the DOE was established, and respondents were not forced to draw a distinction. Of importance is the distinc-

TABLE 7.2

Frequency of Interaction Between Interest Groups and DOE Policy Formulators

Sector	Reported frequency of interaction				Mean frequency[a]
	Frequent	Sporadic	Infrequent	None	
Environmental groups	38% (3)	25% (2)	25% (2)	12% (1)	1.88
Consumer and PIGs	11% (1)	22% (2)	44% (4)	22% (2)	1.22
Petroleum and gas industry	15% (2)	38% (5)	31% (4)	15% (2)	1.54
Electric power	50% (4)	38% (3)	12% (1)	0 (0)	2.38
Conservation and renewable energy	14% (1)	29% (2)	0 (0)	57% (4)	1.00
Labor unions	43% (3)	0 (0)	43% (3)	14% (1)	1.71
Commercial users	15% (2)	8% (1)	46% (6)	31% (4)	1.08
Financial institutions	0 (0)	50% (1)	0 (0)	50% (1)	1.00
TOTALS[b]	24% (16)	24% (16)	30% (20)	22% (15)	1.52

NOTE: "Policy formulators" operationally include the DOE's Office of the Secretary and Office of Policy and Evaluation. The qualitative frequency labels correspond approximately with the following numbers of estimated meetings over the first year of Carter's energy administration: none, 0; infrequent, 1-5; sporadic, 6-11; frequent, 12 or more.

[a] Means are calculated by assigning ordinal scale scores of 0, 1, 2, and 3 to the respective frequencies of none, infrequent, sporadic, and frequent.

[b] Totals do not sum to 73 because of missing data.

tion between this group of formulators and their predecessors in the FEA.

Based on their estimated number of meetings with all designated planners interest groups were classified into four categories, according to frequency of participation. The pattern of consultation between DOE policy planners and interest groups differs dramatically from the pattern that characterized policy formulation at the old FEA (see Table 7.1). The FEA's bias toward the petroleum industry and commercial petroleum users is not in evidence at the new Energy Department. In fact, DOE consultation was not decidedly skewed in any direction. Each sector had several groups that interacted frequently or sporadically with DOE policy makers; no sector was largely shut out. The electric power sector does stand out as the most frequently involved; its mean participation frequency of 2.38 exceeds by 0.5 the interaction rate of the next most active sector. Its participation edge is somewhat overestimated, however, by the sectoral indicator. Unlike the other energy supply sectors, its mean participation is not depressed by the presence of corporate offices or other "smaller" interests in the sector's sample. In sum, the DOE's apparent pattern of planning consultation is consistent with expectations for an agency charged with such a comprehensive problem. Its policy-relevant interactions are rather pluralistic.

The explanation of this pattern lies not only in the initiatives of interest groups but also in the political strategies of the agency. Table 7.3 summarizes in three categories the reported frequencies of DOE approaches toward interest groups. These data give a rather different picture of policy consultation than is revealed by the pluralistic summary of interactions. The DOE evidenced a distinct preference for interacting with some sectors rather than others. Of the eleven groups that reported frequent initiatives from the DOE offices for policy formulation, four are environmental groups and four are representatives of the electric power industries. The DOE did not show nearly the proclivity for interaction with oil producers or users demonstrated by the FEA. Only the API, among oil and gas groups, and the Business Roundtable, among commercial users, were approached frequently by DOE policy makers. Since these two groups are the representatives of the largest firms in their respective sectors, it is apparent that high-ranking DOE policy makers were not prone to solicit help from every relevant interest in Washington. At this level of decision making, executive officials tended to be economical in their outreach efforts; their frequent initiatives were

TABLE 7.3
Frequency of DOE-Initiated Contacts Between Policy
Formulators and Interest Groups

Sector	Frequency of DOE initiatives			Mean frequency [a]
	Frequent	Sporadic	None	
Environmental groups	50% (4)	38% (3)	12% (1)	1.38
Consumer and PIGs	11% (1)	67% (6)	22% (2)	0.89
Petroleum and gas industry	8% (1)	54% (7)	38% (5)	0.69
Electric power	50% (4)	38% (3)	12% (1)	1.38
Conservation and renewable energy	0 (0)	43% (3)	57% (4)	0.43
Labor unions	0 (0)	86% (6)	14% (1)	0.86
Commercial users	8% (1)	31% (4)	62% (8)	0.46
Financial institutions	0 (0)	50% (1)	50% (1)	0.50
TOTALS [b]	16% (11)	49% (33)	34% (23)	0.82

NOTE: "Policy formulators" operationally include the DOE's Office of the Secretary and Office of Policy and Evaluation. The qualitative labels imply the incidence of agency contacts that are agency-initiated meetings: none, 0; sporadic, 1-4; frequent, 5 or more.

[a] Means are calculated by assigning ordinal scale scores of 0, 1, and 2 to frequencies of none, sporadic, and frequent.

[b] Totals do not sum to 73 because of missing data.

confined to a small number of major groups. Only the generous initiatives toward environmental groups violated this pattern. The electric power sector was contacted primarily through four major national associations: the NCA, the APPA, the AIF, and the ANEC. High-level DOE outreach to the consumer community also fit the pattern. The Energy Action Committee, a frequent recipient of DOE initiatives, was represented by James Flug, the most prominent Washington spokesman for consumer interests in energy policy.

Although DOE policy makers did not try frequently to involve more than the largest and most politically vocal groups, they did not ignore the other Washington representatives. The fact that almost half of the groups in the sample were contacted sporadically by DOE policy makers is at least *prima facie* evidence that the DOE recognized the comprehensive nature of its responsibility and the difficult political diversity of its constituency. The proportion of groups not contacted at all (34 percent) is small by comparison with other arenas of administrative policy making. The regulatory and allocation bureaucracies did not even approach involving 66 percent of the sample in their activities. On balance, then, the consultative initiatives of DOE planners were not seriously skewed.

It would be premature to conclude, however, that the behavior of energy policy makers changed dramatically after the formulation of the National Energy Plan. It is necessary first to understand the substance of these pluralistic interactions. The planning offices of the DOE interacted with interest groups for many reasons. For summary purposes, we may consider three general types of interaction: public relations, congressional strategy, and planning or formulation. The upper echelon of any executive agency or department will meet with prominent interest groups within its jurisdiction as a simple courtesy due representatives of a major constituency. Such meetings will have no direct impact upon policy and will result in no agreements to provide political support. They involve general discussions and produce at most mutual understandings. These contacts, often pro forma, are classified as public relations. Other contacts hold greater immediate, substantive significance. Executive policy-making responsibilities do not cease after a proposal is sent to Congress. The agency must sell the proposal to Congress and, to accomplish this, will often seek interest group assistance. Meetings that fulfill this purpose are classified as congressional strategy sessions. Finally, executive planning may involve interest groups in serious, substantive discussions with the potential for significant programmatic contributions. Reported interactions with this potential are labeled planning or formulation.

To summarize interactions with DOE planning offices, each group is classified by the preponderant substance of its meetings and placed in one of the three categories described above, or in a fourth category for those significantly involved in all three activities. The frequencies are reported in Table 7.4.

These data shed very different light on the apparent efforts by the DOE to pluralize its consultation. Of the fifty-three groups that had contact with DOE policy makers, 64 percent essentially engaged in pro-forma, public relations interactions. In fact, public relations was the modal substance of meetings attended by the groups in every sector.[24] The clear majority of interest groups that interacted with DOE policy makers enjoyed no more significant contact than they experienced during the formulation of the National Energy Plan. The DOE frequently invited groups to briefings that did not permit significant substantive input and did not involve serious discussions of political strategy. It fulfilled its obligation to major constituents through equally shallow processes. Ostentatious meetings between Secretary Schlesinger and top corporate or association officials would satisfy many political actors, as a spokesman for the NCA

TABLE 7.4
*Substance of Interactions Between DOE Policy
Formulators and Interest Groups*

Sector	Preponderant substance of interactions				Modal substance
	All three	Planning or formulation	Congressional strategy	Public relations	
Environmental groups	43% (3)	0 (0)	0 (0)	57% (4)	P.R.
Consumer and PIGs	0 (0)	12% (1)	25% (2)	62% (5)	P.R.
Petroleum and gas industry	0 (0)	18% (2)	18% (2)	64% (7)	P.R.
Electric power	38% (3)	12% (1)	0 (0)	50% (4)	P.R.
Conservation and renewable energy	0 (0)	0 (0)	33% (1)	67% (2)	P.R.
Labor unions	17% (1)	17% (1)	0 (0)	67% (4)	P.R.
Commercial users	11% (1)	0 (0)	0 (0)	89% (8)	P.R.
Financial institutions	0 (0)	100% (1)	0 (0)	0 (0)	Planning
TOTALS	15% (8)	11% (6)	9% (5)	64% (34)	P.R.

NOTE: Totals are for less than 73 because groups with no interaction are excluded from the table.

discerningly explained: "The Washington interest group representative is pleased because he has arranged a big meeting for his boss. The corporate executive is pleased because he has rubbed elbows with the powerful. The DOE is pleased because it has at least tried to massage important egos. Everyone is pleased, but the discussions have been nothing more than political rhetoric."[25] For the majority of interest groups, consultation with DOE policy makers amounted to little more than superficial discussions that gave the appearance of accessible policy making but had scant immediate impact upon substantive or political decisions by the department.

A significant minority, however, did engage in serious consultation with DOE planners: five groups primarily on congressional strategy, and six mostly in substantive policy formulation. Finally, eight consulted with DOE policy makers in every manner. While this may seem like very limited consultation for a policy area that concerns so many groups, it is a significant change from the consultation employed in the formulation of the National Energy Plan. Indeed, the changes seem to reflect lessons learned from that initial experience.

The National Energy Act that finally became law in October 1978 bore little resemblance to the ambitious plan recommended in April 1977. Congress opposed the plan for many reasons and ultimately weakened it beyond recognition.[26] Part of the fault lay in the Carter administration's failure to consult seriously with key interest groups during the formulation process. The administration made little effort to assemble a winning coalition of supporters among policy influentials. Perhaps it believed that the eminent logic of the comprehensive proposal, coupled with public support, would be sufficient to ensure enactment. The House of Representatives in May and June 1977 gave the administration reason to believe it had figured correctly and quickly adopted all of the plan, except the "gas-guzzler" tax, with few modifications.[27] This good fortune was not, however, a result of adept administration planning. It was primarily a product of favorably predisposed committees and masterful leadership by House Speaker O'Neill.[28]

When the Senate took up the plan in July 1978, the administration's failing became abundantly clear. The gas-guzzler tax, the crude oil equalization tax, and the natural gas pricing proposal were all rejected—consistent with the well-lobbied preferences of the oil industry and many commercial users. The crude oil and natural gas proposals constituted the very heart of the plan. To the further chagrin of the administration, the Senate passed a bill authorizing deregulation of the wellhead price of natural gas. The administration had grossly underestimated the political strength of opposing interests and the weakness of its own support.

With the start of trouble in the Senate, the administration energy team (and later the DOE) began to change its relations with interest groups. The serious consultation summarized in Table 7.4 reflects this change. Three environmental groups began to cooperate closely with administration lobbyists in an effort to rescue the plan, and administration officials even attended regular strategy sessions held at the Sierra Club's Washington office. After the Department of Energy was established, the cooperation was extended to its regular planning activities. One of the DOE's first major activities was the formulation of a nuclear licensing bill to expedite regulatory procedures without sacrificing environmental and safety objectives. The process lasted nearly a year and included many drafts of prospective legislation, which the environmental groups were invited to review.

Several other public interest groups were similarly involved. New Directions and Ralph Nader's Tax Reform Research Group cooperated with the administration on congressional strategy after the plan began to falter. A new peak association, the Citizen-Labor Energy Coalition, led by liberal Machinist Union president William Winpisinger, also began to enjoy serious policy consultation with the DOE and, along with several environmental groups, worked closely with the DOE during the summer of 1978 on an evaluation of solar energy policy known as the "Domestic Policy Review." The consequence was solar legislation recommended to Congress in 1979.

The DOE also increased its cooperation with industry groups. During the protracted congressional conference on natural gas pricing in 1978 it worked closely with several petroleum and gas industry groups in an attempt to negotiate a compromise and salvage that section of the National Energy Plan. The Natural Gas Supply Committee, the industry's primary representative on the issue, cooperated extensively with the DOE and the administration, and the administration itself consulted frequently with commercial user groups. Ultimately it was the administration and DOE that negotiated the complex compromise, calling for gradual deregulation by 1985, that the conference accepted. The support of commercial users was decisive.[29] This extensive effort to cooperate with interest groups bears a sharp contrast to the insulated formulation process and no doubt reflects an important lesson learned the hard way.

The department also began consulting with industry groups on a new energy plan. To stem criticism of the National Energy Plan for its failure to provide production incentives, Schlesinger promised that the department would quickly propose a Phase II.[30] Proposals were formulated in early 1978 and benefited from the participation of several oil industry groups. Although the Office of Management and Budget intercepted them before they could be recommended to Congress, the 1979 proposal for huge synthetic fuel subsidies had its beginning in the Phase II consultations, which bore fruit in 1980 as the multi-billion-dollar Synthetic Fuels Corporation.[31] The nuclear and coal industries also enjoyed significant consultation. The AIF and the ANEC cooperated with the DOE on the formulation and subsequent (unsuccessful) congressional selling of the 1978 nuclear licensing bill. The NCA reported a great deal of meaningful interaction with DOE policy makers on subjects ranging from synthetic fuels, to environmental obstacles, to coal utilization.

Despite the belated increases in interest group consultation by the DOE, it must be emphasized that very few groups—in fact, not even all the major groups in their respective sectors—ultimately enjoyed some significant interaction with the department. The consultation that a majority of these groups experienced, moreover, amounted to little more than public relations.

In the remaining sectors significant consultation was almost non-existent. Only one conservation or renewable energy group, Consumer Action Now, had effective interactions with policy formulators in DOE. The Washington representative of that group, Susannah Lawrence, was the unofficial coordinator of the congressional solar lobby and worked with some of the DOE planning staff on congressional strategy. In contrast, the president of the SEIA, Sheldon H. Butt, attacked the new department in early 1978 for its lack of cooperation: "At the policy-making level we see the same lack of interest in solar that we saw in ERDA. There's just no visible evidence that Dr. Schlesinger and his policy-making crew ever give a moment's thought to it."[32] Organized labor, which originally provided strong support for the National Energy Plan, was not seriously consulted by the DOE. The United Auto Workers was the only exception, cooperating with the department on lobbying for the plan and on occasional policy proposals. Among commercial users the Business Roundtable, which represents executives of major corporations, was the only group to work effectively with DOE planners. Its relationship, however, hardly provided effective representation for the wide array of commercial energy users such as mass transit, agriculture, or rail transportation.

The Causes and Consequences of "Pluralistic" Planning

If energy policy making during the 1970s had a central objective, it was surely to develop a national plan that would lend foresight and consistency to the existing hodgepodge of energy programs. The key steps toward that goal were a series of bureaucratic reorganizations that eventually centralized energy policy making in the DOE. One measure of progress is the ability of the bureaucracy to mediate the many conflicting interests that had lain dormant or had been separately appeased for so many years. The observed relationships between the energy planners and the attentive interest groups indeed indicate significant change. To what extent we want to characterize this change as progress, however, is a different matter.

When energy policy-making responsibility was centered in the FEA, interest mediation was not occurring in any comprehensive way. Group participation was thoroughly dominated by the oil industry and by the large commercial consumers of its products. The administrator's office of the FEA attended to intra-industry conflicts among oil businesses and oil-consuming businesses, but the larger issues and tradeoffs entailed by energy generally went unaddressed. Ford administration policy initiatives reflected the FEA's preoccupation with problems of oil regulation. In 1975 and 1976 the deregulation of oil was the centerpiece of executive proposals. In effect, then, the first step toward comprehensive energy policy making did not prompt a broader consideration of the interests at stake in national energy problems.

The last step, the creation of the Department of Energy (and the requirement of national energy plans), was more successful. Interest group participation in the DOE planning offices was more competitive than in the FEA. Of the groups in this study 24 percent participated frequently and another 24 percent sporadically. No sector dominated, as happened consistently in the regulation and allocation arenas, and every sector was represented. While the agency's efforts to consult did not mirror the initiatives of its constituents, they did seek a diversity of input. Sixteen percent of the groups were contacted frequently by the DOE, and another 49 percent approached sporadically. Most attention was directed toward major associations such as the API, the Business Roundtable, and the AIF; however, the assistance of several environmental and consumer groups was also frequently solicited. On balance, the DOE's strategy was pluralistic.

The pluralism that ultimately characterized the organizational relationships of energy planning was not, however, the particular variety predicted by the organizational theory. The contributions that most of the participating groups (64 percent) made to national energy planning were insubstantial. The dominant forms of interaction between the DOE and its constituents were informational briefings, at which opportunities for significant input were minimal, and pro forma meetings between DOE leaders and the leaders of major interests. There is nothing necessarily disingenuous about public relations practices of this sort. Agencies commonly hold courtesy meetings with interested constituents to promote goodwill while serious discussions with influential groups go on in greater privacy. What was unusual about the DOE's consultative practices was that so many, and often key, groups were treated to these superficial audiences.

The other unexpected quality of the pluralism of DOE planning was its ad hoc and reactive make-up. Planning agencies are expected to try to establish multiple and fluid bonds with constituent interests, in order to provide flexibility in planning over time and a reservoir of political support for relations with political sovereigns. The significant relationships that the DOE developed were not so motivated; its planners never operated with such political foresight. Their significant relationships emerged as reactions to a series of political circumstances, and not in anticipation of the political requirements of comprehensive planning. The pluralism of planning relationships at the DOE was, in sum, rather shallow and unstable.

How did this imperfect version of pluralism develop? Most of the explanation lies in bureaucratic strategies because interest group initiatives were as competitive as predicted: the expected benefits of participation are high because planning yields legislative proposals with typically large impacts; and the costs are low because technical and legal expertise are not at a premium. The consequently high expected value makes it unlikely that even the poorest groups will be excluded; planning participation is not a tactic that groups would usually regard as marginal. The number of groups with some planning involvement at the DOE confirms that they responded to favorable incentives. Planning at the DOE, unlike regulation and allocation, did not discourage the participation of all but the technically-based, affluent organizations; rather, it stimulated competitive inputs.

The planning bureaucracies were not, however, interested in reinforcing the competitive input pattern. When the FEA held planning responsibility, it was preoccupied with its major implementation responsibility. Oil regulation was so politically controversial and administratively demanding that the agency showed little interest in anything else. The FEA was also living under temporary organic legislation and working for a president who was more interested in eliminating regulation than in creating comprehensive plans. The FEA during the Ford years therefore showed little interest in developing a supportive constituency for long-term policy development. When President Carter took office, the FEA was simply bypassed as a planning body until a new permanent planning bureaucracy could be established. Its oil relationships continued and later moved on to the Economic Regulatory Administration within the DOE.

The new DOE planning offices had more incentive to cultivate an effective planning constituency. The department was given an explicit planning mandate and a comprehensive jurisdiction. Its planners, however, were slow to recognize the importance of interest group relationships; they all but ignored interest groups as they prepared the 1977 National Energy Plan, looking only to the environmental groups favored by President Carter. Not until the plan stumbled badly in the legislative process did the planners and the new department realize the full potential of consultation. Relationships with interest groups then began to be cultivated as political currents dictated. Commercial users and coal producers were asked for assistance in saving the National Energy Plan. Interests omitted from the plan were promised future assistance in exchange for support. A nuclear licensing reform proposal was to make amends to the nuclear industry. Efforts to appease the oil industry occurred later with synthetic fuel initiatives. None of this consultative effort can be attributed, however, to a broad-gauged political strategy. The initial inclination of the planners was to eschew group consultation; their subsequent overtures were merely short-term political expedients.

The group relations of the early DOE planning effort were strongly influenced by the political values and decision-making style of President Carter. The analytical, secretive, and concentrated formulation process that he established for his National Energy Plan structured the politics of the regular planning processes that followed it. The DOE planners never had the chance to establish a comprehensive set of priorities and begin building political support for them. Their interest group relations were immediately dictated by the problems plaguing their initial recommendations. It is, of course, obvious that Congress also played an influential role in pluralizing the planning relationship. All of the interests in this study enjoyed strong support from some segment of Congress, and that support often caused problems for the National Energy Plan. In this bureaucratic setting, unlike in regulation and allocation, congressional demands were effective. They were effective because bureaucratic success depended entirely on legislative approval. It is important to recognize, however, that Congress was not exerting influence through informal ties and understandings between its committees and the permanent bureaucracy. The ability of Congress to manage the energy bureaucracy on a regular basis was nearly as poor for planning as for regulation and allocation.

The relationships that developed between the planning bureaucracy and the interest group population during the DOE's first years will probably undergo considerable change in the years to come. Many groups had access to the planners, but few enjoyed close working relationships. Alliances with key congressional committees did not underpin those relationships that existed. Organizational relationships, rather, showed the clear marks of ephemeral presidential interests and short-term political needs. Most important, the relationships gave no indication that a centralized energy bureaucracy was capable of overcoming and controlling the conflicting interests and independent sources of political support that characterize the modern energy constituency. National energy planning remains a serious political dilemma.

CONCLUSION: ORGANIZATIONAL BIAS AND ENERGY POLICY

The Persistent Subsystems

Prior to the energy crisis of 1973, government policies affecting energy supply and demand were formulated and implemented by political subsystems that more often than not promoted or generously accommodated the interests of major energy producers. Each subsystem was organized around an independent administrative agency with political support from a few major interest groups and, usually, a committee in each house of Congress. The sources of their sustenance were twofold. First, all the subsystem members benefited politically, economically, or organizationally from mutual cooperation and the production of promotional policies. Second, interests excluded from the subsystems were nonetheless mollified by the economic growth and unperturbed by the relatively minor external costs produced by promotional policies. By the early 1970s, however, these sources of subsystem support had weakened considerably.

Several developments in the early 1970s challenged the subsystem approach to energy policy. The scarcity of cheap and environmentally benign domestic energy raised the specter of large economic, distributional, and environmental costs for future energy supplies. These threats motivated interests such as environmentalists, consumers, commercial users, and organized labor, which had long been quiescent on energy issues, to become seriously concerned. The demands of the most diffuse of these interests were expressed with unprecedented vigor by new environmental and consumer lobbies that had organized on nonenergy issues in the late 1960s. Finally, the unanticipated hardships of the first energy crisis awakened political leaders to the inconsistent and nearsighted energy programs that subsystem politics had produced. These developments made the life of subsystems most difficult in Congress. Once prospective subsystem policies began to impose external high costs, and scores of groups began to object, the subsystem approach to policy making became politically infeasible.

Congress responded to the new energy problem, and its heightened political conflict, by acknowledging the need for a national energy policy and reorganizing bureaucratic and legislative authority in the area. The reorganizations were intended to centralize, coordinate, and otherwise rationalize energy policy making. They were also intended to dismantle the subsystems that had long fashioned uncoordinated energy programs. The major purposes of this study were to understand theoretically and empirically how energy politics and policy making became structured in the wake of government reorganization, interest proliferation, and energy scarcity.

Part One of the book developed an organizational theory of political influence to help explain energy policy making. While the theory is intended to inform modern policy making generally, it is particularly pertinent to an area such as energy that has long been dominated by corporate, political, and bureaucratic organizations. Policy subsystems, the theory avers, are a special case of the political relationships that inevitably exist between public authorities and the private interests those authorities affect. Subsystems exist when the relationships exclude all but a few major interests and when political authorities assent to the arrangement. To understand these relationships, the theory suggests, we must explain why affected interests choose to participate or not to participate, and why the bureaucracy chooses to cooperate or not to cooperate with the various interests under its influence. In a policy arena that includes as many interests and organized representatives as does energy, the political behavior of neither the groups nor the bureaucracy is intuitive. Such an explanatory quandary is not new, however, to policy analysis. The pluralist ideas that underpin most political analyses of policy making do not offer explicit hypotheses for deducing the structure of political conflict or accommodation in complex political arenas.[1] The organizational theory proposed an explanation of interest group initiatives and bureaucratic behavior by essentially standing the conventional pluralist model on its head. Rather than search for post hoc explanations of energy policy in the interactions of groups and agencies, the theory proposes explanations of political behavior in terms of the policies at stake and other government variables. Taking a cue from modern corporatist theories of interest group politics, the organizational theory seeks to explain group influence in terms of the incentives, disincentives, cooperation, and resistance provided by the government.[2]

Part Two assessed the validity of the organizational theory by explicating the behavior of the many interests and agencies concerned with contemporary energy policy. The central empirical finding is that strong energy subsystems continue to thrive. The new ones are composed of permanent bureaucracies responsible for particular components of national energy policy allied with the most affluent interest groups within their respective purviews. They prosper on exchanges of technical information about energy production, distribution, and consumption between agency staff and those few groups that can afford to produce relevant expertise. The subsystems discourage the participation of all but the most technically competent groups, and resist political pressure to provide greater interest access.

The most insulated and exclusive of the subsystems was the one that emerged for oil regulation. Interest group initiatives to participate in bureaucratic policy making were nearly monopolized by major oil producers and refiners, while agency strategies mostly reinforced this pattern through co-optation. Interests outside the subsystem relied primarily on congressional lobbying to secure their regulatory goals. In a word, the oil subsystem was a case of capture. That label is also the most accurate for the organizational relationship associated with nuclear regulation. The nuclear subsystem was not as exclusive as that in oil: several environmental groups made frequent attempts to provide policy input and, after 1978, the NRC commissioners significantly pluralized an otherwise co-optive strategy. Nonetheless, the staff of the NRC was decidedly pro-industry; the only groups enjoying working relationships with the agency represented producer interests; and the agency's decision making exhibited the pro-cost-bearer biases of capture. Finally, in energy research and development a contrasting subsystem was found. Group participation was dominated in nearly monopsonistic fashion by the largest and most concentrated industries eligible for R&D assistance, and bureaucratic strategies were cooperative exclusively with these same interests. The bias in this quasi-corporatist subsystem favored the traditional, well-organized beneficiaries.

In comparison to these three stable subsystems, the organizational relationships of national energy planning were fairly unbiased. This is not to say that rich pluralist relationships of extensive consultation and heterogeneous political support characterized energy planning. To the contrary, consultation ranged from nonexistent to disingenuous during the formulation of President Carter's National Energy Plan and expanded only uneasily at the Department of Energy. Nevertheless, interest group efforts to participate in this new, centralized formulation process were by 1978 rather competitive, and the department eventually initiated political and substantive contacts with a variety of groups. Given the strong nonpluralist roots of planning in the Federal Energy Administration and the early Carter White House, the planning relationships that were beginning to develop in the new department represented significant movement toward pluralism. In relative terms, then, the energy planning relationships are best described as protopluralist—albeit tenuous and perhaps temporary in quality.

Theoretical Implications: The Public Mobilization of Bias

The four organizational relationships observed here are basically consistent, as the accompanying figure depicts, with the predictions derived at the end of Chapter 3 for regulation, allocation, and planning activities.[3] The validity of the organizational theory, and its implications for energy policy making, do not, however, hinge on these general relationships. The theory is not based on nominal categories of policy making but rather on a number of continuous variables that determine group initiatives and bureaucratic strategies. The variables tend to assume particular sets of values when policy making involves primarily allocation, regulation, or planning; hence, it is possible to predict the general relationships that the case studies supported. The important theoretical issue, however, is the significance of those variables, mostly under government control, that underlie the general predictions.

Consider first the causes of interest group initiatives. The organizational theory assumed that interest participation depends largely on the nature of the organization that interests are able to assemble to represent themselves. Part of this dependence, as explicated in the economic theories of Olson, Salisbury, and Moe,[4] is that the more

BUREAUCRATIC STRATEGIES

	Corporatist	Pluralist	Co-optive
Monopsonistic	*Corporatism* Research and Development		
Competitive		*Pluralism* Planning	
Monopolistic			Nuclear Regulation *Capture* Oil Regulation

INTEREST GROUP INITIATIVES

The Political Subsystems of Energy Policy, 1980

diffuse an interest, the more it will be plagued by free-rider problems; the greater difficulty it will have in organizing a strong political group; and the more it will need to rely on selective incentives to succeed. Interest group politics will consequently tend to be biased in favor of concentrated interests such as large businesses, and group leaders will tend to be unaccountable to members concerned mostly with nonpolitical benefits.[5] These theoretical tendencies (and others summarized in Chapter 2) raise serious questions about the quality of democracy in pluralist politics. The questions are based, however, on an oversimplified, undifferentiated conception of the political universe that ignores both the comparative advantages enjoyed by different groups in different political arenas and the strong influence exerted by the government over effective interest participation. The current state of economic theorizing is thick with insight into the dynamics of group formation and maintenance, and internal group politics, but is rather thin in perspective on the role of groups in politics and policy making. The organizational theory advanced in this book attempts to fill out that perspective by elucidating the relationships between group structure, political context, and interest participation.

Three relationships were strongly supported by the empirical analysis and merit reiteration. First, the organizational resources that interest groups bring to a policy arena are strongly related to the impacts that actual and potential group supporters experience from policies in the arena. All things being equal, interests experiencing large and concentrated policy impacts—the cost-bearers of oil and nuclear power regulation and the major industrial beneficiaries of R&D subsidies, for example—tend to participate through affluent interest groups while interests experiencing diffuse policy impacts, such as the beneficiaries of oil and nuclear power regulation and the cost-bearers and small entrepreneurial beneficiaries of R&D subsidies, tend to be represented by poor organizations. In between these two poles are the fairly successful organizations, representing interests such as small refiners and independent marketers, whose numerous members absorb moderate policy impacts.

The correlation cannot, of course, be attributed entirely to public policy. A fully specified model of the relationship would also have to include the economic resources of potential group members. Often the concentration of policy impacts is simply a function of the predetermined economic size of the targets. For example, the Emergency Petroleum Allocation Act, which among other things redistributed income from refiners to independent marketers, had on average a larger impact on the former because their firms are larger. Economic factors—making refining a more concentrated industry than marketing—and not the EPAA were the primary cause of differential policy impacts, and an organizational advantage for refiners. Another relevant variable, the number of potential members of a group, and the seriousness of the free-rider problems attendant on increasing numbers, may also operate independent of policy influence. The government can do little, for example, about the dispersion of environmental externalities, consumer costs, or small business impacts that create organizational difficulties for those interests. A fully specified model would have to include, finally, the collective incentives for political organizing other than the rewards and penalties of established policies. Interest groups are also formed and maintained around common interests that arise from social and economic relationships—e.g., producer-consumer, owner-worker—and not from public policy. Because the incentives, number, and size of potential group members can be exogenous to policy impacts and are often colinear with those impacts, the influence of public policy on organizational resources must be ascribed cautiously.

Two important effects of policy on organizational resources nonetheless emerge clearly. Policy impacts may provide the final collective incentive that either awakes potential members to the size of common political stakes or makes those stakes worth defending through collective action. In this study recent energy policy was found to have catalyzed the formation of a number of important groups, including Critical Mass, the Citizen-Labor Energy Coalition, the Energy Policy Task Force of the CFA, the APRA, the Council of Active Independent Oil and Gas Producers, the NOJC, the ANEC, Consumer Action Now, the SEIA, the Electricity Consumers Resource Council, and the PEG. Moreover, many groups augmented their resources in response to energy policy. Without the stimulus of government-imposed costs, or the lure of program benefits, it is likely that many of the new groups would not have formed and many of the established groups would not have enlarged.

Policy impacts determine organizational resources in an important way also by establishing common and opposing interests. Because public policies include specifications of cost-bearers, beneficiaries, and other affected interests, they create classes of interests. The specifications sometimes reinforce established lines of consensus and conflict in society or the interest group arena. Oil price controls that redistribute income from producers to consumers, for example, reinforce a basic line of economic conflict and group opposition. Policies may also specify classes of interests that cross-cut established boundaries. The oil entitlements program, for example, caused a schism among large oil companies; refiners without substantial reserves of cheap, domestic crude oil were required to buy entitlements from, and were thereby thrown into conflict with, companies dependent on expensive, foreign crude. If the cross-cutting impacts are large, they may prompt a formal split in an existing group; the National Gas Supply Committee and the APRA are notable products of that process. A public policy may also establish common interests that are problematic to organize. The EPA, for example, supervises an essentially bipolar conflict between environmental and industrial interests, but the industrial interest includes so many and varied businesses that a single group representing cost-bearing interests has proved impossible to organize.[6]

As these illustrations suggest, the government exercises significant and predictable control over the strength and structure of the group environment of public policies and their bureaucracies. The controls are essentially twofold: first, the more concentrated the impacts of a policy, the more likely that a resourceful interest group will be poised to influence the administration of those impacts; second, the more the concentrated impacts reinforce established common interests, the more formidable the poised group will be. Although these controls may be modified by other factors that influence group participation, in basic form they do explain a significant amount of the variation in interest group alignments.

Much of the variation in the structure and strength of the group environments of regulation, allocation, and planning is explained by the first control. The resourceful, organized constituents of pure regulation will tend to be cost-bearers—and of pure allocation, beneficiaries—because those are the interests experiencing concentrated impacts. In contrast, the group environment of planning agencies will tend to include multiple, resourceful groups because the impacts of plans and policy proposals, though uncertain, are potentially large for many constituents. Within these pure policy types variation is also explained by government controls—especially by the second control. The number and competitiveness of cost-bearing groups in regulation, or of beneficiary groups in allocation, depends on the dispersion of costs or benefits respectively among established interest organizations. If the costs or the benefits are concentrated on a single industry with an established interest group, the group arena will be respectively monopolistic or monopsonistic. The participation imbalances of oil and nuclear regulation were rooted in the single industry purviews of the regulatory agencies. Although the R&D bureaucracy had a multi-industry constituency, its attentive group environment tended toward singularity because only the interests in central electrification and synthetic fossil fuels enjoyed very concentrated benefits; the producers of conservation and solar energy products experienced far more diffuse impacts and were less encouraged to organize.

These problematic group environments are not, however, without remedy—and variations on the government controls offer prescriptions. Multi-industry or multi-interest jurisdictions can promote cost-bearer competition in regulatory bureaucracies and beneficiary competition in allocation bureaucracies if the impacts on different classes of interests are similarly distributed. For example, an environmental regulatory agency that limited pollution by auctioning off scarce pollution rights to a large number of firms could promote competition between cost-bearers that would in turn encourage economic efficiency.[7] Even if cost-bearer competition could not be used to induce efficiency, it would have the salutary effect of discouraging regulatory capture. If, on the other hand, it is infeasible to structure cost-bearer competition into the administrative arena, it may be best to sidestep the regulatory problems of capture and goal displacement through nonregulatory instruments. Such a device works to benefit society by forcing business or industry to provide services that they would not otherwise provide and to incur costs they would prefer to avoid. If it is possible, however, to provide society with the means to acquire those benefits directly, the regulatory goals can be effectively pursued without the problems of regulatory politics. The goals of oil price regulation, for example, might have been approached at least as successfully with temporary, and perhaps progressive, income tax credits based on energy consumption to help consumers adjust to the shock of higher oil prices.[8]

In allocation programs similar principles should guide reform. Multi-interest jurisdictions should be established where benefits can be distributed in like concentrations across the different classes of constituents, but should be avoided where one class would enjoy extra-concentrated rewards and organizational advantages. The latter situation has been problematic in the energy R&D bureaucracy since ERDA was created in 1974. From a political standpoint, more promising ways to implement a multi-pronged R&D strategy would include either two separate R&D agencies—one for "hard" technologies and the other for "soft"—or a nonbureaucratic system of R&D tax incentives. Both would be preferable to the noncompetitive, quasi-corporatist politics of recent energy R&D.

As promising as these remedies may be for encouraging competition between cost-bearers in regulation and between beneficiaries in allocation, they do nothing to promote the participation of regulatory beneficiaries or allocation cost-bearers. These interests tend to suffer a shortage of organizational resources due, among other reasons, to the diffuse policy impacts they usually experience. This organizational disadvantage notwithstanding, their interests need not go unrepresented. Their representation hinges, however, on factors other than policy impacts. It is these factors, moreover, that most enable the organizational theory to integrate economic theories of interest groups with the political environment in which groups organize and participate.

The remaining factors—the net collective benefit of participation and the selective incentive value of participation—combine to form a calculus of participation used by group leaders to assemble lobbying strategies. The calculus is constrained by organizational resources but otherwise permits much wider variation in group politics than economic theories have suggested. The organizational theory proposed that group leaders build political strategies by (1) estimating the expected net value to group members (and nonmembers) of the collective goods that alternative tactics would yield, and the value those tactics might have as selective membership incentives, and (2) cumulating tactics of decreasing collective and selective value until the group's political budget is exhausted.[9] Organizational resources will thus have their greatest impact on forms of participation that promise relatively marginal payoffs and fall somewhere below the top of the list of profitable tactics—forms that often occur in the bureaucracy.

The apparent use of such a strategic calculus was observed time and again in energy politics. It was first observed in the tendency of groups to emphasize legislative over bureaucratic participation. Seventy-four percent of the groups either emphasized congressional over executive lobbying or divided their efforts equally between the two. The degree to which congressional strategies dominated was also found to be strongly related to organizational budgets. The lower a group's resources, the more likely it was to emphasize congressional strategies. These results are a consequence of the lower costs of political as opposed to technical persuasion, and of the greater benefits of most legislation as opposed to most executive decisions. Participation in bureaucratic policy making is therefore generally biased in favor of concentrated interests such as large businesses, while legislative participation is more competitive.

The calculus also emerged as an important determinant of participation differences across bureaucratic arenas. The Nuclear Regulatory Commission discouraged the participation of environmental groups particularly, and of national interest groups generally, by employing formal licensing proceedings to develop regulatory policy in an incremental fashion. The formal proceedings are expensive, and the licensing outcomes of relatively limited significance. Group participation was therefore monopolized by a few nuclear industry associations that were sufficiently organized to afford this marginal approach to nuclear policy influence. Environmental groups emphasized congressional avenues and encouraged ad hoc local citizen groups to intervene. Following an informal procedure of frequent rule making in which the impacts of individual decisions were usually small and the costs of participation inflated by the constant and technical liaison required for success, the oil regulatory agencies also discouraged group participation. Only the major oil interests could justify the low expected returns of constantly cultivating the regulatory staff. The beneficiaries of oil regulation, consumers and small oil businesses, sought assistance mainly through congressional appeals. Participation need not, however, have been discouraged. By addressing more generic issues and providing genuine forums for nontechnical input, energy regulatory agencies could have stimulated more competitive group initiatives. The high costs of technical input also depressed participation in the energy R&D bureaucracy. Only the electric power industry was a regular bureaucratic participant; the advocates of renewable energy and conservation had to rely on Congress. By contrast, the planning bureaucracy, which promised large policy payoffs and imposed low political participation costs, prompted fairly competitive initiatives by energy-attentive groups. This observation underscores a point that was plain in every bureaucracy: the participation incentives supplied by different policy arenas, and controlled by government decision makers, are as important in determining interest group representation as characteristics of the interests themselves.

The point was equally clear in the interaction between government decision-making practices and the selective incentives groups employ to sustain themselves. Group leaders apparently recognize that certain political tactics also provide selective benefits to group supporters, and thereby acquire value above that associated with successful policy influence. This element of the strategic calculus was also observed repeatedly in energy politics. Groups that provided technical information as a selective benefit could afford technical bureaucratic participation—defrayed with membership fees that supporters pay willingly in exchange. Whenever technical expertise was a prerequisite for bureaucratic entrée and influence, trade associations that already produced it had an advantage over groups that did not. This factor was an important cause of both the limited participation of all groups in regulation and allocation arenas and, particularly, the underrepresentation of environmentalists, consumers, commercial users, and organized labor in those arenas. Selective incentive considerations benefited not only the technically based groups, however. Consumer and environmental groups, which rely heavily on purposive or solidary incentives, collected dividends from any political tactic that heightened the visibility of their cause or reinforced member efficacy. These payoffs help account for the tendency of public interest groups to contest bureaucratic policy making through the media, demonstrations, and congressional lobbying.

As long as technical expertise remains crucial to the formulation of energy policy in the bureaucracy, these different organizational needs will continue to encourage direct and cooperative participation by technically based groups, and indirect and combative strategies by nontechnically based groups. The energy field does not demand that policy making be carried on in largely technical terms; however, the bureaucracy's insistence on it ensures that interest participation biases will remain.

Each determinant of interest group initiatives is strongly influenced by government decisions: organizational resources depend on policy impacts, and the strategic calculus depends on the expected collective and selective value of participation options created by the government. One of the major goals of the organizational theory was to demonstrate precisely that—i.e., that contrary to prevailing conceptualizations interest group participation is not a purely exogenous variable in the policy process, and that it is systematically influenced, and often biased, by incentives supplied by the government. The other major goal of the theory was similar, but involved a more direct form of public control over private influence. That is, the theory sought to show also that the involvement of interest groups with the government was manipulated directly by the bureaucracy through its political strategies. In other words, it proposed that bureaucratic agencies need not be pawns of the interest organizations that confront them. Besides being able to affect the incentives and disincentives for group participation, agencies may selectively cooperate or resist cooperating with groups, as best suits their administrative and political needs. This study demonstrated that, in fact, bureaucracies often take the initiative in relationships with interest groups. On the average, between one-third and one-half of the contacts between groups and bureaucratic agencies resulted directly from agency initiatives.

The interest composition of the bureaucratic strategies varied across the policy arenas and generally reinforced the interest group initiatives. The causes of these strategies were hypothesized to lie mainly with the cues and constraints issuing from the political sovereigns of the agencies. The agencies were expected to seek those interest group alliances that would best serve their relationships with Congress, the courts, and the president. Support for those hypotheses was weak. The only cues from political sovereigns with clearly demonstrable impacts came from the White House. President Carter insisted on greater access for consumer, environmental, and conservation groups than President Ford had cared to ensure, and all of the bureaucracies studied began to provide it. These new efforts at cooperation did not, however, involve the entire bureaucratic hierarchy; only the agency leadership offered significantly better access to the previously excluded groups. The cues from Congress were loud, clear, and pluralistic throughout most of the 1973–78 period in each policy arena, yet bureaucratic strategies were biased and exclusive. The cues from the courts were directly relevant only in the regulatory arenas and were more ambiguous than those emanating from Congress, but on balance favored greater pluralism in rule making and adjudication. Again, these cues were substantially unheeded.

The conflicts between the political strategies of the energy bureaucracies and the political preferences of their democratic sovereigns raise serious theoretical questions about processes of democratic accountability. Modern empirical theories of bureaucracy are dominated by conceptualizations of bureaucratic behavior as a function of demands from the political environment. Beginning in the 1950s with the study of subgovernments, porkbarrel politics, and regulatory life cycles—and continuing to the present with theoretical work on the constituency basis of congressional influence, the growth of the public sector, the power of the presidency, and the legalization of public policy—the bureaucracy has been understood primarily through the legislative, executive, and judicial pressures thrust upon it.[10] This work finds the bureaucracy to be a shrewd political bargainer that is nonetheless responsive to some salient subset of the demands from its democratic institutional environment. Why these demands had relatively little influence over the energy bureaucracies is therefore theoretically puzzling.

One solution to the puzzle is an alternative set of specifications for the hypothesized processes of institutional influence. The courts, this study suggests, are unlikely to influence bureaucratic political strategies to the extent hypothesized. Because administrative agencies can often satisfy judicial review by guaranteeing procedural due process to all interests enjoying standing, court action may constrain or enhance only formal participation opportunities. The informal avenues of group access may be unaffected. This was surely the case for environmentalists in nuclear regulation and for consumers in oil regulation. Given that these two interests were among the prime beneficiaries of the liberal, interventionist posture of federal courts in the 1970s, it appears that a more circumscribed role is warranted for judicial constraint in the organizational theory of political influence.

The hypothesized role of Congress may also require refinement. Although Congress was not without influence over the bureaucracy—it continued, for example, to provide significant support for the traditional producing interests favored by the bureaucracy—the institution was not able to coax the bureaucracy away from its biased and exclusive private contacts, and into the more pluralistic relationships represented in congressional oversight structures. It may be that Congress simply had insufficient time to work its will with the bureaucracy. After all, the new regulatory and subsidy programs that it had created to aid environmental, consumer, and alternative energy interests had scarcely taken hold when in 1978 the political winds and its own composition shifted in a conservative direction away from regulation and government spending.[11] It is also possible, however, that Congress is inept at inducing more pluralistic bureaucratic behavior. It may be that by dividing oversight responsibility among multiple committees and subcommittees, and thereby enabling agencies to play the interests of one committee off against another, Congress weakened its ability to discipline the bureaucracy and to encourage pluralistic interest representation.[12] If that is the case, heterogeneous congressional interests should be represented in the bureaucracy not when they are protected by multiple oversight committees, as originally hypothesized, but rather by a centralized oversight committee.

Finally, the potential strength of presidential influence may need rethinking. The behavior of the entire energy bureaucracy was basically consistent with President Ford's preferences, but only the actions of the appointed leadership were supportive of President Carter's policies. Since the energy bureaucracy was already strongly oriented toward the views of Ford when he assumed office, the influence of presidential constraints cannot be easily assessed for his administration. The Carter experience is more informative because the president sought departures from the bureaucracy's energy policy. It is also an important test case of presidential influence because energy was the top priority of the administration, the new Department of Energy was indebted to the president for its creation, and sympathetic Carter appointees headed the new bureaucratic offices. The failure of these aggressive efforts to alter the interest group relationships of the three established subsystems suggests that presidential constraints are a considerably weaker influence on bureaucratic strategies than was hypothesized. While the specific cause of the weakness is unclear, it is probably some combination of civil service impediments, inferior expertise, unmanageable size, and other factors cited as potential curbs on presidential influence.

Although each of the institutional constraint hypotheses can be modified to explain the weak responsiveness of the energy bureaucracy, it would be premature to reformulate a general theory around the evidence of several cases. Political scientists should nonetheless be motivated by this poor record of democratic accountability to question their rather sanguine perspectives on bureaucratic responsiveness, and to conduct systematic empirical research into these relationships in other modern policy arenas. They should also be motivated to consider a potentially important missing piece in the theoretical puzzle of bureaucratic strategies. The organizational theory, and the political environmental tradition of which it is a part, omits causes of bureaucratic behavior that lie *within* bureaucracies. Factors such as organizational structure, professional norms, information flows, and decision-maker capabilities have long been the basis of sociological explanations of bureaucratic phenomena, but political science has tended to deemphasize them.[13] This study likewise made little systematic effort to explore internal factors, yet several emerged as significant.

The permanent energy bureaucracy, whether it was regulating oil prices or designing R&D programs, engaged in highly technical decision making with wide-ranging ramifications. For years prior to the energy crisis of 1973 the predecessors of the current energy bureaucracy had assembled large scientific, technological, and legal staffs, and instituted cautious, incremental decision-making processes. Notwithstanding the many changes in the structure and political environment of the bureaucracy, the energy agencies cooperated most with interest groups that had the expert personnel and the financial resources to contribute to these slow and technical policy-making processes. While the organizational barriers to broader interest representation may be stronger in the energy field than in other policy arenas, political analyses of bureaucracy should not so casually exclude such factors from theoretical and empirical consideration. The bureaucratic subsystems that continue to bias national energy policy making owe their longevity in no small part to the technical approaches that have dominated the government's role in energy problems.

Coming Full Circle

As energy policy making enters the 1980s it appears that the energy bureaucracy may have won its wager with the political forces of change. In the late 1970s the permanent energy bureaucracies were sustaining political subsystems that enjoyed traditional producer support but lacked the historically important assent of Congress. Presidential pressures on the agencies were being dissipated by leadership concessions, but otherwise the pressures from officialdom and the group arena were being resisted. With Republican gains in Congress in 1978 and 1980, the election of President Ronald Reagan in 1980, and the concomitant rise of opposition to government intervention in energy markets, the political pressures for interest pluralism in the energy bureaucracy are weakening. It now seems likely that the expansion of representation caused by the Carter presidency will contract without reinforcement from the Reagan administration. It also seems likely that the tension between Congress and the bureaucracy during the late 1970s will be relieved—by pro-producer congressional turnover rather than by bureaucratic adjustments. With the Reagan administration proposing to dismantle the Department of Energy, it is also probable that the experiment with comprehensive national energy planning will be terminated before it establishes any stable mediation of the many conflicting interests in energy. In the final analysis, the future of traditional, promotional energy subsystems is much brighter in the 1980s than it was in the 1970s. Their survival, should it occur, can be attributed primarily to the tenacious bonds of mutual support between the major, permanent, public and private organizations of energy.

APPENDIXES

APPENDIX A

INTEREST GROUP QUESTIONNAIRE

Organization:

Address:

Interviewee:

Job Title:

Date:

Time:

Description of Offices:

A. I would like to begin by getting some background information on your organization and Washington office.

   1. (For Associations and PIGs only) Could you briefly describe the origin of this organization?

      a. What year was it established?

   2. What year was this Washington office created?
   3. What are the major goals and functions of this office?
   4. (For Associations and PIGs)

      a. What is the current membership of this organization?

         1) Could you please describe those members?

      b. Do you provide services or inducements other than lobbying to attract members?
      c. How is this organization supported financially?
      d. (If necessary) How much are the dues?
      e. Is this organization tax exempt?

   5. How many persons work in your Washington office?

      a. Of these how many are full-time and paid?
      b. How many volunteers, if any, do you use?

6. How many of your staff members (professional and clerical) are involved directly with issues of federal energy policy development or implementation?

    a. How many of these work in congressional liaison?

    b. How many deal with the energy agencies or the executive branch of government? Has the attention grown of late?

    c. What do the remainder do?

7. Do you have any offices elsewhere?

8. Could you give me a rough estimate of this office's annual budget?

    a. (Associations and PIGs) What is the organization's total budget?

9. If this organization takes a position on an energy issue, how does it arrive at that position?

10. Has your organization or staff changed in size over the last five years?

    a. (For PIGs) What are its prospects for survival?

B. Now I would like to ask a few questions regarding your background and responsibilities.

    1. How long have you worked for this organization?

    2. How long have you held this particular position?

    3. What position did you hold prior to joining this organization?

    4. What is your formal education?

C. Energy regulation

1. Over the last four years has your organization been involved on the bureaucratic side of government with any of the many energy regulatory programs?

    a. (If yes) Which ones has this office been involved with, and what is this office's average time commitment to each?

    b. Do other parts or offices of this organization have any involvement in these or other areas? If so, how?

    c. What are this office's major objectives in its dealings with these regulatory programs and agencies?

    d. How do you pursue these goals? I.e., what strategies and methods do you use?

2. Let's take an in-depth look at the one regulatory area you have dealt with most often. Specify _____

    a. Over the last four years how frequently have you participated in the formal regulatory process? I.e., either how many times have you been involved (name the cases), or on what percentage of those regulatory issues of clear relevance to your goals have you participated?

    b. What forms of formal participation have you utilized and how frequently have you utilized them? E.g., written comments, oral testimony, petitions for rule-makings, etc.

    c. Could you rate the effectiveness of these methods on a scale of 1 to

10? Let 1 represent totally ineffective and 10 represent totally effective.

d. Do you have informal contacts with any members of this regulatory agency?

1) Could you describe the types of informal contacts you have? E.g., what do they deal with, and what is their purpose?

2) How frequently do you have these contacts? E.g., day to day, on every relevant rule-making, etc.

3) What proportion of each of these types of contacts are initiated by the agency?

4) What are the agency's motives for initiating these contacts?

5) How do these informal contacts benefit your organization in its pursuit of its goals?

6) Are these informal contacts generally more effective, less effective, or about as effective as your formal regulatory participation?

e. What successes and failures has your organization had before this regulatory agency? E.g., either specific cases or more long-run benefits.

f. In your opinion do other interest groups have more effective access to the regulators than yourselves in the areas in which you are involved? Who, and how are they more effective?

g. If you are dissatisfied with a regulatory decision, what do you usually try to do about it?

h. How knowledgeable are the regulatory people you deal with? That is, are they expert enough to make intelligent decisions without a good deal of outside help?

i. (For petroleum) Has your participation or ability to influence decisions been much different on the so-called Energy Actions? How so? Examples?

j. (If necessary) Do you aid in any way your members in their dealings with this regulatory agency?

k. Which of the following descriptions best characterizes the people in the regulatory administration you usually deal with?

1) Shares our viewpoint and requires little persuasion.

2) Is sympathetic to our viewpoint and may be persuaded to support us.

3) Is neutral and tries to remain that way.

4) Is antagonistic and is not easily persuaded.

3. If these questions have not adequately covered your organization's role in energy regulation, could you describe what other forms of advocacy or strategies of influence you utilize? E.g., do you attempt to influence the appointment of persons to the regulatory agency?

4. What is this organization's position on petroleum product and crude oil pricing and allocation regulations?

5. If these controls were eliminated today, how do you think it would affect the interests (or company) you represent?

D. I would like to turn now to the energy research, development, and demonstration programs handled by ERDA and now by DOE.

1. What is your organization's view of the current R&D effort being mounted by DOE?

2. Are there any areas which deserve more or less emphasis?

3. What is your organization's role in R&D contracting? E.g., do you press for particular contracts or oppose them?

4. Even without awarding contracts, government R&D can be a big help to private industry by sharing the costs and risks of these activities.

  a. How have you participated in decisions leading up to the undertaking of basic applied research by a national laboratory?

  b. How regular or routine is this participation?

  c. How often did ERDA or does DOE contact you for advice on prospective research projects?

  d. Do you often provide advice or consultation *during* projects?

5. What approach do you use in trying to persuade the energy bureaucracy to pursue the R&D effort you favor? For example, do you deal with program area officials or with policy-level people?

6. Could you describe briefly your organization's role in agency decision making leading up to *demonstration or commercial utilization* projects?

  a. What role have you played in the conduct or implementation of those projects?

7. Have you been involved in ERDA or DOE budgeting deliberations or other stages of the agency budgetary process? If so, please elaborate.

  a. What level people do you usually deal with?

  b. Do conflicts between the technical people and the political appointees ever hamper your efforts?

8. What are the major obstacles in the energy bureaucracy to your organization achieving its R&D goals?

9. Has ERDA or DOE ever asked you to support their funding requests in the congressional authorization or appropriation process?

10. How has your ability to influence energy R&D changed since the energy bureaucracy was reorganized?

11. Could you please describe for me any other ways in which your organization interacts with the government's energy R&D bureaucracy, or any other forms of advocacy you utilize in this area to alter the energy R&D effort? E.g., lobby Congress, OMB, or the Executive Office.

12. What do you regard as your organization's major success and failure in R&D interactions with the bureaucracy?

E. The third and final area I would like to probe is planning and policy development by the energy bureaucracy. Prior to last year FEA had these responsibilities in a limited way, and presently DOE has comprehensive responsibilities in these areas.

1. While FEA was in existence how many times would you estimate you dealt with either the administrator's office or the Office of Policy and Program Evaluation on matters relating to the development of policy recommendations or long-range plans?

a. What percentage of these times would you say the agency initiated the meeting?

2. Since the DOE was created, how many times would you estimate you have had contact with Dr. Schlesinger's office on matters of policy development?

a. What percentage of these times did DOE initiate the meeting?

3. Apart from recommending specific policies, FEA and now DOE were mandated by Congress to develop National Energy Plans. How, if at all, has the government involved your organization in their work in this area? I'm referring now specifically to Al Alm's office, and not to the Executive Office planning teams.

a. (If agency failed to initiate) Have you made any attempts to become involved?

b. (If not) Why not; surely this is important?

4. Did your organization play a role in the development of any of the following policy proposals?

a. President Carter's National Energy Plan Phase I? _____
b. President Carter's National Energy Plan Phase II? _____
c. President Ford's energy proposals? _____

1) Which ones?

5. If not, why not?

6. I would like to ask you a series of questions about your participation in these policy development activities.

a. Were you permitted to submit proposals or merely react to agency ideas?

b. Was your participation largely a result of your own initiative or at the agency's invitation?

c. At what stage in the process were you involved?

d. What methods of persuasion did you utilize?

e. Who else would usually be present when you participated? E.g., any other groups or Executive Office people?

f. Did the administration ever compromise with your organization in order to gain your support in the legislature or with OMB or other members of the executive branch?

g. Could you give me an example of an instance or two in which your participation was effective?

h. What were some major points you were unsuccessful in pressing?

i. If you did not participate, did you in any way aid, or coordinate the participation of, your members?

7. Could you fill in any gaps about your participation that these questions missed?

8. Did you feel that other groups besides yourselves had more influence on proposals through their participation? If so, who?

9. Did the administration seek your help in any way as its proposals ran into problems in Congress? If so, when?

10. Political scientists and journalists often point to the vested interests which bureaucrats or private groups sometimes have in federal programs as a major impediment to policy innovation. Commentators have suggested that vested interests in long-established programs in the fragmented energy area may present the greatest obstacle to the development of a comprehensive national energy plan.

a. Do you see this as a problem?

b. If so, how does it intrude?

c. Do you think the reorganization that created the DOE has dislodged these vested interests or are they still a problem?

F. If time permits, several general questions.

1. To what office in DOE does your organization presently have its most effective access?

a. Its worst access?

2. How do you cooperate or act jointly with other groups in your dealings with the energy bureaucracy? What groups?

3. What changes, if any, would you like to see made in the organization, staffing, or procedures of the current energy bureaucracy?

4. How, if at all, have you been able to utilize the extensive network of energy advisory committees to further your organization's interests?

5. What differences are there between your organization's ability to deal effectively with the energy bureaucracy since Carter took office and when Ford was in office?

6. Do you attribute any changes in your effectiveness to the reorganization?

7. Could you fill me in on any other significant activities your organization engages in to influence national energy policy?

THE INTEREST GROUP SAMPLE

Bureaucratic constituencies, as explained in Chapter 2, are most usefully specified in terms of functional representation. It is in this sense that the sample of groups drawn from the energy bureaucracy's constituency can be called representative. The particular functional interests represented are to some degree arbitrary; politics and policy analysis suggest many ways in which the conflicting interests in energy can be categorized. That difficulty notwithstanding, the categories specified here attempt to maximize internal cohesion and minimize external commonalities among groups. Eight functional interests were so identified: (1) environmentalists; (2) consumers and other "public" (or highly diffuse) interests; (3) petroleum and natural gas producers, refiners, and distributors; (4) proponents of centrally generated electricity; (5) designers, producers, and implementers of conservation and renewable energy technologies; (6) labor; (7) commercial energy users; and (8) financial institutions. For each interest a "representative" sample of voluntary advocate organizations was constructed. The operational meaning of representative varies across categories because they differ greatly in population and complexity. The internal representativeness of each category should therefore be judged separately.

Based on association directories, interviews with environmentalists, and phone calls to many environmental organizations that turned out to be nonpolitical, the Washington-based population of environmental advocacy groups numbered about twenty-five. Of these only fifteen pursued issues bearing directly on national energy policy. The nine environmental groups included in the sample are the most active and most concerned with energy matters. Interviews support the conclusion that this function is represented nearly exhaustively by the sample.

The quality of the sample of consumer and other public interest groups is more difficult to evaluate. No more than five organizations in Washington, D.C., were both explicit representatives of consumers and activists in energy politics; these are included in the sample. A number of other diffuse interest groups, however, also claimed to support broad citizen interests in energy policy. Common Cause, the National Taxpayers Union, Congress Watch, and New Directions fall into this category. Again, interviews, directories, and phone calls indicated that the population of such groups did not exceed twenty; the four included in the sample were chosen for their diversity in energy issues, group structure, and constituency.

In 1978 the petroleum and natural gas industry was represented in Washington by twenty-three trade associations. In addition, no fewer than fifty-seven individual corporations in the industry maintained Washington offices for governmental relations.* Many other companies in the industry, and the other energy production industries, retain Washington counsel to represent their interests. Twenty-three of the twenty-five largest petroleum corporations have their own Washington offices. In constructing a sample of this large and diverse population while maintaining a manageably small N, some bias was bound to intrude. I opted to overrepresent the activities of major oil companies so that the role of these private interests—centrally involved in providing the bulk of the nation's energy—would not be obscured. The sample includes five of the seven largest, integrated, multi-national oil corporations, as well as three integrated or semi-integrated oil companies without international production that ranked 11th, 15th, and 31st in sales in 1977. The remainder of the industry is represented in the sample by associations. The natural gas industry is represented by its major trade association, the AGA, and by a deregulation lobbying group, the Natural Gas Supply Committee. Gasoline distributors and retailers are represented by the NOJC and the SIGMA; "wildcat" producers by the Council of Active Independent Oil and Gas Producers; and small and larger refiners by the APRA and the NPRA respectively. The most prominent organization for the petroleum industry as a whole, the API, is also included.

The next function, central electricity generation, includes the electric utilities, the nuclear industry, and the coal producers. While oil is also used to fuel many electrical generators, oil companies are excluded from this function because oil is a more versatile fuel, creating other interests quite beyond the growth of electrical power. Nuclear and coal, however, fit into the energy picture primarily as fuels for electrical generation and are therefore included in a single category with utilities. Moreover, interviews revealed that cooperation among the representatives of these interests is regular. While many utilities, coal companies, and manufacturers of nuclear reactors have their own Washington representatives, time constraints dictated that their interests be represented in the study through their trade associations.† The sample includes the only two national organizations of nuclear production interests, plus the four national associations of electric utilities, which represent the gamut of small and large, and privately and publicly owned utilities. In addition, the sample includes the NCA, repre-

---

*Among these are 30 large oil corporations also represented by the API: Aminoil USA, Arabian American Oil, Ashland Oil, Asiatic Petroleum, Atlantic Richfield, BP, Caltex Petroleum, Champlin Petroleum, Cities Service, Clark Oil, Husky Oil, Kerr-McGee, Marathon Oil, Mobil Oil, Pennzoil, Phillips Petroleum, Shell Oil, Standard Oil of Ohio, Sun, Superior Oil, Tenneco, Texaco, and Union Oil.

† Since the major concern of current energy politics is petroleum, as is the major focus of this study, it is not unreasonable that the only corporate representatives included in the study represent oil companies.

senting the producers, both small and large, underground and surface, of 98 percent of the nation's coal. Rounding out the sample is the American Mining Congress, which represents coal and uranium producers, and the NARUC, which represents the state public utility commissions that set utility rates nationwide. The sample is all but exhaustive of the associational representatives of utilities, nuclear producers, and coal in Washington.

Because energy conservation and renewable energy technologies fulfill the same purpose, i.e., saving traditional, nonrenewable fuels, they are paired as a single function. Under the heading of conservation fall the AIA, the NAHB, the Institute for Local Self-Reliance, and the National Congress for Community Economic Development. The first two are the major representatives of the private interests that will design and implement energy-saving measures in commercial and residential buildings. Unlike commercial users, who also have interests in conservation, the major interest of these two organizations in the energy field is promoting conservation. The other two organizations are concerned with community energy use, and with implementing "soft-path" community self-sufficiency in energy. Consumer Action Now is a public interest group whose primary function is the promotion of solar energy before Congress and government agencies. The sample also includes the SEIA, the only national association of this fledgling industry, and United Technologies, a large industrial conglomerate with the nation's leading research and development expenditures for a variety of alternative (often "hard") energy technologies. This sample by no means encompasses all the many inventors and small companies involved in conservation and renewable or alternative energy. It is, however, reasonably representative of the basic functions, including the most prominent organized advocates of solar energy, "hard" alternative energies, and conservation in buildings.

The remaining three functions were sampled in a straightforward fashion from well-defined populations. The sample of labor unions accounts for the overwhelming proportion of organized labor in the nation, and includes the workers in energy industries. The sample of commercial users of energy includes the country's two peak business associations, the Chamber of Commerce and the National Association of Manufacturers, plus the Business Roundtable, an organization of chief executive officers of the nation's largest corporations. Two special industrial consumer groups, the Electricity Consumers Resource Council and the Industrial Energy Users Forum, and the main organizations speaking for trucking, railroads, airlines, automobiles, public transit systems, petrochemical users, and farmers are also represented. The sample covers all the major commercial energy-consuming interests. The functional sample is rounded out with the associational representatives of the country's main financial institutions, the American Bankers Association speaking for commercial banks and the National Savings and Loan League working for thrift institutions. Both play key roles in financing energy development and conservation.

NOTES

Complete authors' names, dates, and publication data are given in the Bibliography, pp. 301–12. Abbreviations of names of participating organizations and Department of Energy agencies appear in Table 1.1 (p. 14) and Tables 3.1 and 3.2 (pp. 69 and 71) respectively.

Chapter 1

1. Throughout the 1970s, inflation consistently ranked as the "most important problem facing this country today." The "energy crisis," usually among the top several problems, was rated number one in January 1974 by 46%, and in May 1979 by 33%, of the population. *Gallup Opinion Index*, 167 (June 1979): 6–8.

2. Among energy analyses lacking careful attention to politics are Stobaugh and Yergin, *Energy Future*; Commoner, *Poverty of Power*; Kash et al., *Our Energy Future*; Ford Foundation National Energy Project, *A Time to Choose*; Breyer and MacAvoy, *Energy Regulation*; MacAvoy, *Federal Energy Administration Regulation*; Mancke, *Squeaking By*; National Academy of Sciences, *Energy in Transition, 1985–2010*; Rowen, *Options for U.S. Energy Policy*; Lovins, *Soft Energy Paths*.

3. The paucity of theory and the profusion of description and polemics are exemplified in Davis, *Energy Politics*; Rosenbaum, *Energy, Politics, and Public Policy*; Freeman, *Energy: The New Era*; Engler, *Brotherhood of Oil*; Commoner, *Politics of Energy*. Analyses of the international dimension have been more sophisticated: e.g., Vernon, *Oil Crisis*.

4. The most thorough exposition of this thesis is Davis, *Energy Politics*.

5. The justifications for government-induced change in domestic energy supply and demand patterns are basically twofold: the insecurity of foreign oil supplies resulting from political instability in the Middle East, and the stagflationary consequences of increasingly scarce and expensive nonrenewable supplies. For a careful explication, see Stobaugh and Yergin, *Energy Future*, chs. 1, 2.

6. The nonrenewable nature of traditional fossil fuels makes infinite price escalation inevitable and indefinite reliance on them physically im-

possible. For perspective on achieving a renewable energy future, see Commoner, *Politics of Energy.*

7. For historical evidence, see Davis, *Energy Politics*; Engler, *Politics of Oil*; Green and Rosenthal, *Government of the Atom*; Selznick, *TVA*; Wildavsky, *Dixon-Yates*; for the subsystems argument in comparative perspective: Lindberg, *Energy Syndrome.*

8. For the government's role in inflating oil prices, cf. Blair, *Control of Oil*; Mancke, *Failure of U.S. Energy Policy*; Bohi and Russell, *Limiting Oil Imports.*

9. Cf. Oppenheimer, *Oil and the Congressional Process.*

10. The subsystem pattern has also prevailed in other advanced industrial systems; cf. Lindberg, *Energy Syndrome.*

11. Cf. McConnell, *Private Power and American Democracy*, pp. 272–80.

12. On the Bureau of Land Management, see *ibid.*, pp. 205–12; on the Atomic Energy Commission, Green and Rosenthal, *Government of the Atom*; on the Federal Power Commission, Davis, *Energy Politics*, ch. 4; on the Rural Electrification Administration, Childs, *The Farmer.*

13. For commentary on changes in public concern, see Downs, "Up and Down with Ecology."

14. My theoretical framework relies most on organizational models that build on assumptions of rational actors and follow economic lines of reasoning. When assumptions are relaxed to reflect organizational reality and behavioral incentives broadened to include diverse political stimuli, the economic approach provides both theoretical coherence and empirical flexibility. The work of Mancur Olson, Robert Salisbury ("Exchange Theory"), and Terry Moe (*Organization*) on interest groups, and of James March and Herbert Simon (*Organizations*) and Anthony Downs (*Inside Bureaucracy*) on bureaucracy illustrate the potential of this line of organization theory.

15. Bentley's work (*Process*) was a reaction against the formal, institutional political science of his time; he objected to its sterile, legalistic methods, and he urged political scientists to focus instead on observable activity—that is, on the actions of those in and around government. Bentley was not advocating merely a broadening of political inquiry to include pressure groups; he was advocating a sharp epistemological break with the past. His objective was "to fashion a tool." The successors to Bentley included Truman, *Governmental Process*; Schattschneider, *Politics, Pressures*; Bailey, *Congress Makes a Law*; Bauer, Pool, and Dexter, *American Business and Public Policy.*

16. Cf. Halperin, *Bureaucratic Politics*; Allison, *Essence of Decision*; Heclo, *Government of Strangers.*

17. For critiques of the interest articulation model, cf. Eckstein, *Pressure Group Politics*; Macridis, "Interest Groups in Comparative Analysis"; LaPolombara, *Interest Groups in Italian Politics.*

18. Cf. Kvavik, *Interest Groups in Norwegian Politics*; Donald M. Hancock, *Sweden: The Politics of Post-Industrial Change* (Hinsdale, Ill.: Dryden Press, 1972); Cohen, *Modern Capitalist Planning*; Beer, *British Politics in the Collectivist Age.*

19. McConnell, *Private Power*, esp. chs. 7, 8. See also Huntington, "Clientelism"; Bernstein, *Regulating Business*; and Stigler, "Theory of Economic Regulation."

20. Lowi, *End of Liberalism*, esp. ch. 10.

21. Cf. Schmitter, "Still The Century of Corporatism?" and "Modes of Interest Intermediation," especially for comparisons of corporatism and pluralism; and Heisler, *Politics in Europe*.

22. Four interviews (Standard Oil of California, Gulf Oil, Shell Oil, and Clark Oil) were conducted in person in December 1977, and six (National Park and Conservation Association, Consumers Union, Tax Reform Research Group, Council of Active Independent Oil and Gas Producers, United Steel Workers, and Industrial Energy Users Forum) were conducted by telephone.

23. The available methods for case analysis are summarized, and an adapted "correlational" approach recommended, in George, "Case Studies and Theory Development."

Chapter 2

1. On the importance of the market for energy politics, cf. Davis, *Energy Politics*, esp. chs. 1, 8; on its global influence: Adelman, *World Petroleum Market*.

2. Cf., for example, on corporations: Bauer, Pool, and Dexter, *American Business and Public Policy*; on trade associations and unions: Wilson, *Political Organizations*, chs. 7, 8; on public interest groups: Berry, *Lobbying for the People*; and on all groups: Truman, *Governmental Process*.

3. Cf. Olson, *Logic*; Salisbury, "Exchange Theory"; Moe, *Organization*.

4. It is fair to say that "analytical pluralists" tend to deemphasize the organizational problems encountered by political interests and the special role of the government in structuring group politics. For the classic statement of this approach, see Truman, *Governmental Process*.

5. One 1970s estimate places the proportion of federal laws with executive branch origins at 80%: Peter Woll, *Public Policy* (Cambridge, Mass.: Winthrop, 1974), ch. 1. The trend continues in earnest under the Reagan administration, which commanded an unchallenged leadership role in policy initiative during its first six months in office.

6. The main rules governing interest group participation in the bureaucracy are specified in the Federal Advisory Committee Act of 1972 (P.L. 92-463) and the Administrative Procedures Act of 1946.

7. See especially Krislov, *Representative Bureaucracy*.

8. The philosophical competition between these norms extends from guild socialism through modern pluralism and neo-corporatism. Cf. Cole, *Guild Socialism*; Dahl, *Preface*; and Stein Rokkan, "Norway: Numerical Democracy and Corporate Pluralism," in *Political Oppositions in Western Democracies*, ed. Robert A. Dahl (New Haven: Yale University Press, 1966), ch. 3.

9. For a similar distinction, see Theodore Lowi's venerable typology in "American Business." For later commentary: Salisbury, "Analysis of Public

Policy"; Kjellberg, "Do Policies (Really) Determine Politics?"; Ripley and Franklin, *Congress*; George D. Greenberg et al., "Developing Public Policy Theory: Perspectives from Empirical Research," *American Political Science Review*, 71 (December 1977): 1532–43; and finally, by Lowi himself: "Four Systems."

10. Any introductory work on microeconomic theory will clarify these relationships, e.g., Ward, *Elementary Price Theory*.

11. See Mishan, *Economics for Social Decisions*.

12. For the conventional view, see Niskanen, *Bureaucracy*.

13. See McConnell, *Private Power*, pp. 272–80; and Engler, *Brotherhood*, pp. 170–90.

14. Selznick defines the concept as "the process of absorbing new elements into the leadership or policy determining structure of an organization as a means of averting threats to its stability or existence" (*TVA*, introd.).

15. Olson follows the conventional definition of rationality as behavior that seeks to maximize the utility of the individual (*Logic*, ch. 1).

16. As the number of potential members of a group diminishes and the stakes of each potential member increase, the probability of group formation increases. These factors distinguish three types of groups: latent, intermediate, and privileged (*ibid.*, pp. 43–52).

17. On leadership, see Salisbury, "Exchange Theory," and Frolich, Oppenheimer, and Young, *Political Leadership*; on rationality assumptions: Barry, *Sociologists*, ch. 2; Marsh, "On Joining"; and Cyert and March, *Behavioral Theory*; on noneconomic incentives: Wilson, *Political Organizations*, ch. 3; Barry, *Sociologists*, ch. 2; and Moe, *Organization*, ch. 5.

18. For alternative predictions about interest group formation, see especially Moe, *Organization*, chs. 4, 5.

19. The theoretical argument is supported with substantial data on member motivation (*ibid.*, pt. 2).

20. Modifications of information, material incentives, and dues can be incorporated into a mathematical model; important, nonmaterial incentives cannot (Moe, "A Calculus").

21. On public goods generally, see Musgrave, *Theory of Public Finance*.

22. On the role of political efficacy, see Moe, *Organization*, pp. 30–34, 54–57, 213–18.

23. On types of organizational incentives, see Clark and Wilson, "Incentive Systems."

24. The only clear exceptions are Moe, *Organization*; Sapolsky, "Organizational Competition"; and Salisbury, "Exchange Theory."

25. Cf. Edelman, *Symbolic Uses*; and Downs, "Up and Down with Ecology."

26. Cf. Salisbury, "Exchange Theory."

27. It has been argued, for example, that leaders of groups employing selective material incentives have weaker political ties to their members, and therefore greater political leeway, than leaders of groups depending on purposive incentives (Moe, *Organization*, pp. 74–80, 103–4).

28. The familiar criticisms of rational decision making—that it requires too much analytical ability or is overwhelmed by subjective and non-eco-

nomic considerations—are less valid for group leaders who are responsible for substantial economic resources than for prospective group members who are not.

29. Cf. Charles O. Jones, *An Introduction to the Study of Public Policy*, 2nd ed. (North Scituate, Mass.: Duxbury Press, 1977).

30. Benefits may accrue to groups in negative terms, i.e., keeping threatening proposals off the agenda or costly laws off the books may provide benefits to some groups.

31. See Appendix A, question 6.b.

32. See Downs, "Up and Down with Ecology."

33. This relationship is recognized also by Moe (see n. 27, above).

34. For this assumption, see Downs, *Inside Bureaucracy*; Wildavsky, *Politics*; and Niskanen, *Bureaucracy*.

35. For more extensive inventories of congressional powers, see Dodd and Schott, *Congress*; Harris, *Congressional Control*; Ogul, *Congress Oversees*.

36. For a penetrating analysis, see Dodd and Schott, *Congress*, chs. 1–4. Historical studies of greater depth include Gallaway, *History of the House*; Ripley, *Power in the Senate*; and more generally on fragmented power: Burns, *Deadlock*. For studies of congressional committees: Fenno, *Congressmen in Committees*; Manley, *Politics of Finance*; Arnold, *Congress and the Bureaucracy*.

37. Cf. Dodd and Oppenheimer, *Congress Reconsidered*; and Dodd and Schott, *Congress*, ch. 4.

38. See especially Bibby, "Congress' Neglected Function."

39. Congress has become more professionalized through the augmentation or creation of research arms such as the Congressional Research Service, the General Accounting Office, the Office of Technology Assessment, and the Congressional Budget Office; through the addition of personal and committee staff; and through the restructuring of the budgetary process. Cf. Schick, *Congress and Money*; Fisher, *Presidential Spending Power*; Hammond and Fox, *Congressional Staffs*; and Dodd and Schott, *Congress*, ch. 5.

40. Dodd and Schott, *Congress*, pp. 229–35.

41. This is the central thesis of Fiorina, *Congress*.

42. Cf. Parris, "Congressional Program Review Legislation."

43. Aberbach, "Changes in Congressional Oversight."

44. Richard E. Cohen, "Will the 96th Congress Become the Oversight Congress?" *National Journal*, 11 (January 1979): 44–49.

45. Fiorina, "Control of the Bureaucracy."

46. My provision that intentional behavior without impact also constitutes oversight is an addition to the definition by Ogul, *Congress Oversees*, p. 11.

47. Cf. Dodd and Schott, *Congress*, pp. 184–211.

48. Aberbach, "Changes in Oversight," also omits any indicators of quality, though it too emphasizes the importance of the gap.

49. Cf. Fisher, "Presidential Control"; and on presidential fiscal tools, *Presidential Spending Power*.

50. Art. 1, sec. 8, of the Constitution.
51. This is the legal argument in Fisher, "Presidential Control."
52. Cary, *Politics*, p. 8.
53. For pre-reform problems, cf. Heclo, *Government of Strangers*; for post-reform prospects: Davis, "Senior Executive Service."
54. Good theoretical research on presidential power is generally acknowledged to be in short supply. Among the best studies are Cronin, *State of the Presidency*; Neustadt, *Presidential Power*; and George, *Presidential Decisionmaking*. For an insightful evaluation, see Heclo, *Studying the Presidency*.
55. Cf. Orren, "Standing to Sue"; Stewart, "Reformulation"; Gellhorn, "Public Participation"; and Davis, *Discretionary Justice*, ch. 5.
56. Cf. Davis, *Discretionary Justice*, ch. 1.

Chapter 3

1. The economic costs of foreign oil dependence are estimated in Stobaugh and Yergin, *Energy Future*, pp. 41–55.
2. OPEC, in existence since 1960, had threatened to rationalize world oil markets under its control but had hardly shown even hints of effective cooperation before 1973. On its perceived weakness, see Zuhayn Mihdashi, "The OPEC Process," and James W. McKie, "The United States," in Vernon, *Oil Crisis*, pp. 73–90, 203–16. On the 1973 crisis, see Klaus Knorr, "The Limits of Power," *ibid.*, pp. 229–43.
3. For discussion of the early indicators of impending problems, see Joel Darmstadter and Hans H. Landsberg, "The Economic Background," in Vernon, *Oil Crisis*, pp. 39–58.
4. For the politics of individual fuels, cf. Davis, *Energy Politics*.
5. On the oil industry subsidies, see Blair, *Control of Oil*; and Bohi and Russell, *Limiting Oil Imports*.
6. See especially Green and Rosenthal, *Government of the Atom*.
7. On natural gas regulation, see Breyer and MacAvoy, *Energy Regulation*.
8. On promotional foreign policy, see Stobaugh and Yergin, *Energy Future*, pp. 16–31; Chandler, *Visible Hand*; and Sampson, *Seven Sisters*. On electricity promotion, see Davis, *Energy Politics*, ch. 5.
9. For an important cross-national study of the economic growth issue, see Lindberg, *Energy Syndrome*.
10. Wellhead price regulation of interstate natural gas began with *Phillips Petroleum Co. v. Wisconsin* in which the Supreme Court agreed with the Wisconsin attorney general that gas producers were able to charge "excessive" prices at the wellhead and should therefore be subject to FPC rate making. The ambiguity of the decision also caused the dual market in natural gas and the subsequent political conflict between producing and consuming states. See Stobaugh and Yergin, *Energy Future*, ch. 5, and Davis, *Energy Politics*, ch. 4.
11. William Moffat, "Federal Energy Proprietorship: Leasing and Its Critics," in Rowen, *Options*, pp. 211–35, esp. 214–21.
12. See especially Ferejohn, *Porkbarrel Politics*.

13. Prior to World War I government involvement was confined to the great trust-busting confrontation with Standard Oil and a little assistance with foreign exploration. Among other historical accounts, see Sampson, *Seven Sisters.*

14. Davis, *Energy Politics*, ch. 3.

15. Blair, *Control* provides a compelling case for stability and limited competition as the enduring policy goals of the major oil industry. Although the case stands well on its rich data and analytical merits, it is important to note that Dr. Blair served for fourteen years as chief economist for the U.S. Senate Subcommittee on Antitrust and Monopoly, and prior to that for nearly ten years as assistant chief economist of the Federal Trade Commission.

16. *Ibid.*, ch. 8.

17. On oil prorationing, see Mancke, *Squeaking By*, pp. 5–7. My discussion borrows heavily on his account.

18. MacAvoy, *Federal Energy Administration*, p. 3.

19. Mancke, *Squeaking By*, pp. 5–7.

20. Davis, *Energy Politics*, p. 68.

21. Mancke, *Failure*, p. 17.

22. Milton Friedman, "Oil and the Middle East," *Newsweek*, June 26, 1967.

23. Engler, *Brotherhood of Oil*, pp. 57–83.

24. For an incisive account of the early period of executive energy politics, see William A. Johnson, "Why U.S. Energy Policy Has Failed," in Kalter and Vogely, *Energy Supply*, pp. 280–305.

25. *1974 Congressional Quarterly Almanac*, p. 745.

26. *Ibid.*, pp. 746–48.

27. The respective committee reports of the Department of Energy Act were approved with little floor action in the Senate 74 to 10 (May 18, 1977), and in the House 310–20 (June 3, 1977).

28. On the politics of the reform process, see Dodd and Schott, *Congress*, chs. 4, 7; and Davidson and Oleszek, *Congress Against Itself.*

29. *1977 Congressional Quarterly Almanac*, pp. 660–61.

30. The Bolling Select Committee on Committees reported eleven committees with energy jurisdiction in 1974: Agriculture, Armed Services, Banking and Currency, Education and Labor, Government Operations, Interior and Insular Affairs, Interstate and Foreign Commerce, Judiciary, Merchant Marine and Fisheries, Public Works, and Ways and Means. "Committee Reform Amendments of 1974," 93rd Cong., 2nd sess., 1974, H. Rept. 93–916, II, pp. 247–55.

31. Chase Manhattan Bank has maintained an energy analysis department for forty years and has participated publicly in the current energy debate. It is not included in the study because its Washington representatives declined to be interviewed.

32. The American Association of Railroads and the American Transportation Association are the only historical group forces from this sector—and their self-described roles were minor. The Petrochemical Energy Group, created in 1972, is an early member of a subsequent trend toward energy involvement by commercial users.

33. Oil companies reported staff changes in the interviews; interviews

also with AGA spokesperson (July 11, 1978), with AIF spokesperson (June 8, 1978), and with ANEC spokesperson (July 10, 1978).

34. Heclo, "Issue Networks," pp. 87–124.

35. Lindblom distinguishes between three basic methods of social control: authority, exchange, and persuasion (*Politics*), and Wildavsky between "interaction" and "cogitation" (*Speaking Truth*). For distinctions between planning and other policy instruments, similar to the ones I intend, see Benveniste, *Regulation and Planning*.

36. For a similar use of interest diffusion, see Wilson, *Political Organizations*, ch. 16.

37. Cf. Arnold, *Congress and the Bureaucracy*.

38. Cf. Dodd and Schott, *Congress*, ch. 5, and Fiorina, *Congress*.

39. For evidence to the contrary, see Moe, "Independent Commissions."

Chapter 4

1. Stigler, "Theory," pp. 17–18.

2. Because regulatory programs can be defined in various reasonable ways, a definitive count of agencies that regulate energy cannot be made. The count here was offered by the Doub Commission, appointed by President Nixon to study the problem of managerial fragmentation in energy (*Federal Energy Regulation*).

3. Among the major hypotheses treated in other works are: the intermingling of managerial and regulatory responsibilities in one agency (Landis, *Administrative Process*); the atrophy of the supportive regulatory constituency over the "life-cycle" of an agency (Bernstein, *Regulating Business*); the "revolving door" between the personnel of the regulatory agency and the regulated industry (Kohlmeier, *Regulators*, and Cushman, *Independent Regulatory Commissions*); the "capture" of the agency by politically resourceful clients (Huntington, "Marasmus"); the vagueness of regulatory statutes and the concomitant delegation of political discretion (Lowi, *End of Liberalism*, and Jaffe, *Administrative Law*); and the independent, institutional status of many regulatory agencies (Cutler and Johnson, "Regulation"). Revisionist critiques of the "regulatory failure" theories have now begun to appear, with an emphasis on important cases of regulatory success. Cf. Sabatier, "Social Movements"; Weaver, "Regulation"; and Wilson, *Politics of Regulation*.

4. Cf. Davis, *Energy Politics*, ch. 6.

5. On the first fifteen years of the AEC, see Green and Rosenthal, *Government of the Atom*, and Mullenbach, *Civilian Nuclear Power*.

6. Davis, *Energy Politics*, pp. 180–83.

7. Mullenbach, *Civilian Nuclear Power*, p. 285.

8. The following summary of organizational politics draws on the analysis in Ebbin and Kasper, *Citizen Groups*.

9. *Ibid.*, pp. 230–53.

10. The substantive restrictions and guidelines provided by the 1954 Atomic Energy Act gave the AEC considerable discretion in establishing the specific standards for nuclear power plants: "The Commission shall

issue such licenses on a nonexclusive basis to persons applying therefor (1) whose proposed activities will serve a useful purpose proportionate to the quantities of special nuclear material or source material to be utilized; (2) who are equipped to observe and who agree to observe such safety standards to protect health and to minimize danger to life or property as the Commission may by rule establish; and (3) who agree to make available to the Commission such technical information and data concerning activities under such licenses as the Commission may determine necessary to promote the common defense and security and to protect the health and safety of the public" [P.L. 83–703 (1954), ch. 10, sec. 103, b].

11. Ebbin and Kasper, *Citizen Groups*, p. 51.

12. As permitted under AEC *Rules of Practice*, 10 CFR sec. 2.101a.

13. Kingsley, "Licensing," pp. 319–22.

14. The meetings were opened to the public by the 1972 Federal Advisory Committee Act.

15. Ebbin and Kasper, *Citizen Groups*, p. 246.

16. *Ibid.*, p. 254.

17. The Administrative Procedures Act of 1946, which establishes the standards for procedural due process, does not ensure substantive due process. Cf. Stewart, "American Administrative Law."

18. For the AEC's hybrid rule-making procedures, see Bauser, "Rule-making Within the AEC," pp. 165–84.

19. During its early years the AEC employed informal rule making to handle noncontroversial standards, rulings, etc.—which required simply publishing advance notice of decisions and accepting written comments; it did not begin to hold contested hearings until the ECCS issue was designed for generic resolution.

20. Bauser, "Rulemaking Within the AEC," p. 172.

21. Ebbin and Kasper, *Citizen Groups*, pp. 130–38.

22. For the data in the following discussion of the industry's woes, see Rankin, "Troubled Nuclear Power," pp. 621–30.

23. Cf. Arlen J. Large, "Nuclear Power Industry and Agency Seek to Speed Procedures of Licensing Plants," *Wall Street Journal*, July 8, 1981, p. 46.

24. For a discussion of the reasons for the unhealthy state of the industry today, cf. Rankin, "Troubled Nuclear Power," p. 628.

25. This NRC estimate, contained in an agency document dated January 1, 1978, and reported in testimony by Daniel F. Ford and Robert D. Pollard of the Union of Concerned Scientists (UCS) before the Subcommittee on Energy and the Environment of the Committee on Interior and Insular Affairs, U.S. House of Representatives, on June 12, 1978, was provided by the UCS.

26. The transition was specified in the Energy Reorganization Act, P.L. 93–438 (1974).

27. Ebbin and Kasper, *Citizen Groups*, ch. 4.

28. According to a 1981 estimate, oil companies, including Kerr-McGee, Exxon, Conoco, Sohio, Gulf, and Arco, produce 37 percent of the national output of uranium oxide concentrate (the raw material then enriched by

the government). On the basis of a $30-per-pound price for mined uranium oxide, eight firms own about 50 percent of American uranium reserves. Among those eight, six are oil companies, with Kerr-McGee and Gulf Oil ranking one and two (Prast, *U.S. Energy Supplies*, pp. 17–18, 23–32). Despite extensive oil company holdings, the whole industry does *not* take a policy position on nuclear power.

29. Once in operation, nuclear reactors do not provide nearly the jobs-per-capital investment of other energy sources; their construction, however, does provide a large dividend in jobs. On employment payoffs of energy technologies, see R. Grossman, "Energy and Jobs," pp. 68–94.

30. As expressed by a UMW spokesman in a personal interview, June 30, 1978.

31. The picture gleaned from these interviews is a simplified version of industry participation. The general functional map is accurate, but particular details are missing. Time and resource constraints precluded me from exploring the roles of reactor vendors such as Westinghouse, General Electric, and Babcock-Wilcox, which maintain Washington offices, or delving into the activities of individual electric utilities. For corporate behavior, where oil companies become politically active, see below, ch. 5.

32. A spokesman for PIRG estimates that 80% of its political efforts in 1978 related to the NRC. In the past it had devoted a great deal more time to issues involving major oil companies. Personal interview, June 7, 1978.

33. This estimate is based on a comparison of the 1978 budget (reported in a personal interview with a UCS spokesman, July 1978) with a 1976 budget estimate of $139,000 reported in the *Boston Globe*, August 22, 1976.

34. The indicators are subject to two sources of measurement error: (1) underestimation of the governmental relations ability of an organization, e.g., a corporation, that maintains a physically small Washington operation but supplements it vigorously with home-office research, telephone or mail lobbying, and frequent Washington visits by headquarters personnel; (2) overestimation of the effort of an organization, e.g., a trade association headquartered in Washington that expends vast resources providing its members with services other than governmental relations. Nonetheless, these data are superior to the alternative of complete organizational budgets. A group headquartered in Washington is so located because governmental relations is the overriding function of the organization. Otherwise, different considerations would dictate its locations, and it would deal with the government through a Washington office serving only that purpose. The total annual expenditures of the Exxon Corporation, for example, would not provide a comparable indicator of their governmental relations effort. Such data bear on larger questions of political and economic power, and no doubt provide a gauge of supportive resources; however, they grossly overestimate corporate efforts to play administrative politics.

35. McFarland, *Public Interest Lobbies*, p. 68.

36. The environmental groups are Critical Mass, Friends of the Earth, NRDC, PIRG, and UCS.

37. This is particularly true for "informal rule making" that requires

only public notice of a proposed rule and opportunity for public comment (Administrative Procedures Act, 1946).

38. For the hybrid procedures, see Bauser, "Rulemaking Within the AEC," and the symposium articles by Steward, Byse, and Breyer, in "Vermont Yankee," pp. 1804–45.

39. On the propriety of ex parte communication, see White, *Reforming Regulations*, ch. 2; and see Stewart, "Vermont Yankee," pp. 1811–20, on the efforts of the NRC to base its decisions on the formal record.

40. E.g., the "GESMO" hearings of 1976 and 1977, and the nuclear decommissioning hearings of 1978.

41. This policy instrument is very popular with the federal government. By a recent count there were 29 "new style" social regulatory agencies, among them the Environmental Protection Agency, the Bureau of Land Management, the Mine Safety and Health Administration, and the Occupational Health and Safety Administration. Cf. White, *Reforming Regulation*, pp. 36–39.

42. The determination of the need for new generating capacity is left to the electric utilities and the state public utility commissions.

43. Although committees also practice oversight through "private" methods (phone calls, letters, and staff visits), there is no reason to believe that certain committees prefer these methods and that the number of hearings as an indicator of oversight is biased.

44. This figure is not simply half of the 21 hearings noted in Table 4.5 because the data cover only three-fourths of the 94th Congress.

45. The 1954 Atomic Energy Act said only that licenses would be required and that the Administrative Procedures Act should be followed. Nothing was said about the use of generic rule making or about the appropriateness of formal vs. informal procedures. See the Atomic Energy Act of 1954, P.L. 83–703, chs. 10, 16.

46. See Ebbin and Kasper, *Citizen Groups*, pp. 139–61.

47. The composition and governance of the NRC is specified in the Energy Reorganization Act of 1974, P.L. 93–438, Title II.

48. *1976 Congressional Quarterly Almanac*, p. 92.

49. *Ibid.*, pp. 162–66.

50. Cf. Davis, *Energy Politics*, pp. 197–201.

51. In a speech to the plenary session of the International Fuel Cycle Evaluation in October 1977. Cf. *Energy Policy*, p. 121.

52. *Ibid.*, pp. 105–14.

53. A spokesman for the Sierra Club revealed in a personal interview (June 7, 1978) that it had approved, either directly or tacitly, each of the nominations of NRC commissioners.

54. My discussion of standing is based on Karen Orren's "Standing to Sue," pp. 723–41, esp. p. 728.

55. The criterion was fashioned by Justice Douglas, writing for the majority in the decision of *Association of Data Processing Service Organizations v. Camp*, 397 US 150 (1970).

56. Cf. Orren, "Standing to Sue," pp. 727–31.

57. *Ibid.*, p. 733.

58. 354 F.2d 608 (2d Cir. 1965), and 405 US 727 (1972).

59. In *U.S. v. SCRAP* 412 US 669 (1973) the Supreme Court all but eliminated the obstacle of interest *groups* suing on behalf of general rather than individual interests. Cf. Orren, "Standing to Sue," pp. 738–39.

60. 449 F.2d 1109 (1971).

61. For example, in *Newman v. Piggie Park Enterprises* 390 US 400 and *Sims v. Amos* 340 F.Supp. 691, pursuant to the 1964 Civil Rights Act, legal fees were awarded to plaintiffs.

62. *La Raza Unida v. Volpe* 4 ERC 1797.

63. The committee was indicating no prejudice against the policy but rather a preference to permit the NRC to settle the issue itself. In contrast, Congress has explicitly provided for paid public participation at the Federal Trade Commission, the Consumer Product Safety Commission, and the Environmental Protection Agency. Cf. Paglin and Shor, "Regulatory Agency Responses," pp. 140–48.

64. Ruling on the issue of intervenor compensation in 1976, the NRC decided that it should offer compensation only if "it *cannot make* the required determination unless it extends financial assistance to certain interested parties," and "participation is *essential* to dispose of the matter before it" (emphasis added) (see *ibid.*, p. 144).

65. Richard B. Stewart is critical of the Supreme Court's decision ("Vermont Yankee," pp. 1805–22). For dissenting views of the decision, see the other symposium articles by Clark Byse and Stephen Breyer, in *ibid.*, pp. 1823–32 and 1833–45, respectively.

Chapter 5

1. P.L. 93–159 (1973). Although the EPAA passed Congress by wide margins, it owed much of its support to the extant crisis and the provision that it would expire in only sixteen months.

2. See MacAvoy, *Federal Energy Administration*, ch. 1; Willrich, *Administration*, ch. 6; and Mancke, *Squeaking By*, ch. 2.

3. All estimates from *Congressional Quarterly Almanac 1974*, p. 723.

4. P.L. 94–163.

5. Willrich, p. 152.

6. Upper tier oil included, besides new oil, the production from "stripper" wells that produce less than ten barrels per day, and "released" oil that had previously been exempted. The Energy Conservation and Production Act of 1976 (P.L. 94–385) subsequently exempted stripper oil from price regulation.

7. With a few exceptions the staff and leadership of the organizations sampled are accountable to their members. This is not to say that they are strictly democratic, or that all positions are subject to membership approval, although half of the membership organizations do adhere to such procedures. Rather, the organizations are accountable in the general sense that the leadership at least knows the views of the membership and hesitates to take a position unless there is at least a majority—typically, an overwhelm-

ing majority—in favor. The existence of a policy position is evidence, therefore, that the group has an important stake in an issue and wants that stake understood by government decision makers.

8. The Teamsters Union does not take a position, because its membership is divided. Many truck drivers view supply security as their primary goal, and deregulation as the best way of obtaining it; others take low prices as their major objective and therefore favor regulation.

9. The jurisdictional understanding between these groups was explained to me by a spokesperson for the Natural Gas Supply Committee in an interview, July 19, 1978.

10. P.L. 93–275 (May 7, 1954): quotations at sections 7 (i) (1) (c) and 7 (i) (1) (7s).

11. Figures given in congressional testimony by FEA General Counsel Robert Montgomery. Hearings [arranged chronologically in the Bibliography], June 3, 1975, p. 5.

12. Because it is difficult to measure the "quality" of written comments, I have no hard data on this estimate. Nonetheless, examination of reams of comments in the FEA's public reading room leaves the clear impression that the majority of comments are simply statements of demands and preferences, or unsubstantiated predictions of impacts; only a minority of them are supported by careful analysis.

13. The PEG was the only group that regarded formal participation as more influential.

14. The PEG and the NOJC, which believe influence is exerted largely during the period after publication of a hearing notice in the *Federal Register* and before the hearing.

15. Each group assigned only one or two of its executive branch specialists to the FEA or the ERA. The specialists' task was also to maintain contact with the Department of Interior, the EPA, and the Occupational Safety and Health Administration, among others.

16. Hearings, personally attended, before the Committee on Energy and Natural Resources, Senate, 95th Cong., 2nd sess., June 16, 1978.

17. Information supplied by a spokesperson for the Sun Company, an API member firm, in an interview, July 19, 1978.

18. Exxon claimed that it divided its time about equally between political and staff level contacts. The Washington Office of Gulf Oil concentrated its efforts on political administration, while its Houston office interacted with the staff.

19. Cf. Hearings, June 16 and July 10, 1978.

20. See Ch. 4, above, n. 34.

21. The National Congress of Petroleum Retailers was omitted only after repeated efforts to schedule an interview failed.

22. *Federal Register*, 39, no. 187 (Sept. 25, 1974), pp. 34395–96.

23. Because the meeting logs pertain to matters other than rule makings, they are not totally valid measures of informal contacts to influence general rules. If the indicator is biased, however, it should overrepresent the independent sector of the industry that dealt with the agency on thousands of requests for exceptions.

24. He did meet with some representatives of state governments who often advocated consumer interests.

25. Ascertained in interviews with six major oil companies and the API.

26. Because hearings are orchestrated by committee members, interest group appearances are not, strictly speaking, independent variables. Hearings are used, however, to establish a record—and as complete a record as possible. Consequently, it is reasonable to expect that all interested views will be expressed in hearings. See Sharkansky, "Appropriations Subcommittee," pp. 622–28.

27. The actions initiated in 1976 and 1977 were Energy Action: (1) residual fuel oil decontrol; (2) modification of small-refiner entitlement bias; (3) and (4) middle distillate oil decontrol; (5) naphtha, gas-oil, and "other product" decontrol; (6) and (7) naphtha jet fuel decontrol; (8) and (9) motor gasoline decontrol; (10) withdrawal of actions 8 and 9; (11) domestic crude oil composite price adjustment.

28. Hearings, April 1, 1977.

29. The final rule reflected the CFA's view of desirable standards for reimposing price controls and fulfilled their participation objective (interview, July 11, 1978).

30. This estimate is based on oil agency initiatives reported by all groups in the sample.

31. Oil burning utilities also qualify as commercial users vis-à-vis petroleum regulatory programs. Utility representatives had frequent contact with program administrators (see Tables 5.4 and 5.5); however, I found no indication that utilities were important targets of staff initiatives.

32. See Mancke, *Squeaking By*, pp. 21–47.

33. William A. Johnson, "Why U.S. Energy Policy Has Failed," in Kalter and Vogely, *Energy Supply*, p. 300.

34. Sworn testimony at hearing (personally attended) before Committee on Energy and Natural Resources, Senate, 95th Cong., 2nd sess., July 10, 1978. Quotations taken from committee transcript.

35. These remarks were made respectively by Scott Bush, assistant administrator for Office of Regulation and Emergency Planning, DOE, and Peter Holihan, industrial specialist, Division of Oil and Gas, Office of Resource Applications, DOE.

36. The precise effects on prices are hotly disputed by economists, but price reductions of some magnitude are definitely associated with the regulations. Cf. Cox and Wright, "Effects," pp. 1–13, and Phelps and Smith, *Petroleum Regulation*.

37. P.L. 94–163, Title IV, Section 403.

38. See text and n. 27 above. For a dissenting view, see Willrich, *Administration*, p. 195.

39. Calculated from General Accounting Office, *Problems*.

40. *Ibid.*

41. Rycroft, "Bureaucratic Performance," p. 625. The majors were monitored only in the aggregate by periodic checks on the "old-new" national ratio of crude oil runs. This procedure, however, did not permit detection of individual company violations.

42. Quoted in Larry Kramer,"Strike Force Hunts Oil Price Violators," *Washington Post,* July 14, 1978, p. F1.

43. Richard Halloran, "Gulf Oil to Pay $42 Million on Pricing," *New York Times,* July 28, 1978, p. D1.

44. Hearings, Dec. 11, 1974, p. 27.

45. Hearings, June 19 and 20, 1975, p. 13.

46. This position was established by the Ford White House; the inference that it resulted from major oil influence at the FEA is not warranted.

47. Hearings, April 1, 1977, pp. 7–8.

48. In 1977 ten integrated oil companies were among the twenty largest industrial corporations in the United States as measured by sales ("The Fortune Directory of the 500 Largest U.S. Industrial Corporations," *Fortune,* May 8, 1978, pp. 238–60).

49. Consumer: Energy Policy Task Force of the CFA, Energy Action, and the Citizen-Labor Energy Coalition; commercial user: PEG.

50. Energy Action is supported by a small group of philanthropists headed by the film actor, Paul Newman. The Energy Policy Task Force of the CFA and the Citizen-Labor Energy Coalition are small peak organizations of labor unions and other large consuming groups (see Ch. 3).

51. Reasonable estimates of the proportion of agency-group interactions involving consumers or commercial users can be obtained from Tables 5.4 and 5.5, and the reported frequency of interaction between groups and agency staff. Aggregating across Tables 5.4 and 5.5 consumers and commercial users were involved in 5% and 19% respectively of meetings between groups and the political administration. To estimate staff level interaction, assume that: (1) its volume is five times greater than the volume of political level interaction (which is reasonable, given the relatively large size of the staff), and (2) that the proportion of contacts by consumers and commercial users is half that at the political level (which again is reasonable, given the infrequent contacts recalled in interviews). These assumptions yield estimates of 2.5% and 9.6% of total staff contacts occupied by consumers and commercial users respectively. Pooling these estimates with those for the political level, it is reasonable to estimate that consumers and commercial users accounted for 2.9% and 11% of the total group-agency interactions, and the regulated industry for at least 85%.

52. For these changes, see Ch. 3.

53. Cf. Ch. 4, n. 43.

54. See, for example, Hearings, Dec. 11, 1974; April 10, 1974; and especially June 19 and 20, 1975. On obstruction: Hearings, April 9 and 11, May 6, 7, and 8, 1975.

55. See testimony by FEA Administrator John Sawhill in Hearings, Sept. 24, 1974, pp. 6–11.

56. Proposed in Energy Actions (8) and (9), January 1977.

57. Proposed in Energy Action (10), January 1977.

58. Cf. Hearings, Oct. 23, 1975, and April 1, 1977, pp. 7–8.

59. By 1974, when the FEA was created, liberalized rules of standing that emerged through the court decisions discussed in Ch. 4 already enabled all of the constituents of the oil regulators to sue. In addition, P.L. 93–275

explicitly provided for judicial review of all regulatory decisions (sec. 7 (i) (2)). On standing, cf. Ch. 4, text and nn. 56–57.

60. On court challenges, cf. Willrich, *Administration*, pp. 156–58.

61. On the "hard look" doctrine, cf. Stewart, in "Vermont Yankee," pp. 1805–22.

62. *Consumers Union v. Sawhill*, 393 F. Supp. 639 (D.D.C. 1975).

Chapter 6

1. Department of Energy, *Organization Fact Book*, pp. 7–8.

2. The estimated increase is based on actual outlays for energy R&D in FY74 of $739 million, and proposed FY80 budget authority for $4,471 million (*Budget 1976*, p. 93; *Budget 1980*, p. 126).

3. See Ch. 3 for the definition of "allocation" policy.

4. Political scientists are not in agreement on what policies qualify for the often-used label "distributive." The term was first defined by Theodore J. Lowi as part of a typology that also included "redistributive" and "regulatory" policies, and has since been redefined so many times that its meaning is ambiguous at best. This analysis therefore eschews the term in favor of policy benefit/cost characterizations that may or may not fit neat policy types. For the debate over policy typologies, see Ch. 2, n. 10.

5. See Arnold, *Congress*; Ferejohn, *Porkbarrel Politics*; and Rundquist, "Testing a Theory." Of these, Arnold provides the most sophisticated theory and the most appropriate statistical tests of congressional allocation decisions.

6. The oil and gas industry needs methods to increase the yield of domestic oil and gas formations, i.e., tertiary recovery techniques for extracting gas economically from "tight" (low permeability) reservoirs in the Rocky Mountain states and the Midwest. All other means of increasing domestic oil and gas production involve regulatory and economic policy. See Kash et al., *Our Energy Future*, pp. 145–60 and 203–11.

7. "Structure," pp. 83–86.

8. On this distinction, cf. Lovins, *Soft Energy Paths*, ch. 2.

9. The AGA, which claims the highest rate of administrative liaison in this sector, works regularly with DOE on a $30 million coal gasification project. Gulf Oil Corporation, which claims frequent agency intervention, hold nine R&D contracts and attributes most of its liaison to "grantsmanship" work.

10. The only exception is a coal gasification plant run by the NCA for the government.

11. The ANEC is not a trade association but primarily a political interest group. It lacks the analytical capacity and data resources of a trade association, but claims to provide advice at the gestation stage of all relevant projects, and frequently on ongoing projects. Its input is made, however, at a higher level of the hierarchy than the staff level employed by trade associations.

12. Reported by the legislative director of Friends of the Earth (interview, June 12, 1978).

13. On procurement, see C. W. Borklund, "What Makes Procurement Unique at the Energy Department," *Government Executive*, January 1978, pp. 13–17.

14. Multi-million dollar contracts for demonstration projects have been awarded to major corporations such as General Electric, Westinghouse, Babcock & Wilcox, and Gulf Oil, but these are exceptional. See Daniel Guttman, "The Energy Hustle," *New Republic*, March 11, 1978, pp. 16–19.

15. The absence of any definite R&D plan is widely acknowledged. Cf. Kash et al., *Energy Future*; and Holloman and Grenon, *Energy Research*.

16. The research literature on budgeting is voluminous, and the empirical support for incremental short-cuts to budget decisions equally extensive. See especially Wildavsky, *Politics*.

17. See Natchez and Bupp, "Policy and Priority."

18. See Wildavsky, *Politics*, pp. 16–18.

19. This characterization of OMB-agency negotiations is the conventional wisdom in the budgeting literature. See *ibid.*, pp. 35–47, for a cogent explanation.

20. Studies of agency program requests are few, but a recent analysis of the Department of Agriculture indicates that agencies are usually capable of maintaining their priorities by anticipating OMB evaluation routines. See LeLoup and Moreland, "Agency Strategies."

21. For their policy differences, see Chs. 4 and 7.

22. The key federal level support for solar energy is reputedly exercised through an "insiders' lobby" in Congress, composed of key congressional staff, several congressmen, and a variety of interest groups. See "Solar Energy—Will Federal Policy Work to Let the Sunshine In?" *National Journal*, April 15, 1978, pp. 592–95.

23. On market shares, see Duchesneau, *Competition*, p. 75. The first, second, third, fourth, and thirteenth ranked coal producers in 1972 were owned respectively by Kennecott-Copper, Continental Oil, Occidental Petroleum, Standard Oil of Ohio, and Gulf Oil. Other *Fortune 500* corporations among the top twenty coal producers in 1972 included Pittston Coal (ranked 4th), Amax (5th), U.S. Steel (6th), Bethlehem Mines (7th), Eastern Associated Coal (8th), North American Coal (9th), General Dynamics (11th), and Westmoreland Coal (12th). See Duchesneau, *Competition*, pp. 83–85, and *Fortune*, May 8, 1978, pp. 238–60.

24. The concentration levels for uranium milling and mining are for 1971, as reported in Duchesneau, *Competition*, p. 87. Of the numerous firms involved in nuclear plant construction, three—General Electric, Westinghouse, and Babcock & Wilcox—had produced every nuclear reactor in operation in the U.S. as of 1981.

25. Edison Electric Institute, *EEI Pocketbook*.

26. The NCA represents 60 percent of all domestic coal production. The EEI has 200 of the 250 investor-owned utilities as members. The Atomic Industrial Forum and the ANEC are supported by all of the major reactor vendors, nuclear engineering firms, nuclear construction companies, and electric utilities. Even two subsectors, with many small firms, have succeeded in organizing strong associations: the APPA represents 85 percent of the

1,900 municipally owned utilities, and the NRECA represents virtually all 1,000 eligible cooperatives. Both associations, nonetheless, have far easier organizational tasks than do interests with tens of thousands, or even millions, of prospective members.

27. A second, regular bureaucratic participant from this sector, the United Technologies Corporation, is not an interest association and therefore does not operate under the collective action constraints described by the organizational theory. A private firm engages unilaterally in administrative liaison when it is profitable to do so. United Technologies is a large industrial conglomerate, ranked 34th on the 1977 *Fortune 500* list, with large investments in "hard path" renewable energy technologies such as fuel cells and centralized photovoltaic generators. Many large firms in the electric power sector, such as General Electric and Babcock & Wilcox, are also active in bureaucratic politics. Because those firms are not included in the sample of that sector, United Technologies should not be used in this sectoral comparison.

28. See Stobaugh and Yergin, *Energy Future*, ch. 7, esp. pp. 189–90.

29. *Ibid.*, p. 206.

30. See *ibid*, ch. 6; Wilson, *Global Prospects*; Socolow, "The Coming Age," pp. 239–89; and Schipper and Darmstadter, "Logic of Energy Conservation," pp. 41–50.

31. See Kash et al., *Energy Future*, ch. 8, and Stobaugh and Yergin, *Energy Future*, ch. 8, for conservation R&D proposals.

32. Roger Sant, quoted in Stobaugh and Yergin, *Energy Future*, p. 140.

33. See Moe, *Organization*, ch. 8.

34. See below, Ch. 7, for elaboration.

35. Both Friends of the Earth and the Sierra Club reported several opportunities to grant approval of Carter nominations. Further evidence of the administration's courtship of the environmental community is reflected in the 1979 nomination of Denis Hayes, organizer of Earth Day 1970 and Sun Day 1978, to become director of the federal Solar Energy Research Institute.

Chapter 7

1. On this seemingly logical approach to policy making, see especially Braybrooke and Lindblom, *Strategy*; Lindblom, *Politics*; and Wildavsky, *Speaking Truth*.

2. S. Cohen, *Capitalist Planning*, p. xv.

3. For an introduction to coercive planning, most common in socialist systems, see Lindblom, *Politics*, parts VI, VII.

4. On this method, traditionally employed in the French economy, see S. Cohen, *Capitalist Planning*.

5. Advocated by Shonfield (*Modern Capitalism*).

6. If we define planning generously as any long-term, goal-directed policy making, the United States has surely practiced it. But if we adhere to stricter definitions that preserve the analytical integrity of the concept, planning is most uncommon in the national government. Cf. Wildavsky, "Planning."

7. The effects of the liberal ideological tradition on American policy making are analyzed most perceptively in Rimlinger, *Welfare Policy*, part I.

8. P.L. 95–91; Title VIII, section 801.

9. *Ibid.*, Part d.

10. It has been argued that a multi-sector national planning committee would be useful for formulating U.S. energy policy. Such a committee would ostensibly clarify the interdependencies among contending energy interests, reveal mutual interests, and facilitate broad compromise. See Lindberg, *Energy Syndrome*, pp. 373–74.

11. Department of Energy, *Organization Fact Book*, pp. 11, 41.

12. *Energy Policy*, p. 34.

13. An insightful technical critique of the energy model used in the planning process is presented in Commoner, *Politics of Energy*, ch. 2.

14. Cf. Quade, *Analysis*, esp. ch. 1.

15. Cf. Wildavsky, *Speaking Truth*, ch. 10.

16. For these data and the comments summarized below, see Executive Office, *National Energy Plan*.

17. Less than 4 percent of the people polled during the presidential campaign, between October 22 and 25, 1976, considered the energy crisis "the most important problem facing this country today." Six months later (March 18–21, 1977), after no significant change in the situation, the proportion had jumped to 23 percent. *Gallup Opinion Index* 137 (Sept. 1976): 29, and 142 (May 1977): 24.

18. Even with strong public support President Reagan had to court assiduously the support of individual congressmen, and especially conservative Democrats, to achieve victory on the 1981 budget reconciliation bill and 25 percent income tax reduction. Cf. Peters et al., "Reagan Budget."

19. On Carter's congressional relations problems generally, see Ranney, "Carter Administration."

20. The House Commerce and Ways and Means committees had in previous years held favorable hearings on utility rate reform, natural gas pricing, and energy tax proposals similar to those recommended in the National Energy Plan.

21. The sectors allotted mini-conferences included consumer groups; the auto industry; labor unions; builders; architects and planners; financiers, bankers, and investors; coal producers; nuclear energy producers; public utilities commissioners; privately owned and publicly owned utilities; small energy producers (geothermal, solar, wind, hydro-electric, and resource recovery); industrial and business energy users; oil and gas producers; agricultural interests; petroleum retailers and marketers; environmentalists; service industry energy users; state and local officials; education representatives; low and fixed income representatives; state energy offices; and nineteen citizens.

22. The environmental community supported the plan wholeheartedly during 1977 congressional deliberations, but refrained from publicly endorsing it to avoid the appearance of being co-opted. According to a spokesperson for the Environmental Policy Center, environmental groups feared grass-roots criticism of overt cooperation with the administration.

23. See S. D. Freeman, *Energy*, ch. 10.

24. The substance of the interactions of the single financial institution representative cannot be viewed as a sector-wide exception because the sector was not adequately sampled.

25. Paraphrased from NCA interview, June 29, 1978.

26. On the causes of congressional opposition, see *Energy Policy*, pp. 33–37.

27. The National Energy Plan was composed of five major sections consisting of numerous related proposals: (1) natural gas pricing proposals retaining regulation but permitting higher prices; (2) a crude oil equalization tax designed to promote conservation through higher energy prices, but providing revenue to the government, rather than the oil companies, to be used for rebates to low-income consumers; (3) coal conversion proposals to shift utilities and industry from oil and gas to coal usage; (4) conservation taxes and tax credits; (5) utility rate reform. The prolonged conflict centered around the first two sections.

28. Cf. Oppenheimer, "Policy Effects."

29. The group roles were ascertained in interviews, and the conference process analyzed on the basis of the interviews. My interpretation is corroborated in *Energy Policy*, pp. 13–37.

30. See Richard Corrigan, "A Funny Thing Happened on the Way. to Phase II," *National Journal*, May 6, 1978, pp. 708–11.

31. Energy Security Act: P.L. 96–294, June 3, 1980.

32. Richard Corrigan, "The Department of Energy's Continuing, Confusing Shakedown," *National Journal*, Feb. 4, 1978, p. 184.

Conclusion

1. See generally Truman, *Governmental Process*, and specifically D. H. Davis, *Energy Politics*.

2. See Schmitter, "Corporatism."

3. The phrase "public mobilization of bias" in the heading was originated by E. E. Schattschneider in *The Semi-Sovereign People*, ch. 4, esp. p. 71.

4. See especially Olson, *Logic*; Salisbury, "Exchange Theory"; and Moe, *Organization*.

5. Olson and Salisbury first explicated these normative consequences, but important qualifications have been added by Moe.

6. Other multi-industry regulatory agencies that do not face a unified opposition include the FTC, the Occupational Health and Safety Administration, and the Consumer Product Safety Commission.

7. See Ackerman et al., *Uncertain Search*.

8. Although this policy, like price controls, would discourage conservation and encourage imports, the rewards for consumption would be weaker because they would be deferred until income taxes are paid, and the direct subsidy for imports through the entitlement program would be eliminated. To make adjustment to the OPEC cartel equitable, windfall profits on domestic oil could also be taxed.

9. The selective incentive value of strategies should be reflected in greater organizational resources in the future.

10. From the 1950s, see especially J. L. Freeman, *Political Process*; Maass, *Muddy Waters*; and Bernstein, *Regulating Business*. Among recent work on environmental models of bureaucracy see, on congressional influence: Ferejohn, *Porkbarrel Politics*; Fiorina, *Congress*; and Arnold, *Congress*. On bureaucratic bargaining: Niskanen, *Bureaucracy*; Marwick, *Theory*. On presidential influence: Fisher, *Presidential Spending Power*; and Neustadt, *Presidential Power*. On judicial impacts: Bardach and Kagan, *Going by the Book*.

11. In the 1978 national election the Republicans gained 11 seats in the House and 3 seats in the Senate, to reduce the Democratic advantage to 276–159 and 58–41 respectively. This trend continued in 1980 with the Republicans taking control of the Senate 36–46, increasing their House seats to 192 and winning the presidency. The year 1978 also saw the fruition of the tax revolt. In California Proposition 13, an initiative that slashed property taxes to 1 percent of market value, won a large majority at the polls.

12. Cf. Dodd and Schott, *Congress*, ch. 5.

13. Cf. Allison, *Essence of Decision*, and Steinbruner, *Cybernetic Theory*.

BIBLIOGRAPHY

Aberbach, Joel D. "Changes in Congressional Oversight." *American Behavioral Scientist,* 22 (May/June 1979): 493–515.

Ackerman, Bruce A; Ackerman, Susan Rose; and Sawyer, James W., Jr. *The Uncertain Search for Environmental Quality.* New York: Free Press, 1974.

Adelman, M. A. *The World Petroleum Market.* Baltimore: Johns Hopkins University Press, 1972.

Alford, Robert R. *Health Care Politics: Ideological and Interest Group Barriers to Reform.* Chicago: University of Chicago Press, 1975.

Allison, Graham T. *Essence of Decision.* Boston: Little, Brown, 1971.

Almond, Gabriel. "A Comparative Study of Interest Groups and the Political Process." *American Political Science Review,* 52 (March 1958): 270–82.

Arnold, R. Douglas. *Congress and the Bureaucracy.* New Haven: Yale University Press, 1979.

Bachrach, Peter, and Baratz, Morton S. *Power and Poverty: Theory and Practice.* New York: Oxford University Press, 1970.

Bailey, Stephen. *Congress Makes a Law.* New York: Columbia University Press, 1950.

Bardach, Eugene, and Kagan, Robert A. *Going by the Book: The Problem of Regulatory Unreasonableness.* Philadelphia: Temple University Press, 1982.

Baren, Paul A. *The Political Economy of Growth.* New York: Modern Reader Paperbacks, 1957.

Barry, Brian M. *Sociologists, Economists and Democracy.* London: Collier-Macmillan, 1970.

Bauer, Raymond A.; Pool, Ithiel DeSola; and Dexter, Lewis Anthony. *American Business and Public Policy: The Politics of Foreign Trade.* Cambridge: Aldine, 1972.

Bauser, Michael A. "The Development of Rulemaking Within the AEC: The NRC's Valuable Legacy." *Administrative Law Review,* 27 (Spring 1975): 165–84.

Beer, Samuel H. *British Politics in the Collectivist Age.* New York: Knopf, 1969.

Bentley, Arthur F. *The Process of Government.* Chicago: University of Chicago Press, 1908.

Benveniste, Guy. *The Politics of Expertise.* Berkeley: Glendessary Press, 1972.

————. *Regulation and Planning.* San Francisco: Boyd & Fraser, 1981.

Bernstein, Marver H. *Regulating Business by Independent Commission.* Princeton, N.J.: Princeton University Press, 1955.

Berry, Jeffrey M. *Lobbying for the People.* Princeton, N.J.: Princeton University Press, 1977.

Bibby, John F. "Congress' Neglected Function." In *Republican Papers*, edited by Melvin Laird, pp. 477–88. New York: Praeger, 1968.

Blair, John M. *The Control of Oil.* New York: Vintage Books, 1976.

Bohi, Douglas R., and Russell, Milton. *Limiting Oil Imports.* Baltimore: Johns Hopkins University Press, 1978.

Braybrooke, David, and Lindblom, Charles E. *A Strategy of Decision.* New York: Free Press, 1963.

Breyer, Stephen G., and MacAvoy, Paul W. *Energy Regulation by the Federal Power Commission.* Washington, D.C.: Brookings Institution, 1974.

Brown, David S. "The Management of Advisory Committees: An Assignment for the 70s." *Public Administration Review*, 32 (July/August 1972): 334–42.

Bryson, Lyman. "Notes on a Theory of Advice." *Political Science Quarterly*, 66 (1951): 321–39.

Budget of the United States Government, 1976, 1977, 1978, 1979, 1980. Washington, D.C.: U.S. Government Printing Office.

Burns, James McGregor. *Deadlock of Democracy.* Englewood Cliffs, N.J.: Prentice-Hall, 1963.

Cameron, Juan. "James Schlesinger in Dubious Battle." *Fortune Magazine*, Feb. 27, 1978, pp. 36–44.

Campbell, Angus, et al. *The American Voter.* New York: Wiley, 1960.

Cary, William L. *Politics and the Regulatory Agencies.* New York: McGraw-Hill, 1967.

Cater, Douglas. *Power in Washington.* New York: Random House, 1964.

Chandler, Alfred D., Jr. *The Visible Hand.* Cambridge, Mass.: Harvard University Press, 1977.

Childs, Marquis. *The Farmer Takes a Hand.* Garden City, N.Y.: Doubleday, 1952.

Clark, Peter B., and Wilson, James Q. "Incentive Systems: A Theory of Organizations." *Administrative Science Quarterly*, 6 (Sept. 1961): 129–66.

Cockrell, William F., Jr. "Federal Regulation of Energy: Evolution of the Exceptions Process." *Administrative Law Review*, 27 (Summer 1975): 233–53.

Cohen, Bernard C. *The Political Process and Foreign Policy.* Princeton, N.J.: Princeton University Press, 1957.

Cohen, Stephen S. *Modern Capitalist Planning: The French Model.* Berkeley: University of California Press, 1977.

Cole, G.D.H. *Guild Socialism Restated.* New York: Frederick A. Stokes, 1921.

Committee on Interior and Insular Affairs, United States Senate. 93rd Congress, 1st session, 1973. *History of Federal Energy Organization.*

Commoner, Barry. *The Politics of Energy.* New York: Knopf, 1979.

———. *The Poverty of Power.* New York: Bantam Books, 1977.

Congressional Quarterly Almanac 1974, 1976, 1978. Washington, D.C.: Congressional Quarterly, Inc.

Cox, James C., and Wright, Arthur W. "The Effects of Crude Oil Price Controls, Entitlements and Taxes on Refined Product Prices and Energy Independence." *Land Economics,* 54 (Feb. 1978): 1–13.

Cronin, Thomas E. *The State of the Presidency.* Boston: Little, Brown, 1980.

———, and Thomas, Norman C. "Federal Advisory Processes: Advice and Discontent." *Science,* 171 (Feb. 26, 1971): 771–79.

Cushman, Robert. *The Independent Regulatory Commissions.* Revised edition. New York: Octagon Books, 1972.

Cutler, Lloyd N., and Johnson, David R. "Regulation and the Political Process." *Yale Law Journal,* 84 (June 1975): 1395–1418.

Cyert, Richard M., and March, James G. *A Behavioral Theory of the Firm.* Englewood Cliffs, N.J.: Prentice-Hall, 1963.

Dahl, Robert A. *A Preface to Democratic Theory.* Chicago: University of Chicago Press, 1956.

———. *Who Governs? Democracy and Power in an American City.* New Haven: Yale University Press, 1961.

Davidson, Roger H., and Oleszek, Walter J. *Congress Against Itself.* Bloomington: Indiana University Press, 1977.

Davis, David Howard. *Energy Politics.* 2nd ed. New York: St. Martin's Press, 1978.

Davis, Kenneth Culp. *Discretionary Justice.* Urbana: University of Illinois Press, 1971.

deCarmoy, Guy. *Energy for Europe: Economic and Political Implications.* Washington, D.C.: American Enterprise Institute, 1977.

Department of Energy. *Organization and Functions Fact Book.* Washington, D.C.: United States Department of Energy, 1977.

Dodd, Lawrence, and Oppenheimer, Bruce I., eds. *Congress Reconsidered.* Washington, D.C.: Congressional Quarterly Press, 1981.

Dodd, Lawrence, and Schott, Richard L. *Congress and the Administrative State.* New York: Wiley, 1979.

Downs, Anthony. *Inside Bureaucracy.* Boston: Little, Brown, 1966.

———. "Up and Down with Ecology: The Issue Attention Cycle." *The Public Interest* (1972): 38–50.

Drew, Elizabeth. "The Energy Bazaar." *New Yorker,* July 21, 1975, pp. 35–72.

Duchesneau, Thomas D. *Competition in the U.S. Energy Industry.* Cambridge, Mass.: Ballinger, 1975.

Ebbin, Steven, and Kasper, Raphael. *Citizen Groups and the Nuclear Power Controversy.* Cambridge: MIT Press, 1974.

Eckstein, Harry. *Pressure Group Politics: The Case of the British Medical Association.* Stanford, Calif.: Stanford University Press, 1960.

Edelman, Murray. *The Symbolic Uses of Politics.* Urbana: University of Illinois Press, 1964.

Edison Electric Institute. *EEI Pocketbook of Electricity Industry Statistics.* New York: Edison Electric Institute, 1978.

Eidenberg, Eugene, and Morey, Roy D. *An Act of Congress: The Legislative Process and the Making of Education Policy.* New York: Norton, 1969.

Elvander, Nils. *Interest Organizations in Sweden Today.* Lund: Gleerups, 1969.

"Energy Advisers: An Analysis of Federal Advisory Committees Dealing with Energy." Subcommittee on Reports, Accounting, and Management of the Committee on Governmental Affairs, United States Senate. 95th Cong., 2nd sess., March 1977.

Energy Policy. Washington, D.C.: Congressional Quarterly, Inc., 1979.

Engler, Robert. *The Brotherhood of Oil.* Chicago: University of Chicago Press, 1977.

————. *The Politics of Oil.* New York: Macmillan, 1961.

Executive Office of the President/Energy Policy and Planning. *The National Energy Plan: Summary of Public Participation.* Washington, D.C.: U.S. Government Printing Office, 1977.

Federal Energy Regulatory Team. *Federal Energy Regulation: An Organizational Study.* U.S. Government Publication (April 1974).

Federal Register, 39, no. 187, pp. 34395–96. Washington, D.C.: Government Printing Office, Sept. 25, 1974.

Fenno, Richard F., Jr. *Congressmen in Committees.* Boston: Little, Brown, 1973.

————. "U.S. House Members in Their Constituencies: An Exploration." *American Political Science Review,* 71 (Sept. 1977): 883–917.

Ferejohn, John. *Porkbarrel Politics.* Stanford, Calif.: Stanford University Press, 1974.

Fiorina, Morris P. "The Case of the Vanishing Marginals: The Bureaucracy Did It." *American Political Science Review,* 71 (March 1977): 177–81.

————. *Congress: Keystone of the Washington Establishment.* New Haven: Yale University Press, 1977.

Fisher, Louis. *Presidential Spending Power.* Princeton, N.J.: Princeton University Press, 1975.

Ford Foundation National Energy Project. *A Time to Choose.* Cambridge, Mass.: Ballinger, 1974.

Freeman, J. Lieper. *The Political Process.* New York: Random House, 1955.

Freeman, S. David. *Energy: The New Era.* New York: Vintage Books, 1974.

Frolich, Norman; Oppenheimer, Joe A.; and Young, Oran R. *Political Leadership and Collective Goods.* Princeton, N.J.: Princeton University Press, 1971.

Froman, Lewis A., Jr. "The Categorization of Policy Contents." *Political Science and Public Policy.* Ed. Austin Ranney. Chicago: Markham, 1968.

Gallaway, George. *History of the House of Representatives.* New York: Crowell, 1962.

Gellhorn, Ernest. "Public Participation in Administrative Proceedings." *Yale Law Journal,* 81 (Jan. 1972): 359–404.

General Accounting Office. *Problems in Federal Energy Administration's Compliance and Enforcement Effort.* Washington, D.C.: Government Printing Office, 1974.

George, Alexander L. "Case Studies and Theory Development: The Method of Structured, Focused Comparison." In *Diplomacy: New Approaches in History, Theory, and Policy.* Ed. Paul Gordon Lauren. New York: Free Press, 1979.

_____. *Presidential Decisionmaking in Foreign Policy: The Effective Use of Information and Advice.* Boulder, Colo.: Westview Press, 1980.

Gilmour, Robert S. "Political Barriers to a National Energy Policy." In *Proceedings of the American Academy of Political Science 1973–75,* 31 (Dec. 1973): 183–94.

Green, Harold P., and Rosenthal, Alan. *Government of the Atom.* New York: Atherton, 1963.

Grossman, Joel. *Lawyers and Judges: The A.B.A. and the Politics of Judicial Selection.* New York: Wiley, 1965.

Grossman, Richard. "Energy and Jobs." In *Sun!,* pp. 68–94. Ed. Stephen Lyons. San Francisco: Friends of the Earth, 1978.

Grupp, Fred W. "Personal Satisfaction Derived from Membership in the John Birch Society." *Western Political Quarterly,* 24 (1971): 79–84.

Hacker, Andrew. "Pressure Politics in Pennsylvania: The Truckers vs. the Railroads." In *The Uses of Power: Seven Cases in American Politics.* Ed. Alan Westin. New York: Harcourt, Brace and World, 1962.

Hall, Donald R. *Cooperative Lobbying: The Power of Pressure.* Tucson: University of Arizona Press, 1969.

Hall, Robert E., and Pindyck, Robert S. "The Conflicting Goals of National Energy Policy." *The Public Interest,* Winter 1977: 3–14.

Halperin, Morton H. *Bureaucratic Politics and Foreign Policy.* Washington, D.C.: Brookings Institution, 1974.

Hamilton, Walton. *The Politics of Industry.* New York: Knopf, 1957.

Hammond, Susan W., and Fox, Harrison W., Jr. *Congressional Staffs: The Invisible Force in American Lawmaking.* New York: Free Press, 1977.

Harris, Joseph P. *Congressional Control of Administration.* Washington, D.C.: Brookings Institution, 1964.

Hearings: Before the Subcommittee on Communications and Power of the Committee on Interstate and Foreign Commerce. "Emergency Petroleum Allocation Act Extension." House of Representatives, 93rd Congress, 2nd session, Sept. 24, 1974.

_____ Before the Subcommittee on Reorganization, Research, and International Organizations of the Committee on Government Operations. "Enforcement and Compliance of FEA Oil Regulations." U.S. Senate, 93rd Congress, 2nd session, December 11, 1974.

_____ Before the Subcommittee on Oversight and Investigations of the Committee on Interstate and Foreign Commerce. "FEA Enforcement Policies." United States House of Representatives, 94th Congress, 1st session, April 9 and 11, May 6, 7, and 8, 1975.

_____ Before the Subcommittee on Investigations of the Committee on Government Operations. "FEA Enforcement Activities." U.S. Senate, 94th Congress, 1st session, April 10, 1975.

_____ Before the Committee on Interior and Insular Affairs. "Oversight—Federal Energy Administration Programs." U.S. Senate, 94th Congress, 1st Session, April 18 and May 19, 1975.

_____ Before the Subcommittee on Separation of Powers, the Committee on the Judiciary. "Congressional Oversight of Administrative Agencies (FEA)." U.S. Senate, 94th Congress, 1st session, June 3, 1975.

_____ Before the Subcommittee on Administrative Practice and Procedure, Committee on the Judiciary. "FEA: Enforcement of Petroleum Regulations: Hearings." U.S. Senate, June 19 and 20, 1975.

_____ Before the Subcommittee on Interior and Related Agencies of the Committee on Appropriations. U.S. Senate, 94th Congress, 1st session, Oct. 23, 1975.

_____ Before a Subcommittee of the Committee on Government Operations. "Proposed Presidential Consumer Representation Plans." U.S. House of Representatives, 94th Congress, 2nd session, Feb. 23 and Mar. 9, 1976.

_____ Before the Subcommittee on Administrative Law and Governmental Relations of the Committee on the Judiciary. "Government in the Sunshine." U.S. House of Representatives, 94th Congress, 2nd session, Mar. 24 and 25, 1976.

_____ Before the Subcommittee on Administrative Law and Governmental Relations of the Committee on the Judiciary. "Public Participation in Agency Proceedings." U.S. House of Representatives, 95th Congress, 1st session, March 30 and 31, and April 1, 27, and 28, 1977.

_____ Before the Committee on Interstate and Foreign Commerce. U.S. House of Representatives, 95th Congress, 1st session, April 1, 1977.

_____ Before the Subcommittee on Energy and Power of the Committee on Interstate and Foreign Commerce. "FEA Authorization—Fiscal Year 1978." House of Representatives, 95th Congress, 1st session, April 1, 1977.

_____ Before the Committee on Energy and Natural Resources. U.S. Senate, 95th Congress, 2nd session, June 16 and July 10, 1978.

Heclo, Hugh. *A Government of Strangers: Executive Politics in Washington.* Washington, D.C.: Brookings Institution, 1977.

_____. "Issue Networks and the Executive Establishment." In *The New American Political System.* Ed. Anthony King. Washington, D.C.: American Enterprise Institute, 1978.

_____. *Modern Social Politics in Britain and Sweden.* New Haven: Yale University Press, 1974.

_____. *Studying the Presidency: A Report to the Ford Foundation.* New York: Ford Foundation, 1977.

Heisler, Martin O., and Kvavik, Robert B. "Patterns of European Politics: The 'European Polity' Model." In *Politics in Europe.* Ed. Martin O. Heisler. New York: David McKay Co., Inc., 1974.

Henry, Nicholas. "Paradigms of Public Adminstration." *Public Adminis-tration Review*, 35 (July/August 1975): 378–86.

Herring, E. Pendleton. *Group Representation Before Congress*. Baltimore: Johns Hopkins University Press, 1929.

House of Representatives. "Committee Reform Amendments of 1974." 93rd Congress, 2nd sess. (1974). House of Representatives Report 93–916, pp. 247–55.

Huber, Hans. "Swiss Democracy." In *Democracy in a Changing Society*. Ed. Henry W. Ehrmann. New York: Praeger, 1964.

Hunter, Floyd. *Community Power Structure: A Study of Decision Makers*. Chapel Hill: University of North Carolina Press, 1953.

Huntington, Samuel P. "Clientelism: A Study in Administrative Politics." Ph.D. dissertation, Harvard University, 1950.

—————. "The Marasmus of the ICC: The Commission, the Railroads, and the Public Interest." *Yale Law Journal*, 61 (April 1952): 467–509.

Jaffe, Louis L. *Administrative Law*. Englewood Cliffs, N.J.: Prentice-Hall, 1959.

Kalter, Robert J., and Vogely, William A., eds. *Energy Supply and Govern-ment Policy*. Ithaca, N.Y.: Cornell University Press, 1976.

Kariel, Henry. *The Decline of American Democracy*. Stanford, Calif.: Stanford University Press, 1961.

Kash, Don E., et al. *Our Energy Future*. Norman: University of Oklahoma Press, 1976.

Kent, Paul G. "Energy Supply." In *The Political Economy of Energy Policy: A Projection for Capitalist Society*. Ed. Jeffrey R. Hammarlund and Leon N. Lindberg. Madison, Wis.: Institute for Environmental Stud-ies, 1976.

Key, V. O., Jr. *Public Opinion and American Democracy*. New York: Knopf, 1961.

Kingsley, Sidney G. "The Licensing of Nuclear Power Reactors in the U.S." *Atomic Energy Law Journal*, 7 (Fall 1965): 309–52.

Kjellberg, Francesco. "Do Policies (Really) Determine Politics? And Even-tually How?" *Policy Studies Journal*, 5 (Special Issue, 1977): 554–69.

Kohlmeier, Louis. *The Regulators*. New York: Harper and Row, 1970.

Krislov, Samuel. "The Amicus Curiae Brief: From Friendship to Advoca-cy." *Yale Law Journal*, 72 (1963): 694–721.

—————. *Representative Bureaucracy*. Englewood Cliffs, N.J.: Prentice-Hall, 1974.

Kvavik, Robert B. "Interest Groups in a Cooptive Political System: The Case of Norway." In *Politics in Europe*. Ed. Martin O. Heisler. New York: McKay, 1974.

—————. *Interest Groups in Norwegian Politics*. Oslo: Universitetsvorlaget, 1976.

Landau, Martin. "The Concept of Decision-Making in the 'Field' of Public Administration." In *Concepts and Issues in Administrative Behavior*. Ed. Sidney Mailich and Edward H. Van Ness. Englewood Cliffs, N.J.: Prentice-Hall, 1962.

Landis, James. *The Administrative Process*. New Haven: Yale University Press, 1938.

308   *Bibliography*

Latham, Earl. *The Group Basis of Politics: A Study in Basing Point Legislation.* Ithaca, N.Y.: Cornell University Press, 1952.

LeLoup, Lance T., and Moreland, William B. "Agency Strategies and Executive Review: The Hidden Politics of Budgeting." *Public Administration Review,* 38 (May/June 1978): 232–39.

Lindberg, Leon N., ed. *The Energy Syndrome: Comparing National Responses to the Energy Crisis.* Lexington, Mass.: Heath, 1977.

_____. *Stress and Contradiction in Modern Capitalism.* Lexington, Mass.: Heath, 1975.

Lindblom, Charles E. *Politics and Markets.* New York: Basic Books, 1977.

Livingston, William S.; Dodd, Lawrence C.; and Schott, Richard L., eds. *The Presidency and the Congress.* Austin: Lyndon B. Johnson School of Public Affairs, 1979.

Lockhard, Duane. *New England State Politics.* Princeton, N.J.: Princeton University Press, 1959.

Lorwin, Val R. "Segmented Pluralism: Ideological Cleavages and Political Cohesion in Smaller European Democracies." *Comparative Politics,* 3 (Jan. 1971): 141–75.

Lovins, Amory B. *Soft Energy Paths: Toward a Durable Peace.* Cambridge, Mass.: Ballinger, 1977.

Lowi, Theodore J. "American Business, Public Policy, Case Studies and Political Theory," *World Politics,* 16 (1964): 676–715.

_____. *The End of Liberalism.* 2nd ed. New York: Norton, 1979.

_____. "Four Systems of Policy, Politics, and Choice." *Public Administration Review,* 32 (July/August 1972): 298–310.

Maass, Arthur. *Muddy Waters.* Cambridge, Mass.: Harvard University Press, 1951.

MacAvoy, Paul. *Federal Energy Administration Regulation.* Washington, D.C.: American Enterprise Institute, 1977.

McConnell, Grant. *Private Power and American Democracy.* New York: Knopf, 1966; Vintage Books, 1970.

_____. *Steel and the Presidency—1962.* New York: Norton, Inc., 1963.

McFarland, Andrew S. *Public Interest Lobbies.* Washington, D.C.: American Enterprise Institute, 1976.

Mancke, Richard B. *The Failure of U.S. Energy Policy.* New York: Columbia University Press, 1974.

_____. *Squeaking By: U.S. Energy Policy Since the Embargo.* New York: Columbia University Press, 1976.

Manley, John F. *The Politics of Finance.* Boston: Little, Brown, 1970.

March, James A., and Simon, Herbert A. *Organizations.* New York: Wiley, 1958.

Marmor, Theodore. *The Politics of Medicare.* Chicago: Aldine, 1970.

Marsh, David. "On Joining Interest Groups." *British Journal of Political Science,* 6 (1976): 257–72.

Marwick, Donald P. *A Theory of Public Bureaucracy.* Cambridge, Mass.: Harvard University Press, 1975.

Meijer, Hans. "Bureaucracy and Policy Formulation in Sweden," *Scandinavian Political Studies,* 4 (1969): 103–16.

Milbraith, Lester W. *The Washington Lobbyists*. Chicago: Rand McNally, 1963.

Mishan, Edward J. *Economics for Public Decisions*. New York: Praeger, 1973.

Moe, Terry M. "A Calculus of Group Membership." *American Journal of Political Science*, 24 (Nov. 1980): 593–632.

———. *The Organization of Interests*. Chicago: University of Chicago Press, 1980.

———. "Regulatory Performance and Presidential Administration," *American Journal of Political Science*, 26 (May 1982): 197–224.

Mullenbach, Philip. *Civilian Nuclear Power*. New York: Twentieth Century Fund, 1963.

Musgrave, Richard. *The Theory of Public Finance*. New York: McGraw-Hill, 1968.

Natchez, Peter B., and Bupp, Irvin C. "Policy and Priority in the Budgetary Process," *American Political Science Review*, 64 (Sept. 1973): 951–63.

National Academy of Sciences, National Research Council. *Energy in Transition, 1985–2010*. San Francisco: Freeman, 1980.

Neustadt, Richard E. *Presidential Power: The Politics of Leadership with Reflections on Johnson and Nixon*. New York: Wiley, 1976.

Niskanen, William A., Jr. *Bureaucracy and Representative Government*. Chicago: Aldine, 1971.

Odegard, Peter H. *Pressure Politics: The Story of the Anti-Saloon League*. New York: Columbia University Press, 1928.

Ogul, Morris S. *Congress Oversees the Bureaucracy*. Pittsburgh: University of Pittsburgh Press, 1976.

Olson, Mancur, Jr. *The Logic of Collective Action*. Cambridge, Mass.: Harvard University Press, 1965.

Oppenheimer, Bruce I. *Oil and the Congressional Process*. Lexington, Mass.: Lexington Books, 1974.

———. "Policy Effects of House Reform: Energy Legislation." Paper presented to the Annual Meeting of the American Political Science Association, New York, August 31–September 3, 1978.

Ornstein, Norman J., and Elder, Shirley. *Interest Groups, Lobbying and Policy-making*. Washington, D.C.: Congressional Quarterly Press, 1978.

Orren, Karen, "Standing to Sue: Interest Group Conflict in the Federal Courts." *American Political Science Review*, 70 (Sept. 1976): 723–41.

Ott, David J., and Ott, Attiat F. *Federal Budget Policy*. 3rd ed. Washington, D.C.: Brookings Institution, 1977.

Paglin, Max D., and Shor, Edgar. "Regulatory Agency Responses to the Development of Public Participation." *Public Administration Review*, 37 (March/April 1977): 140–48.

Palamountain, Joseph C., Jr. *The Politics of Distribution*. Cambridge, Mass.: Harvard University Press, 1955.

Peters, Jean, et al., "The Reagan Budget," *PS*, 14 (Fall 1981): 731–66.

Phelps, Charles E., and Smith, Rodney F. *Petroleum Regulation: The False Dilemma of Decontrol*. Santa Monica: Rand Corporation, 1977.

Piven, Francis Fox, and Cloward, Richard A. *Regulating the Poor*. New York: Vintage Books, 1971.

Polsby, Nelson W. "Legislatures." In *Handbook of Political Science*, vol. 5, pp. 257–320. Ed. Fred I. Greenstein and Nelson W. Polsby. Reading, Mass.: Addison-Wesley, 1975.

Prast, William G. *Securing U.S. Energy Supplies*. Lexington, Mass.: Lexington Books, 1981.

Quade, Edward S. *Analysis for Public Decisions*. New York: Elsevier, 1975.

Rankin, Bob. "Troubled Nuclear Power Industry Looks to Government for Assistance." *Congressional Quarterly Weekly Report*, March 11, 1978: 621–30.

Ranney, Austin, ed. *The American Elections of 1980*. Washington, D.C.: American Enterprise Institute, 1981.

Rimlinger, Gaston. *Welfare Policy and Industrialization in Europe, America, and Russia*. New York: Wiley, 1971.

Ripley, Randall B. *Power in the Senate*. New York: St. Martin's Press, 1969.

_____, and Franklin, Grace A. *Congress, the Bureaucracy, and Public Policy*. Homewood, Ill.: Dorsey Press, 1976.

Rose, Arnold M. *The Power Structure: Political Process in American Society*. New York: Oxford University Press, 1956.

Rosenbaum, Walter A. *Energy, Politics and Public Policy*. Washington, D.C.: Congressional Quarterly, 1981.

Rothman, Stanley. "Systematic Political Theory: Observations on Group Theory." *American Political Science Review*, 54 (March 1960): 15–33.

Rowen, Henry S., ed. *Options for U.S. Energy Policy*. San Francisco: Institute for Contemporary Studies, 1977.

Rundquist, Barry S. "On Testing a Military Industrial Complex Theory," *American Politics Quarterly*, 6, no. 1 (Jan. 1978): 29–55.

Rycroft, Robert W. "Bureaucratic Performance in Energy Policy-Making: An Evaluation of Output Efficiency and Equity in the FEA," *Public Policy*, 26 (Fall 1978): 599–627.

Sabatier, Paul. "Social Movements in Regulatory Agencies: Toward a More Adequate and Less Pessimistic Theory of 'Clientele Capture,'" *Policy Sciences*, 6 (1975): 301–42.

Salisbury, Robert H. "The Analysis of Public Policy: A Search for Theories and Roles." In *Political Science and Public Policy*, pp. 151–78. Ed. Austin Ranney. Chicago: Markham, 1968.

_____. "An Exchange Theory of Interest Groups," *Midwest Journal of Political Science*, 13 (1969): 1–32.

_____. "Interest Groups." In *Handbook of Political Science*, vol. 4: *Nongovernmental Politics*, pp. 171–228. Ed. Fred I. Greenstein and Nelson W. Polsby. Reading, Mass.: Addison-Wesley, 1975.

_____. "Peak Associations and the Tensions of Interest Intermediation—or Why No Corporatism in America." Paper presented to the Annual Meeting of the American Political Science Association, Washington, D.C., September 1-4, 1977.

_____, and Heinz, John. *A Theory of Policy Analysis in Political Science*. Ed. Ira Sharkansky. Chicago: Markham, 1970.

Sampson, Anthony. *The Seven Sisters*. New York: Viking, 1975.

Sapolsky, Harvey M. "Organizational Competition and Monopoly," *Public Policy*, 17 (1968): 355–76.

Schattschneider, E. E. *Politics, Pressures and the Tariff*. Englewood Cliffs, N.J.: Prentice-Hall, 1935.

———. *The Semi-Sovereign People*. New York: Holt, Rinehart and Winston, 1960.

Schick, Allen. "Complex Policy-making in the U.S. Senate." *Policy Analysis on Major Issues*. Commission on the Operation of the Senate, 94th Congress, 2nd session, 1977

———. *Congress and Money*. Washington, D.C.: Urban Institute, 1981.

Schipper, Lee, and Darmstadter, Joel. "The Logic of Energy Conservation," *Technology Review*, 80, no. 3 (Jan. 1978): 40–50.

Schmitter, Philippe C. *Interest Conflict and Political Change in Brazil*. Stanford, Calif.: Stanford University Press, 1971.

———. "Still the Century of Corporatism?," *Review of Politics*, 36 (Jan. 1974): 85–131.

———, ed. "Corporatism and Policy-making in Contemporary Western Europe," *Comparative Political Studies*, 10 (April 1977): 7–38.

Scoble, Harry. "Organized Labor in Electoral Politics: Some Questions for the Discipline," *Western Political Quarterly*, 16 (1963): 666–85.

Seidman, Harold. *Politics, Position and Power*. New York: Oxford University Press, 1970.

Selznick, Philip. *TVA and the Grass Roots*. Berkeley: University of California Press, 1949.

Sharkansky, Ira. "An Appropriations Subcommittee and its Client Agencies: A Comparative Study of Supervision and Control," *American Political Science Review*, 59 (1965): 622–28.

Shonfield, Andrew. *Modern Capitalism: The Changing Balance of Public and Private Power*. London: Oxford University Press, 1965.

Simon, Herbert A. *Administrative Behavior*. 2nd ed. New York: Free Press, 1976.

Socolow, Robert H. "The Coming Age of Conservation," *Annual Review of Energy*, 2, (1977): 239–89.

Steck, Henry J. "Private Influence on Environmental Policy: The Case of the National Industrial Pollution Control Council," *Environmental Law*, 5 (1975): 241–81.

Steinbruner, John D. *The Cybernetic Theory of Decision*. Princeton, N.J.: Princeton University Press, 1974.

Stewart, Richard B. "The Reformulation of American Administrative Law," *Harvard Law Review*, 88 (June 1975): 1669–1837.

Stigler, George J. *The Citizen and the State*. Chicago: University of Chicago Press, 1975.

———. "The Theory of Economic Regulation." *Bell Journal of Economics*, 2 (Spring 1971): 3–21.

Stobaugh, Robert, and Yergin, Daniel, eds. *Energy Future*. New York: Random House, 1979.

"The Structure of the U.S. Petroleum Industry: A Summary of Survey

Data." Special Subcommittee on Integrated Oil Operations of the Committee on Interior and Insular Affairs, U.S. Senate, 94th Cong., 2nd sess., no. 94–37, 1976.

Truman, David B. *The Governmental Process: Political Interests and Public Opinion.* 2nd ed. New York: Knopf, 1971.

Ulman, Lloyd, and Flanagan, Robert J. *Wage Restraint: A Study of Incomes Policies in Western Europe.* Berkeley: University of California Press, 1970.

U.S. Energy Outlook: Oil and Gas Availability. Washington, D.C.: National Petroleum Council, 1973.

Verba, Sidney. "Organizational Membership and Democratic Consensus." *Journal of Politics,* 27 (1965): 467–98.

_____, and Nie, Norman H. *Participation in America: Political Democracy and Social Equality.* New York: Harper and Row, 1972.

"Vermont Yankee Nuclear Power Corp. v. Natural Resources Defense Council, Inc.: Three Perspectives," *Harvard Law Review,* 91 (1978): 1804–45.

Vernon, Raymond, ed. *The Oil Crisis.* New York: Norton, 1976.

Vogel, David, and Nadel, Mark. "Who Is a Consumer? An Analysis of the Politics of Consumer Conflict," *American Politics Quarterly,* 5 (Jan. 1977): 27–56.

Vose, Clement E. *Caucasians Only: The Supreme Court, the NAACP, and the Restrictive Covenant Cases.* Berkeley: University of California Press, 1959.

Walsh, Edward. "Carter Rips Oil Firms, Defends Energy Plan," *Washington Post* (October 14, 1977): A1, A8.

Ward, Benjamin. *Elementary Price Theory.* New York: Free Press, 1967.

Watson, Richard, and Downing, Randall. *The Politics of Bench and Bar.* New York: Wiley, 1969.

Weaver, Paul H. "Regulation, Social Policy, and Class Conflict," *The Public Interest* (Winter 1978): 45–63.

White, Lawrence J. *Reforming Regulation: Process and Problems.* Englewood Cliffs, N.J.: Prentice-Hall, 1981.

Wildavsky, Aaron. *Dixon-Yates: A Study in Power Politics.* New Haven: Yale University Press, 1962.

_____. "If Planning Is Everything, Maybe It's Nothing," *Policy Science,* 4 (1973): 127–53.

_____. *The Politics of the Budgetary Process.* 3rd ed. Boston: Little, Brown, 1979.

_____. *Speaking Truth to Power.* Boston: Little, Brown, 1979.

Willrich, Mason. *Administration of Energy Shortages: Natural Gas and Petroleum.* Cambridge, Mass.: Ballinger, 1976.

Wilson, Carroll, ed. *Global Prospects 1985–2000.* New York: McGraw-Hill, 1977.

Wilson, James Q. *Political Organizations.* New York: Basic Books, 1973.

_____, ed. *The Politics of Regulation.* New York: Basic Books, 1980.

Zeigler, Harmon, and Baer, Michael. *Lobbying: Interaction and Influence in American State Legislatures.* Belmont, Calif.: Wadsworth, 1969.

INDEX